# THE WIRE

THE COMPLETE VISUAL HISTORY

# THE WIRE

## THE COMPLETE VISUAL HISTORY

## WRITTEN BY D. WATKINS

CONTRIBUTIONS FROM
Siddhant Adlakha, Eric Deggans, Brandon Easton,
Jesse Einhorn, Justine Elias, Nathaniel Friedman,
Melanie McFarland, Chris Prince, Nikki Stafford,
Robert Thompson, and Natalia Winkelman.

**TITAN BOOKS**

*London*

# CONTENTS

PAGE 2 *The Wire* actors Sonja Sohn and Dominic West pose for a publicity still.

PAGE 4 (*top*) Crouched over a corpse, detectives Lester Freamon (Clarke Peters, *left*) and Jimmy McNulty (Dominic West, *right*) get to work, as their colleagues Shakima "Kima" Greggs (Sonja Sohn, *center background*) and William "Bunk" Moreland (Wendell Pierce, *right background*) take notes. (*bottom*) Stickup man Omar Little (Michael K. Williams, *right*) with his partner Renaldo (Ramón Rodríguez, *left*).

We made a great many mistakes. For one thing, we had little interest in entertaining anyone. If we had, we would not have settled our narrative in Baltimore or in any other second-tier post-industrial city. Nor would we have accepted that city's reality as a majority-Black metropolis as being the necessary stage for our drama. Too many people who come across television fare with more than a handful of Black faces think to themselves, well, this is not my story, and then change the channel. We certainly would not have constructed a seeming police procedural in which viewers would not only be denied the bad guy being caught before the end credits, but instead urged to question who the bad guys even were or whether catching them could ever matter.

By the standards of the entertainment industry in which we found ourselves, we made a purposeful point of doing those things that neither build nor gratify an audience. It was as if, having been handed millions in cash and a remarkable opportunity by a premium cable television network, we were trying to fuck things up at every turn.

OPPOSITE The creator of *The Wire*, David Simon. Photograph by Krestine Havemann.

TOP Baltimore detectives Bunk (Wendell Pierce, *left*) and McNulty (Dominic West, *right*).

ABOVE Location photography shows a typical Baltimore street.

My late friend and collaborator, David Mills, once told me after too many drinks that the reason *The Wire* was *The Wire* was simply because the people in charge didn't care whether the show lived or died. At the time, I thought he was greatly overstating things. All of us knew, relatively early in the run, that we were doing something different, that it was a bit special, that if given the time to run out its full story, our narrative might, in the end, stand. But David, with whom I penned my first television script and with whom I had journeyed from campus daily to big-city newspapering and then, improbably, into television drama, was adamant. By then, he was living in Los Angeles and entrenched in the industry. By then, he thought he understood why *The Wire* could even be.

"Every motherfucker out here is trying to keep the plates in the air spinning, to get a show up and get enough of an audience so that the show gets renewed and renewed again and then syndicated. Everyone is willing to tell whatever story they can in order to get their show up and keep it up. And you don't give a shit if you fall down. You'll just go back to journalism."

He was right about that much. Even then, three seasons into *The Wire*, I was still talking to people as if this strange sojourn as a dramatist was

a digression, as if there was a newspapering career that would at some point inevitability resume. And it stood to reason—not in the back of my mind, but as a matter of complete consciousness—that at some point, HBO was going to realize that we didn't know the first thing about writing a television drama, much less a hit. On this project, too many of us were trying to have an argument.

Ed Burns had been a police detective in the city as well as a school-teacher. George Pelecanos, Richard Price, and Dennis Lehane were novelists scratching at the political and socioeconomic fault lines of urban America. William F. Zorzi was a newspaperman covering local politics and Rafael Álvarez the same, but with an eye to Baltimore's port. None of us contemplated a future as television writers. All of us had other gigs. And all of us arrived in that writers' room intent not simply on telling a good story you hadn't heard before, but on making an argument about why it had come to this: Why was this vastly rich society no longer able to recognize or solve its basic problems? Why were we so utterly divided against each other? Where does power and money route itself so that the Baltimores all remain as they are?

We didn't choose to write about Baltimore specifically, any more than we chose to write for a majority Black cast or chose to center ourselves on the unrelenting and utterly dystopic drug prohibition that was doing so much to destroy American cities. We had no real choices when we began. We simply wrote what we knew, maybe all that we truly knew up to that point. And we did it, by and large, out of love for and anger at the city both.

Most of all, we wanted the argument joined more than we wanted to be enjoyed or savored, more even than to be honored or remembered as storytellers. If folks acquired *The Wire* and took to debate, and we managed to move the needle a bit away from drug warring, mass incarceration, and police militarization, many of the people engaged in the project would have considered the years and effort well spent.

Here's hoping that, twenty years on, the work can still contribute to that argument.

David Simon
Baltimore, Maryland
April 2022

"Where does power and money route itself so that the Baltimores all remain as they are?"

OPPOSITE TOP Detectives of the Major Crimes Unit: (*left to right*) Lester Freamon (Clarke Peters), Kenneth Dozerman (Rick Otto), Shakima "Kima" Greggs (Sonja Sohn), Leander Sydnor (Corey Parker Robinson), and Jimmy McNulty (Dominic West).

OPPOSITE BOTTOM A wiretap prop from the show.

TOP LEFT The offices of the Major Crimes Unit.

TOP RIGHT Location photography from season two shows an area used for shooting scenes set at Baltimore's docks.

# PREFACE

by D. Watkins

Supporting a mentee who was a scrappy street poet from around the way landed me in the throes of an awful West Baltimore spoken word event—the kind where each and every artist shares the same delivery, style of dress, collection of beaded bracelets, cadence, and sob story. But I'm a good sport, so I showed up anyway, fully alert from the last row, rocking back in my chair until it pressed against the wall.

"There's so many dope artists in the house tonight!" a short brown emcee named Miss Tee spat in a muffled tone, her mouth too close to the microphone. "We are so much more than *The Wire*!"

Her comment forced me to sit up straight with a raised eyebrow. People were clapping to the left and the right and hooting in front of me. *What in the fuck is wrong with them?*

"Oh, I see the book writer D. Watkins in the house," the emcee continued over the noise. "He's more than *The Wire*. You are seeing a *New York Times* best-selling example of Black Excellence!"

More cheers followed. The spotlight slid from the stage directly to my mug, forcing me to cover my eyes. People were still clapping, some even

OPPOSITE Baltimore-raised author D. Watkins. Photograph by Devin Allen.

TOP In "The Target," the first episode of *The Wire*, officers Robert "Bobby" Brown (Bobby J. Brown, *left*) and Bunk Moreland (Wendell Pierce, *center*) examine the corpse of William Gant (Larry Hull), a key witness murdered by the Barksdale organization.

rising from their seats. I waved off the praise.

"Come on, D.! You not *The Wire*!" Miss Tee bellowed. "Tell the people something good!"

"Peace," I responded with a shrug to the happy onlookers, "Umm . . . I actually like *The Wire*, like a lot. It's my favorite show."

Another segment of the crowd clapped and cheered in agreement as the spotlight was yanked away from my face and back toward the stage.

"Really, D.? You like *The Wire*?" Miss Tee said in a chuckle. "I'm gonna have to school you on that negative copaganda, my brova. Let's get the next poet onto the stage . . ."

I looked back at the stage, shrugged again, rocked my chair back against the wall, and patiently waited for this lesson on *The Wire*, hungry to see what Miss Tee could teach me about a show I had watched and studied religiously. To be clear, *The Wire* consists of about two days and twelve hours of programing—which I watched five times, giving me over roughly three hundred hours of *Wire* knowledge.

I was prepared to explain this to Miss Tee, but for her to fully understand me, I would start by taking her back to the year—no, to the day—I saw a spindly woman named Ronnie get slapped across the face by a man named Kelly, a bony, light-brown crack dealer with fuzzy zigzag cornrows wrapped around his head. "Ronnie burned me tew many times!" Kelly claimed to us bystanders, in a poor attempt to justify his violence.

(Being burned or burnt could mean a number things in Baltimore: being set on fire, literally; being shot, like, "Jay got burned up!"; contracting an STD, like, "she burnt me"; or someone stealing your drugs. "I gave him a pack to sell, and he ran off, can you believe he burnt me?")

Their relationship was personal and professional: Kelly was having sex with Ronnie, and sometimes she was his corner man. Nowadays the progressive approach would be to specify "corner woman" or use the inclusive "corner person," but back in 2008, if you worked the corner for the person running the block, you were their corner man, regardless of your gender.

After Kelly slapped Ronnie, Ronnie slapped the cement. Instantly Roy, Lil Jesse, and I leaped off the porch as a collective, landing blows and elbows and boots and spit and pain on Kelly's face and back. The task was easy because Lil Jesse didn't like Kelly and had been talking about beating on him for months. Roy did whatever Lil Jesse did, so there's that, and I never liked men hitting women, so I snapped and, not for the last time, inserted myself into a domestic that had nothing to do with me.

"You see how I did his face?" Lil Jesse laughed at Kelly. "Yo, look like that ugly fucked-up-ass junkie off *The Wire*."

"*The Wire*?" I asked. "You watch *The Wire*?"

"Boy, that's the best fuckin' show that ever came out!" he said. "Of course I watch it—are you stupid?"

And it wasn't on that day, and not that month, but eventually I caught an episode of *The Wire* during a marathon on HBO. It was "Game Day," from the first season, the one where Avon Barksdale (Wood Harris) loses his mind because he bets a huge amount of cash with Proposition Joe (Robert F. Chew) that his Westside basketball team can beat some Eastside dudes in a full court game, and loses. *The Wire* wrapped its final season that year, 2008. How could I have missed it? The characters played on a court where I played sometimes; they moved through blocks I lived near. My childhood

TOP The Barksdale organization circa season one: (*left to right*) Avon Barksdale (Wood Harris), Anton "Stinkum" Artis (Brandon Price), D'Angelo Barksdale (Lawrence Gilliard Jr.), and Russell "Stringer" Bell (Idris Elba).

OPPOSITE BOTTOM In the season one episode "Game Day," detectives Ellis Carver (Seth Gilliam, *left*) and Thomas "Herc" Hauk (Domenick Lombardozzi, *right*) watch a basketball game set up by rival gangs: the Barksdales on the Westside and Proposition Joe's crew on the Eastside.

friend Andre Poole, aka Silk, Baltimore's version of Vince "Half Man Half Amazing" Carter, was the star of "Game Day," leading the Eastside team to victory. How'd we make it all the way to HBO, and I totally missed it?

I went to a record shop in Fell's Point called the Sound Garden and bought the box set, and for the first time I binge-watched a show. That first DVD went in, and I didn't stop until I watched the last episode of season five and then preceded to watch them all again—not just for the amazing storytelling, but also the lessons.

Miss Tee, who did not grow up in Baltimore City, but Annapolis—a Maryland suburb that is close to an hour away—may not have done the necessary research to understand why a person like me would connect with the show. If she came up in the streets of Baltimore, she would know that despite having some good teachers, the school system is still messed up; she would know the drug trade is going to have a negative impact on your family and neighborhood; she would know a lot of the politicians are in it for themselves; and she would know exactly how crooked police officers can be. Over five seasons, *The Wire* would have brilliantly weaved all those realities together for her, giving her context on why these problems exist—or, at least, that's what it did for me. The show shifted

"That first DVD went in, and I didn't stop until I watched the last episode of season five . . ."

OPPOSITE TOP (*Left to right*) Barksdale organization enforcers Roland "Wee-Bey" Brice (Hassan Johnson) and Stringer Bell (Idris Elba) meet with D'Angelo Barksdale (Lawrence Gilliard Jr.) and his corner boys, Malik "Poot" Carr (Tray Chaney) and Preston "Bodie" Broadus (J. D. Williams).

OPPOSITE BOTTOM Wee-Bey (Johnson) attends court under the watchful eye of Stringer Bell (Elba).

BOTTOM Location photography from the streets of Baltimore.

the argument away from disingenuous individuals and taught us to look at failed, outdated systems. *The Wire* clearly explains how a person with good intentions and a pure heart can get a big city job or be elected to office and completely fail because the system in place forces him or her to do so. The show blew my mind, and my perspective evolved.

TOP Shooting a scene on location in Baltimore: (*left to right*) Dominic West, Seth Gilliam, Domenick Lombardozzi, Sonja Sohn, Ryan Sands as officer Lloyd "Truck" Garrick, Benjamin Busch as Anthony "Tony" Colicchio, and Corey Parker Robinson.

OPPOSITE Filming a scene in which Avon Barksdale's safehouse is raided at the end of season three. On set are prop master Mike Sabo (white shirt), director Ernest Dickerson (orange shirt), technical adviser Jim Rood (gray T-shirt), first assistant director Anthony Hemingway (red shirt), assistant director Xanthus Valan (cap), plus actor Anwan Glover, who plays Slim Charles (next to Hemingway). On the right are Sonja Sohn, Dominic West, and Corey Parker Robinson.

Two years later, I had become that guy: "Yo, you never watched *The Wire*? Are you crazy?" An unofficial ambassador for writer-creator David Simon and writer-producer Ed Burns' brand. And I didn't even think critically about the writing or the craft of the show; I just loved the hell out of it, from the gritty rawness of season one, to season two, which brilliantly broke down crime at Baltimore's ports—even though my friends wanted the focus back on the streets—to season three, which was my favorite until season four, which tied in the horrors of our school system. And then season five perfectly merged everything together. Season five was a bittersweet watch, because the storytelling had me locked, but there was no season six. It was the end of a beautiful era.

In 2014, I published an essay on Salon.com about how so many people in Baltimore were too poor for pop culture. It went viral, gaining me thousands of followers and a platform to share my writing. Almost instantly I became a popular voice in Baltimore. And into my inbox, in a sea of opportunity, offers, praise, and hate mail, came an email from David Simon. "Great work!" he told me.

I wasn't the same kid from 2010—back then I was just a fan who loved the show. By this point, I had consumed all of Simon's work—combed through his *Baltimore Sun* articles and read the book he wrote with Burns, *The Corner*, twice. Getting a stamp from him meant the world to me. In Baltimore, it felt like a rite of passage: the legend reaching out to the rookie.

"If you ever need a writer, I'm free!" I responded.

Years later, I'm a (*New York Times* best-selling) author of three books—relaxing in the back of this horrible spoken word event, waiting for the host to school me on why I should have a problem with the greatest television show in American history. We never had the conversation. She came to greet me, and we took a picture. While she checked out our image on her phone, making sure the lighting was right, I asked, "So what's up with *The Wire*?"

"Oh, I didn't really watch it?" she said. "It's too negative, and I can't give it my energy."

"So why the hard opinions? I mean, if you never saw the show, how do you know it's so negative? How do you know it's not funny and creative and informative?

The young lady didn't have an answer for me. Not only was she not from the city, but she didn't even watch *The Wire*. I imagine that someone who also probably did not see the show shared their opinion with her, and

TOP In the season one episode "The Buys," D'Angelo Barksdale (Lawrence Gilliard Jr., *center*) teaches Wallace (Michael B. Jordan, *left*) and Bodie (J. D. Williams, *right*) how to play chess.

OPPOSITE TOP On the case: (*left to right*) Bunk (Wendell Pierce), McNulty (Dominic West), Kima (Sonja Sohn) and Lester (Clarke Peters).

OPPOSITE BOTTOM In season one, the detail assigned to surveil the Barksdale organization gather in their basement headquarters: (*left to right*) detectives Carver (Seth Gilliam), Sydnor (Corey Parker Robinson), Patrick Mahon (Tom Quinn), Augustus Polk (Nat Benchley, *seated*), Greggs (Sonja Sohn, *standing*), Herc (Domenick Lombardozzi), Roland "Prez" Pryzbylewski (Jim True-Frost), Michael Santangelo (Michael Salconi), McNulty (Dominic West), and lieutenant Cedric Daniels (Lance Reddick).

because she may have had trust for that person, she carried their argument as if it were her own. Seeing a person stand on their own critique of something they'd never seen is extremely scary, so scary that I wanted to know more. *What other things do you have baseless opinions on?* But, lucky for her, we were pulled in different directions by other people who wanted to catch up with us and, of course, take more pictures. I tried to find her as the venue started to clear out, but she was gone.

If I could have caught Miss Tee, I would've explained that *The Wire* is the exact opposite of copaganda. The phrase *copaganda* definitely deserves to be attached to many television shows and movies that only portray officers as pure heroes, hungry to save citizens in a way that is unimaginable to the average person living in an urban area. Simon and *The Wire*'s writers took time to detail the complexities that exist inside the police department. You had cops that wanted to be heroes and tried to do their jobs, and you had cops that were beyond lazy. You had officers who were racist but didn't know they were racist. You had officers who were flat-out racist. You had officers who were extremely intelligent. You had officers that were extremely stupid. There were officers with good hearts who made bad decisions and officers with bad hearts who made good decisions. The officers were Black, white, fit, little, or wildly out of shape.

Every single officer was carefully developed with an unprecedented amount of authenticity. How can you use a word like *copaganda* when the horrors of their brutality and their inability to put down cases were on

front street in multiple seasons of the show? I would also tell her that the only two officers who really made a difference did so after they left or were kicked off the force: Major Howard "Bunny" Colvin (Robert Wisdom), who adopted serial delinquent Namond Brice (Julito McCullum), and Officer Roland Pryzbylewski (Jim True-Frost), who, after becoming a middle school teacher, brought his grossly neglected student Duquan "Dukie" Weems (Jermaine Crawford) clean clothes and snacks to eat from time to time.

I'd also address Miss Tee's comments about the negative depiction of Black people for two reasons. The first being how one views that negativity is solely based on a matter of perspective. If you grew up in an affluent neighborhood or even a lower-middle-class neighborhood, then there's a good chance you didn't have an experience like the Black people in the neighborhoods depicted on the show did. Unlike the bulk of people attending that spoken word event, I actually spent time in multiple housing projects throughout the city of Baltimore for a good chunk of the 1990s and 2000s and took no offense at any of the portrayals. Contrary to what many may believe, some of us actually live or lived exactly like the characters including Preston "Bodie" Broadus (J. D. Williams), Poot Carr (Tray Chaney), and Wallace (Michael B. Jordan), who came from Lexington Terrace, McCulloh Homes, and Poe Homes in West Baltimore.

The second side of that argument would deal with the diversity of the Black experience inside the show. At the time of filming, *The Wire* had one of the most diverse casts in television, with Black actors playing more than just downtrodden street dwellers. While there were Black drug dealers and addicts, there were also Black news reporters, Black lawyers, Black cops on every level, Black politicians, Black teachers, Black coaches, Black businessmen, and Black entrepreneurs, just like there are in the real Baltimore.

But you would have to watch the show to know that. If I could go back to that event, my only response to "We more than *The Wire*" would have been "I'm from Baltimore, and I am *The Wire*."

> "At the time of filming, *The Wire* had one of the most diverse casts in television, with Black actors playing more than just downtrodden street dwellers."

OPPOSITE Officer Roland "Prez" Pryzbylewski (Jim True-Frost), whose journey in *The Wire* takes him from cop to middle school teacher.

TOP Baltimore location photography shows a row of houses in a state of neglect.

# SEASON

# 1

# AN INTRODUCTION TO SEASON ONE

By D. Watkins

Initially people didn't really get *The Wire*. We were all used to the kinds of cop shows that exposed us to crimes committed during act one and then guaranteed that the case would be closed before the closing credits, allowing viewers to feel infinitely safe. *The Wire* hit television like a missile, showing the world that we were everything but safe.

For starters, *The Wire* introduced viewers to the complexities of police officers. Officers, like most citizens, come in all shapes and sizes, are of many different ethnicities, and can be as talented or as worthless as people in any other city-run outfit. We have geniuses like Lester Freamon (Clarke Peters), drunks like James "Jimmy" McNulty (Dominic West), and boneheads like Thomas "Herc" Hauk (Domenick Lombardozzi): The necessary

> "*The Wire* hit television like a missile, showing the world that we were everything but safe."

OPPOSITE McNulty (Dominic West) in his natural environment, a Baltimore murder scene.

TOP The Barksdales head to court: (*left to right*) Wee-Bey (Hassan Johnson), Anton Artis (Brandon Price), D'Angelo Barksdale (Lawrence Gilliard Jr.), Stringer Bell (Idris Elba), and Savino Bratton (Chris Clanton).

personalities that mirror the makings of a real police department, all united in an effort to take down the Barksdale organization led by Avon Barksdale (Wood Harris) and Stringer Bell (Idris Elba).

And we got a firsthand look at the inner workings of the Barksdale organization. Most shows at the time glossed over or completely ignored the streets; *The Wire*, however, bravely took us to the other side. We meet front-line foot soldiers like Bodie (J. D. Williams), underbosses like D'Angelo Barksdale (Lawrence Gilliard Jr.), and ruthless muscle like Roland "Wee-Bey" Brice (Hassan Johnson). And then there is Wallace (Michael B. Jordan), who introduces the world to the more delicate side of the streets—he could have been anything in the world if he had been born into different circumstances, but he wasn't. Wallace is another kid who isn't cut out for the drug game but has to play because he is charged with the task of raising his younger siblings. Eventually, his shortcomings cost him his life. In the midst of all this chaos, we meet Omar Little (Michael K. Williams), one of the best antiheroes in television history. Omar is a gay gangster in a trench coat, straight from a '40s Western movie, who pops in and out of crumbling, boarded-up row houses to rob the biggest dope dealers in the city. He has everyone in the streets of Baltimore shook, and we loved it.

And then adding Reginald "Bubbles" Cousins (Andre Royo) to the mix provided a very important perspective that had never been fully fleshed out in television—the plight of an addict with a personality so easy to love. What does it look like when a guy wakes up every day in search of money just to buy narcotics, when you know he has the kind of social aptitude that would allow him to excel in many professions?

In creating a show that is going to make an honest argument about the war on drugs, we have to consider the most vulnerable players. Including all these personalities and perspectives was extremely important in painting a full picture because it gave us the opportunity to see the number of people involved in a dense investigation: from the cops to the target to the snitch. Cases aren't just open and closed—they are extremely complicated. We learn how cops can be assets or liabilities or both.

We also learn that there are many different mechanisms that street guys implement to derail law enforcement, ultimately showing us how even the perfect investigation can fail.

TOP Officer Herc (Domenick Lombardozzi) on the job.

BOTTOM Omar coming: Michael K. Williams as feared stickup man Omar Little.

OPPOSITE TOP McNulty (Dominic West, *left*), D'Angelo (Lawrence Gilliard Jr., *center*), and Bunk (Wendell Pierce, *right*) have an informal chat. This scene was shot on location at West Baltimore's McCulloh Homes, often referred to in the show as the "Pit."

OPPOSITE BOTTOM D'Angelo (Gilliard Jr.) makes a call, unaware that the Major Crimes Unit is closing in on his activities.

# DAVID SIMON

## Interview by Brandon Easton

A journalist at the *Baltimore Sun* for twelve years, David Simon won acclaim for his 1991 book *Homicide: A Year on the Killing Streets*, which documented the work of the Baltimore Police Department's homicide unit. Simon's book was later adapted into the successful NBC series *Homicide: Life on the Street*. Simon adapted his next book, *The Corner: A Year in the Life of an Inner-City Neighborhood* (1997), cowritten with Ed Burns, into HBO's six-part miniseries *The Corner* (2000), a project that directly led to him becoming the creator, showrunner, writer, and producer of *The Wire*, which ran for five seasons between 2002 and 2008. Since the international acclaim of *The Wire*, Simon has gone on to create several other shows for HBO, including Iraq war drama *Generation Kill* (2008); *Treme* (2010–2013), which looked at the impact of Hurricane Katrina on a New Orleans community; and *The Deuce* (2017–2019), an ensemble drama that explored New York City's role in the rise of pornography from the late '60s onward. In 2022, Simon returned to the streets of Baltimore with HBO miniser es *We Own This City*, which dramatized real-life police corruption in the BPD.

**You've been asked questions about *The Wire* for 20 years because it's stood the test of time for filmmakers and even criminologists. With so much hindsight, has your perspective on the show and its legacy changed at all given the past two decades?**

There have been other people who've weighed in on what happened with the culture of the drug wars and mass arrests. There have been other works of journalism that I've admired. I think in some respects we were correct. First, regarding the idea that not only is this not achieving its goals in terms of reforming anybody's life with regard to drugs or crime or anything like that. Having written *The Corner* as a work of journalism, Ed and I were very [against] the idea of a drug war. I don't think we understood just how destructive to the culture of law enforcement these things were going to be.

And we thought that to be tragic and sad. We were cynical about what the drug war was. We needed to take a few steps deeper because over time, the existential crisis of this kind of policing has [worsened]. So our critique of the drug war, and of a sort of a city that can't even admit to its own problems, much less address any of them—it only got darker. So that's how I sort of feel about it now.

We certainly acknowledged police brutality. We acknowledged you saw cops stealing cash. You saw guys going into people's pockets. But I don't think I could have contemplated in 2008 a plainclothes unit working citywide and, you know, kicking in doors without warrants and just taking shit. That was a generation off. But, hey, we ended up there because nobody put the brakes on this thing.

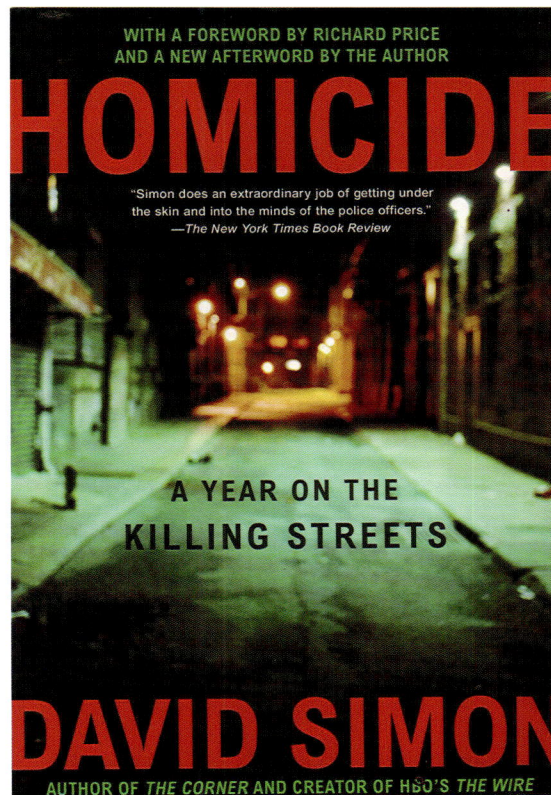

**During the developmental process, how did you decide to focus on a cross-section of the police, the government, and the drug game on the street? Were you ever concerned that you were taking on too big of a story?**

Yeah, that concern came up when we decided to [focus on Baltimore's ports] in season two, and we were halfway through filming season one when we made that decision. I had to sell it to HBO, because at first, they were reluctant purchasers of a crime show. They thought, "Oh, man, the networks do this [type of show]," and they were very wary of the fact that they

OPPOSITE David Simon, the man behind *The Wire*. Photograph by Krestine Havemann.

CENTER The cover for Simon's 1991 book, *Homicide: A Year on the Killing Streets*, published by Picador.

were no longer counterprogramming classically. They weren't doing worlds that the networks couldn't do.

But we made the argument that if you do them in such a way that network television wouldn't, by addressing topics they wouldn't cover, you would be counterprogramming. Network television was not going to be critical of policy, of policing policy, or of the war on drugs as a classist or racist exercise. We eventually sold them on that, and having bought that much, I had to go a season later and say, "Now we're going to build a city shard by shard. First, we're going to do the working class and the death of work, then we're going to do the political infra-structure, then we're going to do the educational system, and then we're going to do the media culture."

I remember sitting in the room with Chris Albrecht [CEO and chairman of HBO at the time]

and Carolyn Strauss [then president of HBO's entertainment division] and making the pitch for why we should now do the working class and the death of work, to layer that over the top of it, to show you that the drug culture we depicted in season one was the only viable factory still standing in terms of industrialization. And I remember Chris turning to Carolyn and saying, "Is that what we bought?" He was a little bit . . . *What*?!

So there was a little bit of faith extended as we marched forward. That was such a dramatic change when we went into season two, in terms of characterization, worlds, and world building, that I think everything after that was quickly forgiven—you know, when we added politics. There was never another moment when they said, "Okay, we don't get it." At that point, they knew that every season was going to take on some other aspect of civic infrastructure and policy.

**The post-industrialization of Baltimore City had a massive impact on Black working classes. Were you ever concerned, or did you ever hear any pushback, about negative stereotypes of Black people in the show because so much of the story was rooted in the drug trade?**

Sure. I mean, I certainly did. We sort of anticipated it.

We had taken a bite of that apple with *The Corner*. Ed and I had gone to a drug corner in '93. We had followed the people there. The open-air drug markets of Baltimore were predominantly located in Black communities. We actually chose the community we did because we wanted the audience to see the white drift from Pigtown and Morrell Park. People from external communities came there to buy, sometimes to fire up, but the drift told you that demand was multicultural. But for a variety of reasons—including industrialization and because police would respond aggressively if you set up a drive-through drug corner in a working-class white neighborhood—the drug culture had centered itself in Black communities, and we knew this going in.

When *The Corner* came out, Ed and I had this pregnant moment where we waited for our heads to get handed to us, you know, as these two white guys who had written this book. That could have happened. But very quickly a couple of people vocally supported what we had done, and one of them was the Reverend Frank Reid III from Bethel A.M.E., the preeminent Black church in West Baltimore. He invited us on to *Book Notes*, [a show] he hosted on cable TV at the Sanctuary of Bethel, to discuss the book. He read it early. His church was centered in the problems of the drug war and he was rigorous in his

EPISODE 101

1  Baltimore Circuit Court, Pt 23: A jury trial in progress, a drug-involved homicide case Judge Clifford Watkins, black, middle-aged, vaguely wearied, presiding as a young prosecutor struggles to keep witnesses from backing up on their grand jury testimony. The second row of seats in the half-empty courtroom is filled with some rough-looking characters, all staring intently at the prosecution witnesses, who are clearly frightened. One of those in the second-row -- Stringy Bell -- is better-dressed, more studious-looking. He writes on a legal pad as each witness answers questions. The defendant is young, black, trying to look hard but clearly nervous. The jury is mostly black, as is the prosecutor. In the back of the room, a rumpled, worn Irish face stares at the proceedings impassively.

Prosecutor. "Mr. Mitchell, did you or did you not tell the grand jury.. "

Witness "I can't remember now. I don't know that I told anyone anything.. "

The witness looks up at the Bell twenty feet away  Bell eyefucks him coolly, writes something on his pad. The rumpled Irishman exhales, gets up, leaves. On Judge Watkins, watching him go.

2  State's attorney's office, Violent Crimes Unit. We follow the Irishman into the office  He greets the secretaries, moving toward the rear offices as if he owns the place. He sees another cop, also white, on the phone, his feet up on a prosecutor's desk. The Irishman nods, listens. His fellow detective is arguing with a contractor about the cost of pressure-treated lumber

The Irishman sits. His pager goes off. He scans the number, frowns

The other detective hangs up, looks to the Irishman

"Fucking thieves."

"You putting a deck up?"

"Not for eight thousand I'm not. Fucking thieves."

The detective picks up the phone again, ready to do battle. The Irishman interrupts him. "You talked to Hansen lately?"

"I'm with Hansen in Part 23 right now. The Marando Bennett case "

"I know that  I was just in there."

"Yeah?" asks the detective, not really giving a shit.

"Yeah. Your case is falling apart."

"The fuck it is "

The Irishman shrugs  "Last two witnesses just backed all the way up."

"The fuck you say."

"You got Stringy Bell and his crew sitting in the second row staring them down  They're backin' up like bad sewer pipe."

"What's Hansen doing?"

The Irishman shrugs. The detective mulls the news over for a second, picks up the phone, calls a second contractor, seeking another estimate

defense of our book. He kind of shut down the local wariness and actually introduced a lot of people to it. After that, we were remarkably well received.

We went through the same thing on a national level when *The Wire* premiered. It was like, "Okay, here we come . . ." I expected a certain amount of criticism. But in our heads—and I think this remains true—we weren't writing a book about race, and we weren't depicting the Black experience in Baltimore, never mind nationally. Nothing we were doing was saying, this is the Black experience. There are whole tracts of middle-class [life] that are not included in *The Wire*. People living quotidian lives of functionality are not the subject of the show, whether they're white or Black or Latino or anything else. And we were aware of this.

I think in some respects, you always know there's the racially collapsed viewer who's going to take it in and say, "Well, this is all Black people." You can't fix that guy, and you can't write for him. He's unreachable with any narrative you might construct that has meaning. So at some point you've just got to go, "I'm writing to the sentient and to the intelligent viewer, and I can't think about that other guy because I can't write anything that's going to fix him." And I'm still at that point.

Conversely, there are some portrayals in here that are tough to watch. I can't help because I either have to tell the truth, or I don't. I remember my own

grandmother reading the New York papers, often in Yiddish, and whenever somebody Jewish had been charged with a crime she would circle it. Like a *shanda* for the goyim: "Look how we look." And you know, that's how that looks. That's the interior sense of minority vulnerability that says, "How can you show that and not have it hurt us?"

In some respects, the greater question is: How can there be a war on drugs that is basically attacking the fundamentals of being poor in America, especially if you're poor and in a community of color; and if you're targeted, how do you stay silent about it? That's the preeminent war going on in my city that I covered as a reporter and am now writing about as a dramatist—how do I not speak to it? How do I not address the situation as it actually is? And in some respects, over time, if you watch the show, your sympathies and your understanding of what people's choices are and what people's actions are rooted in become paramount. And at that point, I think you're okay. I don't think I can make this argument to the people who glimpsed ten minutes of it. If you watch the show, I think, the actual intent bleeds through fundamentally and throughout. But there were people who I was going to lose, and I was going to lose them no matter what, even if I'm on the same side as them.

When you put something out in the world, some people are going to understand it for what it actually

OPPOSITE A page from the document that David Simon created to help pitch *The Wire* to HBO. The pitch mentions a character called "Stringy Bell." The "Irishman" is an early version of the McNulty character.

TOP David Simon (*far right*) works with the cast on location, including Marlo Stanfield actor Jamie Hector (*seated*).

TOP David Simon (*left*) with Bubbles actor Andre Royo (*center*) and Leo Fitzpatrick (*right*), who plays Bubbles's best friend, Johnny Weeks.

is, and other people are going to strain it through their ideologies. We're writing human beings, and if you're not picking up on it, maybe you're not watching it. It's like everybody saw what they wanted to see and would refuse to see anything else that was there. And as the people making the show, making the drama, we had to accept that. You can't fix your audience. You just have to hope it finds some people the right way.

**Can you shed some light on the casting process for *The Wire*? It was surprising to find out that Idris Elba and Dominic West were not Baltimoreans. Why did you or the network opt for so many performers from the UK?**

I think it was pretty random. We used Alexa Fogel in New York. She's been our casting director for a number of projects, but that was the first one

where we got really involved with her. And she's always hungry to find stage actors who haven't yet hit screens. She'll keep an eye on London, and she'll keep an eye on the West Coast. I mean, we wanted a lot of people from the East Coast just because we didn't want to pay for the hotel rooms. You've got to remember, we were making this—by comparison to other HBO shows—on a shoestring, so we took a minimum of people from LA. Money mattered.

Alexa would find these people who had just arrived in New York, like Idris, who were trying to find work in America, and she would clock them. Listen, a good actor who has not been entirely exposed is a precious thing if you're trying to create a documentarian feel to a show, if you're trying to get people to watch it not as a star turn, but as a narrative about a real-world place and argument. So Idris read well. His accent did not peek through. I didn't hear

any East London coming at me. And then, afterward, he stayed in character during the few words that we said as we congratulated him on his reading. It was only at the second meeting where he dropped the [American] accent. At that point, it was too late for us. That was exactly the way to play it.

**Considering that you brought in such a disparate cast of actors from different places in the world, were there any challenges in creating the necessary chemistry?**

With the adult actors, no. They're professionals: You show them the scripts, and they get where they're supposed to be in the hierarchies. Interestingly, we did a show with very little interaction between some of the people in the police world and some of the people on the street. But that wasn't the case for William "Bunk" [Moreland], [Jimmy] McNulty, or

Bodie, because there were early encounters. And Michael K. [Williams, as Omar Little] was always interacting with cops because he had such value in terms of his information that he would engage with McNulty, [Shakima "Kima"] Greggs, and others.

But, for example, the guys who played people higher up in the chain of command would very rarely interact with people on the street. The show was so disparate that there were actors who went their whole run and never got to work a scene with someone else. I remember one of the episodes very late in the run when the actor who played Jay Landsman, Delaney Williams, had a scene with Bubbles, played by Andre Royo. The show had gone on for four years, and Delaney was like, "I finally get to work with you." It was that kind of show.

The only time that we had actors where we tried to do some synthesis of their relationship before we

TOP LEFT David Simon (*left*) with *The Wire* set costumer DaJuan T. Prince (*right*). Photograph by Paul Schiraldi.

TOP RIGHT Simon (*left*) with actor Dominic West (*right*) during shooting.

TOP The Baltimore police department's top brass pose with captured narcotics: (*left to right*) Deputy Commissioner of Operations Ervin H. Burrell (Frankie Faison), Commissioner Warren Frazier (Dick Stilwell), Major William A. Rawls (John Doman), and Narcotics Unit Commander Raymond Foerster (Richard DeAngelis).

turned the cameras on were the kids in season four. And credit there to Ed Burns, who knew we needed it because they were younger actors and not as experienced, but they were being asked to create a dynamic between the four of them from the jump. So running scenes in advance of turning on the cameras was valuable. Robert F. Chew, a great local actor who played Proposition Joe, was their acting mentor. He did a lot of theater here in Baltimore. He was an actor's actor who never left town, and he took on the role of being the teacher for the four kids we featured that year.

**While you were shooting on location across town, were there any things about filming in Baltimore that surprised you? Anything that you didn't expect to happen on or around set?**

I came to very much credit what we were doing because of the different reactions we got from hierarchical Baltimore, political Baltimore, and people on the street, and it became more and more apparent as the show aged. Once *The Wire* had a presence

on TV, somebody from the *New Yorker* wrote that the show seemed to have a strange audience. At the time, everyone was watching *The Sopranos*. Meanwhile, the people who watched *The Wire* when it was on air were sociologists and academics on one end—to argue about policy and stuff—and people from the inner city on the other.

We weren't selling to the American middle class for a long time. Where we started to penetrate sort of normal viewers was in Europe. England jumped in on it fast, and then France. Once it started airing overseas, I think they credulously watched it as if it was just another HBO show like *The Sopranos*. Whereas in America, because of the racial and class disparities in terms of how people watch television, there were a lot of people who clicked it on, saw what it was about, saw the world in which it was set and said, "Oh, that's not my show." And they moved on. But people in West and East Baltimore and in Park Heights and Cherry Hill watched the show. They were like, "Wow, somebody finally made a show about my world." By season four, people like Andre or Wendell—or especially Michael K. or Idris—would come out of their trailers on Monroe Street or on Evanston Road to film a scene, and they would be mobbed by local fans.

There was a lot of sensibility about what the actors were doing. Every now and then someone would come out of a row house with a pie for Idris—there was a real affection, as if the show belonged in some way to everybody in Baltimore.

Meanwhile, the mayor hates the show. The Chamber of Commerce hates the show. They were furious, but there was nothing I could do about that. I'm critiquing a policy that has gone awry. I'm basically saying, "You guys are overpolicing the city in a brutal way that can't work, and that is wasting lives and resources. And you're underpolicing the city in the cases when we actually need to respond to violence. You're doing this, you're in charge, and this is what's happening to your city," and they did not like it. So we were told from the hierarchical Baltimore that we were unfair, and what we were doing was unnecessary, and we should stop. And we were being told from the streets of Baltimore, "Thanks for doing a show about us, and about our world, and about what we're experiencing." The duality of that was weirdly gratifying, as you might imagine.

**After covering all the ground explored in the show's run, what other aspects of Baltimore life would you have liked to cover if you'd had a sixth season?**

Well, it would not have been a season six, but it would have been a sixth season. After season three, David Mills came up with an idea. He was somebody I knew from college, and we worked on the University of Maryland paper together, and we wrote our first script together for *Homicide*. David was a Black writer who I also worked with on *Treme*. He died way too young, at forty-eight of a brain aneurysm. I always wanted him on staff for *The Wire*, but I couldn't get him because he was trying furiously to get a network show up. I don't think he quite believed in HBO, even as I was telling him, "No, this is a home. This is the home you want to be in." He was still trying to get stuff up at NBC, so I could never get him on staff, but I could get him to write a few episodes here and there.

Anyway, at some point, he said, "You know, the thing you should be doing is . . ."—and this was after he walked around Southeast Baltimore, Fell's Point, where he noticed that Baltimore, which was very late to having a Latino immigrant culture, suddenly had one, largely from Central America. He thought that

was fascinating because he had spent time in Chicago and Washington, DC, cities that had experienced this before Baltimore. The city was encountering it for the first time, and it has continued.

*The Wire* world that we had depicted had a very minimal sense, an almost nonexistent sense, of a Latino community. And David said, "You should do something on immigration, on the dynamic of the people coming into this country. That's the part that would be fresh." And as soon as he said it, I realized, yep, we should. And that was about the exact same week that HBO agreed to let us continue the show, because we were sort of canceled after three seasons. Chris Albrecht had said, "Okay, go plan seasons four and five." And four and five were linked by the Marlo story and the bodies and the vacant lot at the end of four.

TOP Actor Robert F. Chew, who played Proposition Joe on the show and also worked as an acting coach for the child actors on season four.

Because once you start season four, you've got to do season five, and season five had to be the media. The last one had to be about media culture. Also, here I was having sold HBO on two more seasons by the skin of my ass. I begged, and they gave me two more seasons. I couldn't very well go back and go, "Wait, wait, wait. Can I insert this one season about immigration before I start the Marlo season, and then end on media culture?" And the last question we wanted to ask was: When all these problems were inherent, what did we bother ourselves with? That's why we wanted to critique the media culture last.

So the suggestion came just a hair too late. We weren't in any position logistically to pick it up and run with it, because that would have been season four, and then seasons four and five would have been five and six. That's the only way I could have added something.

BOTTOM (*Left to right*) Writer and director Tim Van Patten, assistant props master Bob Spore, and David Simon.

OPPOSITE A call sheet from the production of the season one episode "One Arrest."

**Looking back on all your experiences, what kind of changes happened to you personally? Did you become more optimistic about the future, or were you rooted in pragmatism about how to fix the problems in Baltimore?**
Nationally, I will confess, I had a moment of great optimism when we elected Barack Obama because I thought, Maybe there is some post-racial horizon for this country. And, you know, maybe all the inherent fears that come from white America only being a plurality in this country and coalition politics being our future, if we're to survive and solve problems, maybe that moment is upon us—especially when he was elected a second time. I could obviously sense the furious and residual racism from some quarters, but the numbers seemed to be with the future. Did I think Obama was getting to all the problems? No, I did not. Did I think Congress was any more functional than it's been for the last thirty years, since Newt Gingrich? No, I did not, but I did have a moment of [thinking], maybe we're growing up.

Nope. I don't think I anticipated the glories of voter suppression and the vagaries of the Electoral College, so that whatever I thought was a horizon event in 2008 or 2012 now seems further away than I thought. I think I was a little bit of an optimist there.

**I've seen critical acclaim centered on the portrayal of women in *The Wire* as three-dimensional characters with both flaws and virtues. What can you tell us about these roles on the show? Were some of the characters based upon real women in the legal and political structure of Baltimore City?**

# THE WIRE

## "A MAN MUST HAVE A CODE" - Ep. # 107

## Revised Blue Schedule (4/30/02) \ Pink Script (4/30/02)

D.1

| # | Scene | Pages | Script pgs |
|---|-------|-------|------------|
| 1 | INT DETAIL OFFICE - WIRETAP ROOM - Day 1<br>Teaser: Prez happily helps decipher the taped conversation from last night | 2 7/8 pgs.<br>Stage - 3711 E. Monument Street | 1, 12, 13, 15, 16 |
| 2 | INT HOMICIDE OFFICE - Day 1<br>Rawls wants Santangelo to rat on McNulty | 1 6/8 pgs.<br>Police Headquarters Set - 100 N. Charles Street, 5th FL | 9, 42 |
| 3 | INT DETAIL OFFICE - Day 1<br>Freamon, Greggs, Herc & Carver discuss their plan of attack | 1 3/8 pgs.<br>Stage - 3711 E. Monument Street | 4, 12, 13, 15 |
| 4 | INT MITCHELL COURTHOUSE - JUDGE'S CHAMBERS - Day 1<br>McNulty gets graded on his wiretap reports by Judge Phelan | 2 7/8 pgs.<br>111 N. Calvert St. (b/t Fayette & Lexington Sts.), 2nd FL | 1, 10, 23, 60 |
| 5 | EXT PRESTON STREET / WEST BALTIMORE - Day 1<br>Stinkum and his Runner drive past Greggs & Sydnor | 1/8 pgs.<br>Preston Street (b/t Pennsylvania & Druid Hill Aves.) | 4, 17, 24, 41 |
| 6 | INT GREGGS' UNMARKED CAR / PRESTON STREET - Day 1<br>Greggs eyes Stinkum's SUV - radios to Herc | 3/8 pgs.<br>Preston Street (b/t Pennsylvania & Druid Hill Aves.) | 4, 17, 24, 41 |
| 7 | INT CARVER'S UNMARKED CAR / DRUID HILL (MOVING) - Day 1<br>Herc & Carver spot Stinkum & follow him; Turns into a hi-speed chase | 6/8 pgs.<br>Druid Hill Ave. (@ Preston St.) | 12, 12x, 13, 13x, 24, 24x, 41, 41x, 100 |
| 8 | EXT LOW-RISE PROJECTS - COURTYARD - Day 1<br>Herc chases Runner;Greggs cuts him off;Sydnor & Carver join for the tackle | 1 3/8 pgs.<br>Druid Hill/Preston-McCulloh-Hoffman-Druid Hill-"The Pit" | 3, 4, 12, 13, 14, 17, 24, 100 |
| 9 | INT MITCHELL COURTHOUSE - JUDGE'S CHAMBERS - Day 1<br>McNulty & Judge Phelan discuss the effect his case is making on Rawls | 1 4/8 pgs.<br>111 N. Calvert St. (b/t Fayette & Lexington Sts.), 2nd FL | 1, 23 |
| 10,13,15,<br>17,19,21pt | EXT HIGH-RISE PROJECTS - COURTYARD - Day 1<br>Stinkum a nervous wreck at the payphone | 7/8 pgs.<br>McCulloh Homes - Dolphin St. (@ Etting St.) | 6, 41 |
| 11 | INT DETAIL OFFICE - WIRETAP ROOM - Day 1<br>Freamon sees Stringer's pager number appear on the monitor | 1/8 pgs.<br>Stage - 3711 E. Monument Street | 15 |
| 12 | EXT DRUID HILL AVENUE - Day 1<br>The Runner is in the wagon; Greggs receives a call; Sydnor races off | 4/8 pgs.<br>Druid Hill (@ Stoddard Lane) | 4, 12, 13, 17, 24 |
| 14 | EXT CHURCH SOCIAL HALL - Day 1<br>Sydnor arrives outside the church and runs inside | 1/8 pgs.<br>Sharp Street - 1206 Etting St. (b/t Dolphin & Lafayette Sts.) | 17 |
| 16 | INT CHURCH SOCIAL HALL - STAIRWELL - Day 1<br>Sydnor races up the stairs | 1/8 pgs.<br>Sharp Street - 1206 Etting St. (b/t Dolphin & Lafayette Sts.) | 17 |
| 18 | INT CHURCH SOCIAL HALL - STAIRWELL - Day 1<br>Sydnor runs up the last flight of stairs | 1/8 pgs.<br>Sharp Street - 1206 Etting St. (b/t Dolphin & Lafayette Sts.) | 17 |
| 20 | EXT CHURCH SOCIAL HALL - ROOFTOP / POV OF HIGH-RISE - Day 1<br>Sydnor reaches the roof and spots Stinkum; He phones Freamon | 1/8 pgs.<br>Sharp Street - 1206 Etting St. (b/t Dolphin & Lafayette Sts.) | 17, 41 |
| 21pt | INT DETAIL OFFICE - WIRETAP ROOM - Day 1<br>Freamon gets a call from Sydnor; He monitors Stinkum's conversation | 2/8 pgs.<br>Stage - 3711 E. Monument Street | 15 |
| 22 | EXT CHURCH SOCIAL HALL - ROOFTOP / POV OF HIGH-RISE - Day 1<br>Sydnor observes Stinkum | 1/8 pgs.<br>Sharp Street - 1206 Etting St. (b/t Dolphin & Lafayette Sts.) | 17, 41 |
| 23 | INT HOMICIDE OFFICE - Day 1<br>Santangelo struggles w/ his case;Landsman gives him Madame LaRue's card | 1 5/8 pgs.<br>Police Headquarters Set - 100 N. Charles Street, 5th FL | 25, 28, 42 |
| 24 | EXT AMITY STREET / WEST BALTIMORE - Day 1<br>McNulty & Bunk recanvass the Gant crime scene | 1 2/8 pgs.<br>Stoddard Lane (b/t Druid Hill Ave. & McCulloh St.) | 1, 5, 29 |
| 25 | INT DISTRICT COURT - COURTROOM - Day 1<br>Greggs helps to get Johnny off on probation | 3 pgs.<br>110 N. Calvert St. (b/t Fayette & Lexington Sts.), 4th FL | 4, 11, 32, 38, 55, 58 |
| 26 | INT LOW-RISE PROJECTS - RESIDENT'S APARTMENT - Day 1<br>McNulty & Bunk question the Resident about the Gant murder | 1 6/8 pgs.<br>1012 Stoddard Lane (b/t Druid Hill Ave. & McCulloh St.) | 1, 5, 29 |
| 27 | EXT AMITY STREET / WEST BALTIMORE - Day 1<br>Bunk & McNulty feel that they have good evidence on Bird | 4/8 pgs.<br>Stoddard Lane (b/t Druid Hill Ave. & McCulloh St.) | 1, 5 |
| 28 | INT DETAIL OFFICE - Day 1<br>The unit joyfully processes Johnson & the drugs; Prez recognizes Johnson | 6/8 pgs.<br>Stage - 3711 E. Monument Street | 2, 12, 13, 15, 16, 24 |
| 29 | INT DETAIL OFFICE - DANIEL'S OFFICE - Day 1<br>Prez tells Daniels who Johnson is | 3/8 pgs.<br>Stage - 3711 E. Monument Street | 2, 12, 13, 15, 16, 24 |

I knew a prosecutor named Eileen Nathan who worked on a lot of murder cases. I met her when I was doing the *Homicide* book and put some of her pragmatism and demeanor into Rhonda Pearlman [Deirdre Lovejoy]. But Rhonda Pearlman was also a combination of other things, including traits that Deirdre brought. There were no female detectives on the shift I was on, but Bertina Silver was a female detective in the homicide unit on the other shift. I didn't know her as well as I would have liked, but I did talk to her at times about what it was like to be the only woman left in the unit, and I brought some of that into early scenes involving Greggs.

But to be honest, a lot of the narrative for Greggs came from stuff that male police had delivered for us in my memory. I think she talks about the time she had to wrestle a suspect down when she was a rookie, and a veteran cop basically hands her the handcuffs when she's finally got the guy subdued. She feels like she's arrived. But that was a story that [Baltimore detective] Gary Childs gave me about Charlie Smoot, a veteran cop who helped break him in. So it was a true story that I basically borrowed from a male cop. In truth, I don't think we wrote the women as caricatures, but we were definitely writing a male-oriented world. It was a world where there could be girlfriends of gangsters, but there were no

female gangsters in the organized Baltimore drug culture. And many of the aggressive street police in the districts or in the plainclothes units who were women were openly lesbians. Two or three of them come to mind.

**You mentioned the street culture of Baltimore City, so we should talk about Snoop actress Felicia Pearson and how she joined the show. Felicia had been a drug dealer on the streets of Baltimore and served time in prison for second-degree murder. Despite having no prior acting experience, she stood out on *The Wire* and became one of the most popular characters in the series.**

She's *sui generis*. When she came to us as Snoop, we wrote toward the character that she presented. We wrote a few scenes to see what she could do with them and how the camera addressed itself to her, and then we knew how to write a little bit more. By the end, I thought we were in the pocket of who our fictional version of Snoop was. Not to say that it was the real Snoop, but we certainly wrote it as a young woman who was out as a lesbian. Her character was someone who had come up hard, so she sounded like someone who had come up in East Baltimore would sound. It was like a tape loop where she was reading our words, and we were listening to her read our words, and she was changing our words, and our words were changing her. That was just a very symbiotic relationship.

**Did her unique circumstances create any additional challenges? Was it difficult integrating her into the production culture, or did she just naturally glom onto it?**

No, she had to work hard. In the beginning, we let her read scenes and then ad lib a lot. Then there came a moment—I guess it was the beginning of season four, with that scene in the hardware store—where she had to read a metaphor for the whole season. So I very much wanted her to stay on book and read the words I had written. And I said to her, "Okay, you want to be an actor? The time for us giving you a lot of leeway about your lines is over. You know, you have a week and a half, two weeks, to study this big scene that's going to begin the season. The reason you have to say the words the way we want them is that it's a very explicit analogy, a metaphor for what we're trying to say about education with the whole season. It needs to come out just as it is on the page, so go to work."

And she was a little bit doubtful about her own abilities, but I think Gbenga [Akinnagbe, who played Snoop's partner-in-crime, Chris Partlow] read lines with her and got her to the point where she was going to get it.

I remember she came off set that day exhilarated because she had done something she felt like she hadn't done before when we introduced her in season three. It was a growth process for her, and I was very proud of her and the work she did, and how committed she was to it. But I think she even surprised herself in the beginning, because she had not been trained as an actor and was just trying to be in the moment. And part of being in the moment for her was getting to say things her way. Sometimes, at a certain point, the writer has to insist on the writing, and that was a big moment for her. I was very proud of her that day. She got there.

**The Wire managed to walk a tightrope between the gritty and the refined. And that generally has a lot to do with the directors of photography. Were the DPs given the freedom to come up with the visual palette of the show, or were you more hands-on in defining the cinematographic elements of the show?**

The credit for the original palette belongs to the late Bob Colesberry [executive producer of *The Wire*]. He picked the DP, Uta Briesewitz, who is magnificent. Her camera movements are so delicate and smart and languid and directed, and she did a few things with the camera that I'll never forget. She had this German camera system called the Panther, which she operated herself—she understood that system so well and made it work beautifully. There's one scene where she basically delivered a 360 from the Panther and ducked out of the way of the shot at the last minute. In the scene, McNulty is at a phone booth and sees Stringer coming to the block, so he turns back to the phone booth, and then he comes the other way as Stringer passes him. It's a magnificent move, and you don't see her. There were a dozen moments like that. . . .

Now, the visual template of the show was created by Bob Colesberry. I wanted to shoot 16mm, because I'd shot it at home, and you move faster—well, at the time you did. What I didn't understand was that 35mm was becoming easier and more mobile. I didn't want to lay a lot of track; I wanted to shoot fast. I like the guerrilla style of *Homicide*, but that was all I knew. And Bob was like, "No, we can shoot this 35mm. This can be much more filmic and still feel like the streets." And he was right, so that was the template we had.

There came a moment after Bob died, after season two, when I realized I was going to have to step up, be on set more, and think more about shot composition, as well as performance and dialogue. It was an adjustment. Before that, I'd been there for performance and words, while Bob worried about shot composition and coverage. Then suddenly Bob was gone. There was a moment during the shooting of the first episode of season three when I saw us settling into a director's choice that I couldn't abide. And I had to think hard about the fact that something was bothering me about the shot, or what I was being left with in terms of a shot choice and that I needed more coverage in a certain way. But I didn't have the vocabulary to explain myself like somebody who'd been to film school. Still, I knew what was wrong, and I knew what I needed to make it right.

I explained it to the director at the time, and he got me the extra shots. Later, somebody in the camera unit came up to me and said, "So you've read *Hitchcock* by François Truffaut," and I said, "What?" But then I went back and read those interviews [between Alfred Hitchcock and Truffaut] and realized I had internalized those principles just from being on set on *Homicide* and from the first couple of years of *The Wire*, from *The Corner*, and from watching Bob. I had a sense for what worked and what didn't,

and what was bothering me was that the camera knew too much. The camera move was not being motivated by the actions of the characters on screen. The camera move was the filmmaker knowing too much and chasing it. [Characters would be] squatting, talking, making a plan in an alley. Then the character standing over them had a clever line, and the camera went up to catch the clever line. And I realized the issue: How did the camera know that Herc was about to say something? Or that it was worth listening to?

And I said, "No, at that point, you have to be in for coverage. You can't fish for it. You have to cut." Well, that's Hitchcock and Truffaut. That's them talking about what creates suspense. So I looked through the monitor and started to realize that I could have more of an impact—and that I had to, because Bob was gone. That was sort of transformational. But the template belonged to Bob. And after that, we were just chasing it. We were just trying not to fall off the wagon as he had structured it.

**Did the production design team face any specific challenges when re-creating the look of a battered urban landscape? Or were they just able to find the right locations because of Baltimore's urban blight?**

A little of both. I think we didn't get enough credit for how much design was involved because it had such a documentarian feel; people thought we just turned on the cameras and filmed—but that's not the case. I think they may have also assumed that about the actors, the performances. But no, there was more effort than that.

That said, Baltimore did have block after block of urban blight. But the city falls down more beautifully than any other place I've ever been in, save for possibly a couple of quarters of New Orleans. I say that as a Baltimore resident with a sense of the tragedy involved. There's a lot of heartbreak when you point your camera at some places in Baltimore, but it's sort of a beautiful heartbreak in a weird way.

**You've said there were some people within the new political infrastructure of Baltimore City who were unhappy with the show. With the passage of time, have any of your old detractors changed their position or reached out to you with words of praise about what you were able to accomplish?**

No, no. The people who got what we were doing got what we were doing, and the people who didn't get what we were doing were convinced of the surety of their position. But I also think some measure of the opposition had to do with people having different agendas. And the developers I knew were very upset about the show. We were not making it easy for them to flip real estate in Baltimore City. The people who wanted to be credited with having created miracles where no miracles had occurred must have been very disappointed with our narrative. As for the people who were drug warriors—we were never going to get these people to agree that we were arguing for anything.

TOP LEFT "Murdaland" graffiti created by *The Wire*'s art department, led by art director Halina Gebarowicz.

TOP RIGHT Baltimore City Hall, where much of *The Wire*'s political skulduggery takes place.

To them, we were just entertainers who were trading off Baltimore's struggles. We were trying to have a political argument about what had gone wrong, and we were never going to convince those people that we were earnest because we weren't helping them. And by "them" I don't mean their hopes for the city, because I think time has proved us correct: I don't think the city gets appreciably better or reaches that next stage of progress until you actually assess the problems for what they are and begin to address them. And we haven't done that in Baltimore, which is why we're in the place we're in now, twenty years later.

When I say their agendas were not ours, I don't want to suggest that they can claim that their agenda was a better Baltimore. They were there. They had come there ostensibly to do good, but really they were there to stay and do well for themselves. So no, I never reached that point where somebody came to me and said, "I get what you're doing now, I get why, and you know, sorry I tried to stand in front of your trucks." That has never happened.

**How did Method Man, aka Clifford Smith Jr., from Wu-Tang Clan end up in *The Wire*?**

He read. And that's it. He was on a tape with twenty other auditions, and he read really well. At the time, a lot of rappers would basically have their agents call us and say, "So-and-so is ready to be on your show." We'd let them know that so-and-so needs to get to a casting agent and read if they're going to be an actor. I don't give a fuck how many records you've sold. I need to know if the camera can work with you and if you can work with a page.

So I had this tape with twenty-five actors on it reading for the part of [Melvin] "Cheese" [Wagstaff]. Obviously it said "Method," and I was aware of Wu-Tang Clan, and I thought, "Well, that's cool." But he was also good enough to call back. And when we called him back, he was good enough to be the best in the room. And that's a level of professionalism that people will probably not credit Cliff with. They'll probably look at it and go, "He gets to do what he wants because, you know, Wu-Tang Clan." But the truth was, he took the game very seriously and very

BOTTOM Clifford Smith Jr. (*center*), aka Method Man, meets with fans while shooting scenes as Melvin "Cheese" Wagstaff on location in Baltimore. To Smith's left is Perry Blackmon, the show's security supervisor who also played Barksdale bodyguard Perry in the show.

professionally. It's why we cast him again in *The Deuce*—because I knew I had an actor there.

**My favorite scene is in the final episode, when Cheese is screaming and howling about Baltimore and then gets shot by Slim Charles.**

Yeah, let's credit Cliff with that because [originally] he got popped without venting. He got popped a little quicker than that by Slim Charles, and he was like, "Come on, man, after all this time you got to give Cheese his due." And he called me up. It was the only time I ever got a note from him. He was like, "I see how I'm going out, and I'm going out as a punk, and I can act that, but you got to give me a little to work with." And I said, "All right, let me take a look at it." Then I sat down and wrote that little speech that gets interrupted. And when I went to set that day, he was like, "Now I can chew on this, you know?" And he was right. That scene got a lot better because he gave me a note.

And understand that that was his last day of work, and it was the only time he came to us and gave us a note. I love Cliff. I feel like I got to watch him become an actor, and he got to watch me become a TV producer, all in the same breath.

**There are so many characters in the show that viewers can relate to in different ways. What do you think happened to some of these characters ten-plus years down the line? For example, did you envision McNulty landing somewhere else as a cop or private investigator?**

I don't know. I mean, there have been other universes to visit since we finished *The Wire*, and everyone's like, "Oh, can you spin this off? Can you do this? Can do that?" You can do anything. But there are so many other worlds to depict and political arguments to make that I've never actually sat down face-to-page and seriously considered any other endings. I know that when we realize that McNulty and Freamon were out of the police department, that was a level of skill—of investigative skill—that was off the page now. I thought those two motherfuckers would make a great detective agency. There were little moments where I thought it would be funny to play them as private investigators.

But the idea was that 80 percent of their cases were either matrimonial or industrial. So it was all like a misery for both of them. They couldn't give a fuck. Like, whenever they got one that was interesting, it was like, "We can stop drinking for a little bit." Especially McNulty. McNulty doesn't have his pension, so he has to do more for the money. Freamon can be a little more of a dilettante because he has his police pension intact. It might be fun to do that, but the reality of having other storylines and other universes to create, having that be effectively more important, at least in terms of the message, I don't think I ever seriously considered going back to explore those options. I never got around to it, anyway, to writing a word.

And as far as where everybody else ended up, there's a certain amount of the city that stays the same. It's sort of built into the DNA of the show.

**What are your thoughts on the evolution of television as a medium in the current streaming environment? Where do you think things are going to go? Will there still be space for stories like *The Wire*?**

If you're asking me if TV got better, I don't think so. I think there's more of it. There's more really good TV. More good TV narratives. There's more middling TV narratives. And there's more shit. The best thing I can say about it is that it's hungry for more content, so more people are working, and the chance of somebody who has a good idea finding purchase and being funded is good. Now, as for the chances of them getting a huge audience and breaking out from the field of other programming, well . . . people find shows over time. Which makes the current streaming climate more of a lending library than appointment television. I think that's harder and harder. I mean, the numbers you see for the average cable show are minuscule compared to what it was when there were three or four networks.

When I was working on *Homicide*, we were getting twelve and thirteen shares on a Friday night. And we were a mess. They were like, "Why can't you beat *Nash Bridges*?" We were in third place at NBC, and they were not happy with us. That was a twelve share. In the fractured TV universe of today, a twelve share would be like an astonishing hit. It beats *M\*A\*S\*H*.

But it's that fracturing that has allowed idiosyncratic television that isn't relatable in Nielsen ratings to be made. In contrast, buzz is related to: How long do viewers keep talking about your show? How many months or years afterward do they pull it from the shelf and keep watching it? And how long does it drive some of their subscription base? And that's a much better model for people like me, because I'm never writing a hit, and I know it. So if it can be a lending library, I've got a shot of doing this kind of work. But the moment it goes back to Nielsen ratings, I'm fucked.

**It's been twenty years since the show premiered. What do you believe or what would you like the ultimate legacy of *The Wire* to be?**

Years ago, I was asked, "What did I want people to say about the show?" We were still on the air at the time, so I'm wondering if it still holds, but I said, "I would like it said that we didn't lie." Because everything in TV drama is a shortened, heightened way of telling a story. You know reality is often anti-drama, but we're dealing in a place where an inordinate amount of lies have been told to the American public when it comes to American dramas.

First of all, most dramas are not about the other America—the America that got left behind. They're about hyperbolized America where great evil and great good are battling, and things are blowing up—or it's a half-hour comedy, or the shows have an earnestness and simplicity like *Father Knows Best* and *The West Wing*. I mean, we really were writing a show about what had gone wrong in our little city of Baltimore. Ed had policed it, I'd covered it. Zorzi had covered it. These novelists that we hired had been writing about it in other cities. We wanted to have an argument—a political argument—so if we lied about what we had in front of us, we would've wasted the opportunity.

HBO gave us a remarkable sinecure and left us alone. So we felt the last thing we should do is waste the opportunity. We wanted to have a political argument. If we started from a premise of making a hyperbolic version of Baltimore, or solving problems by having people be larger than the problems, or by having our heroes and villains be larger than the system, then we would've wasted a rare opportunity. Years ago, when they asked, "What do you want people to say?" I said: that we didn't lie—that we came to it as people from Baltimore who wanted to say, "This is what's gone wrong, and this is why." I think that still holds up. Certainly, I'm not saying we got everything right. I'm just saying we weren't lying. If we got something wrong, it was because we didn't know any better.

TOP (*Left to right*) Baltimore cops Herc (Domenick Lombardozzi), Sydnor (Corey Parker Robinson), Kima (Sonja Sohn), and Carver (Seth Gilliam).

# SONJA SOHN

## Interview by Nikki Stafford and Robert Thompson

A former slam poet, Sonja Sohn began her acting career in award-winning 1998 indie film *Slam*. After parts in films including *Bringing Out the Dead* (1999), directed by Martin Scorsese, and action remake *Shaft* (2000), Sohn landed the key role of Detective Shakima "Kima" Greggs in *The Wire*. She appeared in all five seasons as the hard-nosed, openly gay officer.

**How did the role in *The Wire* come to you in the first place?**

The opportunity comes in through your folks. My manager sent me the appointment, and I thought the character, a lesbian detective, was very interesting. I was more concerned about playing a cop than I was about playing a lesbian—it was going to take some work on my part to embody that. And that was a challenge, but as actors, we like challenges.

**Many police roles are one-dimensional, but Kima has more elements to her backstory. She's a more rounded character than the standard police officer in a show.**

Right. And she had more of a story than some of the other cops. We don't get a close look at the other cops. Until Carver, for instance, strikes up that

relationship with Randy [in season four], we don't go home with the other cops. So Kima's story was important and exciting.

**Did you know that your character was originally going to be killed at the end of the first season?**

No! There's a whole story about it. It was my first show, so I didn't know how it worked. You sign these five-year contracts, and you think you have a job as a series regular. But the day before I was supposed to shoot my last scene in the pilot, Melanie Nicholls-King, who played my partner, came into town.

She said she heard that my character was going to be killed off in the final episode. And that just stopped me in my tracks. She said, "Oh, you didn't know?" Like, "Oops!" And I was like, "No!" So I went down to the set to discuss this with David Simon, but

OPPOSITE Sonja Sohn as Kima.

TOP Kima (Sohn, *left*) at home with her partner, Cheryl (Melanie Nicholls-King, *right*), and their baby boy.

luckily I went through the makeup trailer first and met with Debi Young [makeup department head on *The Wire*].

Debi is the spiritual godmother of the show. [The artists in the] hair and makeup trailer are the people you see every morning, and they're an incredible team effort. You can't just show up on the set and get your job done. The people in those trailers are really important: They support your efforts and your excellence. Debi did that for everybody on set. She taught me the impact of people in those positions.

So when I wandered through the trailer on my way to David, she told me, "Listen, that's something you heard. This is just the pilot. Nobody knows what's happening. Don't get ahead of yourself."

I hold on to my principles very tightly. I'm very radical in terms of my feelings about capitalism, materialism, vanity, and all of that. That's the biggest challenge to being in this business: I must be careful about holding principles too tightly because they will sink me. And Debi prevented that from happening. She kept me from questioning David and the script.

I was asking, "What is this? What's the intention here? Where are we going? I need to know!" But I grew over the years to realize that it was the most magnificent, glorious intention that could be poured into the show. For a police drama! The intention was so high.

**The writing and the language are so important to *The Wire*. Did you have a sense of the larger vision from the start?**

Not until a few episodes in, once I had a chance to see the compassion in the depiction of the people from the street. It was so refreshing to me; it warmed my heart. I wasn't from Baltimore, but I was familiar with that kind of life. They're people I've known. My brother was involved in those kinds of activities as a young man. So it just made sense to me. I was able to fully buy in.

I think that some of us were feeling that on some level. This is a good crew. There was magic. We connected as people and bonded during that pilot. And that hasn't happened on any other project I've been on since.

Dom West and Wendell Pierce were so friendly and outgoing, too, and that really made a difference.

**You've been very involved in social activism. It's been twenty years since *The Wire* started, and one could make an argument that nothing has changed or that things are in fact worse than they were. Are you surprised that the social structure that *The Wire* portrays over those five seasons is essentially untouched all these years later?**

I do believe I disagree with that on some level. I understand what the stats say, but when I walk through Baltimore today, I see the difference. The

TOP Kima (Sonja Sohn, *left*), Sydnor (Corey Parker Robinson, *center*), and McNulty (Dominic West, *right*). Kima often works closely with McNulty on the Barksdale case.

OPPOSITE TOP Sonja Sohn (*center*) during shooting of season one's, "The Buys," in which the Baltimore police department raids the Barksdale organization's operation at the Pit. Also pictured (*left to right*): Lance Reddick as Lieutenant Cedric Daniels, Corey Parker Robinson, Seth Gilliam, and Michael Salconi as Officer Michael Santangelo.

OPPOSITE BOTTOM The prop ID badge for Kima used in the show.

number of Black-owned restaurants has increased, and they're not all on Pennsylvania Avenue selling just lake trout and pit beef. Young people run that city now. The Baltimore Children & Youth Fund is a million-dollar fund that was developed because young Black activists in the city forced the city to create it and divvy it out to organizations. And charter schools are exploring creative ways of educating kids. We don't see the results yet—the numbers aren't there yet—but Baltimore isn't the same place it was when I was there.

And I'm part of that. I'm participating in the emerging Baltimore. There is a Black arts district on Pennsylvania Avenue that has gotten a national historic registration. Wendell and Clarke told us about the talent that used to come through and perform at the Royal Theater there. So we—myself, Andre Royo, Jamie Hector—started imagining what we could do and asking questions. Why is all the money down in the harbor? Why aren't they developing this? We're asking these questions in our downtime. What is going on in this neighborhood while the harbor is glistening?

But now we're speaking with the next generation. There's a young woman who is probably in her early thirties who was just twelve years old when *The Wire* first aired. And now she's leading the effort with the neighborhood folks, bringing in funding to redevelop it and build a big arts center. And some of us are going to be a part of the fundraising effort. That's what's different.

## So that suggests to you that there is more hope coming out of Baltimore now?

Absolutely! Look at the talent you have coming out now! D. Watkins is writing on *We Own This City*, and he's a son of Baltimore. One of the things I really respect about David Simon is that he's able to live according to his principles and do this job. Which means he employed people in this city. I know people in Baltimore who became a part of the *Wire* machine, whose lives were changed—because that's what [David] wanted! He could have moved to LA. But that's what you do when you care about a place: You stay rooted; you build it up and help it evolve.

Through the job, I think I found a calling. I had no idea this show was going to resonate so many years into the future and bring me back to Baltimore after I left. I had no idea I was going to be so impacted and feel so connected. Now, through being on that show, I'm showing up for something much bigger than an acting job in my life. And I'm grateful for that.

The Wire

Greggs'
ID Badge
TV PROPS
0507

#181890

BALTIMORE POLICE DEPARTMENT

NAME: SHAKIMA GREGGS
TITLE: DETECTIVE
DIVISION: NARCOTICS
DISTRICT: C.I.D.

# THE WIRE SEASON ONE: AN ACT OF WITNESSING

by Siddhant Adlakha

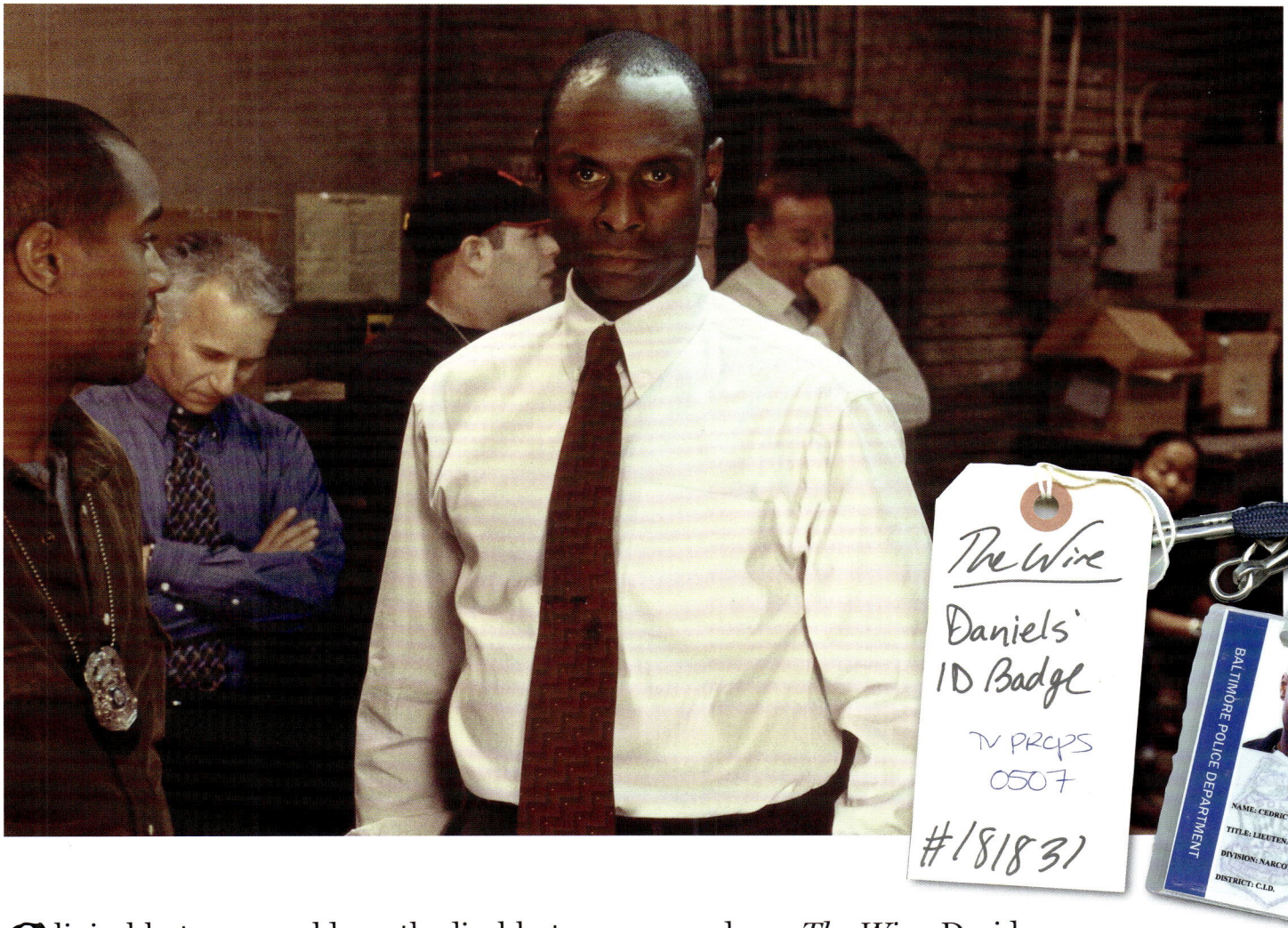

*The Wire*
*Daniels'*
*ID Badge*
TV PROPS
0507
#181831

BALTIMORE POLICE DEPARTMENT
NAME: CEDRIC DANIELS
TITLE: LIEUTENANT
DIVISION: NARCOTICS
DISTRICT: C.I.D.

**C**linical but never cold; methodical but never mundane: *The Wire*, David Simon's television magnum opus, is always exacting, even when it captures events unfurling at a distance. This visual approach is twofold. It occurs when its lead characters are the dramatic subjects of a scene: Cops or drug dealers often argue in enclosed rooms, framed in relaxed medium shots that allow for easier parsing of the information they discuss. It also occurs when the faces and bodies captured on screen are the objects (and objectives) of those subjects, filmed from rooftops and behind tinted car windows from across the street, as their actions are voyeuristically observed and recorded for later use. The first season, as the show's title suggests, is about surveillance, and in many of its scenes, people are the information. But while these two aforementioned visual modes—which keep the audience at arm's length—are the show's dominant lingua franca, they're occasionally interrupted by piercing close-ups and moments of intense subjectivity. When stitched together, these two opposing methods result in dramatic precision.

OPPOSITE Stringer Bell (Idris Elba) attends court in "The Target," the first episode of *The Wire*.

TOP Lance Reddick as the ambitious, no-nonsense lieutenant Cedric Daniels.

INSET The prop ID badge created for the Daniels character.

TOP McNulty (Dominic West, *left*), D'Angelo (Lawrence Gilliard Jr., *center*), and Bunk (Wendell Pierce, *right*) at the Pit.

ABOVE Herc (Domenick Lombardozzi) on left and Carver (Seth Gilliam) on right stake out the Barksdales.

OPPOSITE TOP LEFT McNulty (West) attends a court hearing.

OPPOSITE TOP RIGHT A prop ID badge for McNulty.

OPPOSITE BOTTOM Michael B. Jordan as ill-fated corner boy Wallace.

The very first shot of *The Wire* (in the pilot episode "The Target," directed by Clark Johnson and photographed by Uta Briesewitz) hovers over a trail of blood. It's illuminated both by dim streetlamps cutting through the night air and by the flashing lights of nearby police cars, before the episode switches to a more languid and conversational scene in which Detective James "Jimmy" McNulty (Dominic West) questions a witness. Without wasting a second, the visual language of classic cinema—of wordless evocations of mood, time, and place—transitions toward that of classic television, of stories told through dialogue. But the show's stylistic journey isn't as simple as juggling two different forms of popular entertainment. Before long, its first season becomes a volatile balancing act between visual storytelling and two other vital kinds of information that form the series' bedrock: journalism and surveillance.

While the two mediums have markedly different functions in the public sphere—at least in the United States, whose Constitution guarantees a nominal freedom of the press—their overlap as narrative tools is something *The Wire* frequently wields to its advantage. They are, in an idealistic sense, "objective" in the ways they convey information. As confidential informant Bubbles might say: There's a thin line between them.

*The Wire* is, in essence, about the act of witnessing—about what is seen, and, perhaps just as important, what often can't be seen. The plot of its first thirteen episodes, in which an underdog police task force spies on a ragtag group of drug dealers in Baltimore's projects, finds its forward momentum via snippets of information gathered from phone calls and snapped through long camera lenses. There are moments in which the audience sees the world through these still cameras, with just enough

The Wire
McNulty's
ID Badge
TV PROPS
0507
#181808

BALTIMORE POLICE DEPARTMENT

NAME: JAMES McNULTY

TITLE: DETECTIVE

DIVISION: HOMICIDE

DISTRICT: C.I.D.

shaky movement (from the show's 35mm film camera) to make the viewer feel as if they're in control of what, and who, is being seen. This floating, handheld approach appears and reappears, not only when criminals are seen through the eyes of observant detectives—the likes of Kima Greggs (Sonja Sohn), Thomas "Herc" Hauk (Domenick Lombardozzi), and Ellis Carver (Seth Gilliam)—but from supposedly more objective points of view, which are untethered from any one character's perspective. For example, early in episode one, the camera watches McNulty and the elusive kingpin Stringer Bell seated calmly in a courtroom, its long lens peering in on them from a distance, as if hidden away somewhere behind the judge's bench.

These images are the "facts": They portray character dynamics that are publicly or semi-publicly seen and are then meticulously recorded as the police build their case. What the police do not see, however, are the moments fear and self-reflection appear on the faces of lower-level lieutenants like D'Angelo Barksdale (Lawrence Gilliard Jr.), a young man recently released from prison, and his optimistic sixteen-year-old drug runner Wallace (Michael B. Jordan), as they wrestle with what the drug game, and the resulting violence, does to their souls. These are intimate moments, not heard through words, but felt in one's bone marrow.

These moments are best exemplified by a perturbing visual contrast in the Clement Virgo–directed fourth episode, "Old Cases" (during which *The Wire* arguably goes from a good show to a truly great one). In this chapter of the story, the plot's pieces finally begin falling into place, as McNulty and his partner William "Bunk" Moreland (Wendell Pierce) investigate an unsolved murder

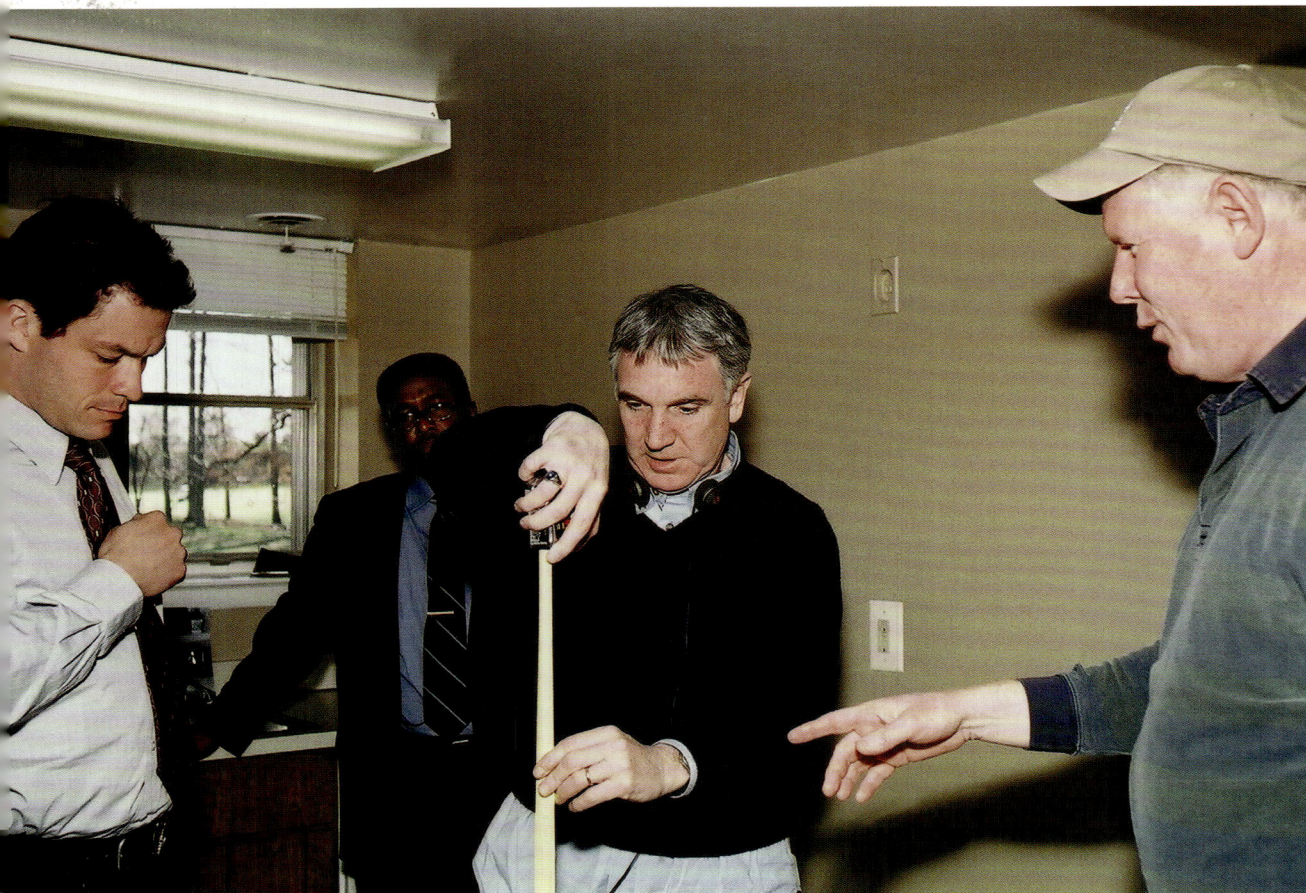

that may or may not be connected to D'Angelo. On the one hand, the two cops retrace the grisly crime scene, laying out and reconsidering each clue while they converse using only a pair of profanities—"fuck" and "motherfucker," spoken in different tones each time they're uttered—as the camera hangs back and captures their comfort not only with each other, but also with bloodshed and bodies. On the other hand, when D'Angelo has his masculine bona fides jokingly questioned by his subordinates, he begins to regale Wallace, Poot, and Bodie with a recollection of that very same killing. And while the show eventually reveals that it was not his doing (though he was forced to witness it), his narration serves a distinct spiritual purpose: He wants desperately to command respect, even if it means boasting about a murder he didn't commit.

As D'Angelo tells his tale, the camera enters a slow and steady dolly zoom, a hyper-calculated yet deeply subjective technique popularized by cinematic masters like Steven Spielberg and Alfred Hitchcock. The background shifts further into view without changing D'Angelo's position in the frame; the space around him seems to morph and expand, but it leaves him feeling more diminutive—lonelier and more childlike—with each passing second. In both reconstructions of this murder—the cops' clinical examination and D'Angelo's chilling recollections—the spoken words clash wildly with the visual mood of each scene. Were one to transcribe either sequence in the vein of a surveillance log, the text alone would thoroughly fail to capture the subtext and humanity unearthed by the camera. The key difference between the two scenes, however, is that the cops are men who can afford to behave like boys, given the long rope provided to them by their institutions, while D'Angelo is a boy who wants, and needs, to be seen as a man, because it's the only way he'll climb the

TOP LEFT Shooting the "fuck" sequence: Dominic West and Wendell Pierce stand by as Robert F. Colesberry (*center*) and Ed Burns (*right*) block out the scene.

OPPOSITE McNulty (West, *left*) and Bunk (Pierce, *right*) in the "fuck" scene with case file photographs strewn across the floor.

ranks of his uncle's organization and survive. But as the frame contorts around him, it leaves him looking and feeling like a helpless child crying out for comfort.

From their positions of authority, McNulty and Bunk can afford to casually reconstruct events and motives, blissfully unaware of who D'Angelo is and what he's going through, beyond the snippets of factual evidence in their thin beige folders. This duality of perspective isn't limited to either side of the law. For instance, all McNulty knows about his new teammate, Lester Freamon (Clarke Peters), are the facts: that he belongs to the low-stress, low-activity pawn shop unit of Baltimore PD, and that he keeps to himself. Yet when Freamon's methods of crime-solving prove to be quick and effective, the camera punches in on a lingering close-up of McNulty—the kind of close up often reserved for the likes of D'Angelo—as the brash detective comes to a silent understanding of Freamon's unassuming facade, and the wisdom it conceals. It's during moments like

"...the two cops retrace the grisly crime scene, laying out and reconsidering each clue while they converse using only a pair of profanities..."

these that one of *The Wire*'s central questions comes to the surface: How much can we really glean from factual details?

Although *The Wire* is about American institutions on the surface — from police, to government, to education, to journalism—it's really about the way people behave when the walls of those institutions surround them from all sides. While its first season depicts the ins and outs of police wiretapping, the story it tells takes a more top-down view of the act of surveillance: It surveils surveillance itself, as it were, embodying the age-old question of "*Quis custodiet ipsos custodes*?"—who watches the watchers?

Season one captures not only the act of seeing, but also the act of being seen, as characters like Bell and his partner Avon Barksdale grow increasingly concerned about the way their methods are being deciphered by the police. Their subsequent hyperawareness and the way they tiptoe around conversations are befitting of the era, both as an extension of fears about technological surveillance as cell phones grew more prominent, and, as a perspective presaging the US PATRIOT Act of 2001. The first episode, though conceived before the September 11 attacks, was shot two weeks afterward and correctly predicted that the FBI's focus on counterterrorism would leave the war on drugs wanting for resources.

*The Wire* may not have been a response to subsequent invasions of privacy, but its grounding in existent real-world paranoia allows it to function as a time capsule. In the season's latter half, the drug ring's

OPPOSITE TOP Defense attorney Maurice "Maury" Levy (Michael Kostroff, *left*) advises his clients Stringer Bell (Idris Elba, *center*) and Avon Barksdale (Wood Harris, *right*).

OPPOSITE BOTTOM Freamon (Clarke Peters, *left*), Kima (Sonja Sohn, *center*), and Prez (Jim True-Frost, *right*) work the Barksdale case.

BELOW Wallace (Michael B. Jordan, *left*) and D'Angelo (Lawrence Gilliard Jr., *right*) at the Pit.

BOTTOM Levy (Kostroff, *left*) defends D'Angelo (Gilliard, *right*) at trial. Actor Michael Kostroff is the brother of *The Wire* producer Nina K. Noble.

TOP All the pieces matter: Sydnor (Corey Parker Robinson, *left*), Freamon (Clarke Peters, *seated*), and Herc (Domenick Lombardozzi, *right*) close in on the Barksdales.

OPPOSITE BOTTOM At the Pit: (*left to right*) Wallace (Michael B. Jordan), Poot (Tray Chaney), D'Angelo (Lawrence Gilliard Jr.), and Bodie (J. D. Williams).

PAGES 60-61 D'Angelo (Lawrence Gilliard Jr., *left*) and Stringer (Idris Elba, *right*), a relationship that will end in betrayal and murder.

upper crust don't merely find themselves on the run, but they also find themselves questioning every comrade, every cell phone and pager, and even every wall, as their eyes begin shifting around each room with suspicion—a logical extension of discussions in earlier episodes where they establish a litany of "rules" to evade prying eyes and ears. Their own rules have failed them, and the police have closed in, leaving them feeling unmoored.

Each season of *The Wire* reaches such a point eventually, where structures—legal or otherwise—fail each character, leaving them in the wind, as the camera discards its distant approach in favor of something more traditionally "cinematic" via close-ups, creeping pans across lateral space, and slow push-ins that box the characters in. It is in these moments that the tension between different forms of "truth" becomes most overt: the "objective" truths, or the narratives strung together by words, and the "subjective" truths, conveyed through silent moments of haunting realization. Despite the contrasting natures of these truths—the former based in facts and observations, the latter in opinions and interpretations— *The Wire* rarely leaves the "subjective" in dispute, given the show's distinct emotional clarity: In moments of contemplation, the camera imbues such scenes with unambiguous meaning. Meanwhile, "objective" narratives, as told by police, reporters, and politicians, are framed as extensions of characters themselves; records are frequently massaged to suit personal and political goals.

In the first season, D'Angelo Barksdale is the lynchpin around whom the surveillance unit's case is initially built, and through whose words and actions they're able to unveil the entire Franklin Terrace drug operation. This place D'Angelo occupies in the plot helps establish *The Wire* as an intricate exploration of police and political machinery. But D'Angelo is also the season's emotional centerpiece, around whom the camera slowly pivots as vital plot points unfold. His conflicted conscience— which remains unreflected in the police unit's reports and recordings— is what establishes the show as an emotional powerhouse, rife with moments that draw the viewer in, well past its police procedural surface and into the conscience of its characters. It offers a peek into the ways Baltimore's men, women, and even children are defined not just by the slivers of their lives entered into public records—criminal, journalistic, or otherwise—but by corrosive circumstances that constantly challenge their morality.

D'Angelo's young drug runner Wallace, for instance, is rattled by the crimes in which he's forced to participate, including the violent, homophobic slaying of the thief Brandon Wright (Michael Kevin Darnall). When Brandon is killed, the frame doesn't depict his final moments, but instead cuts to the computer screens on which the surveillance unit monitors the many calls and pager beeps used to organize his murder. The camera may capture the grisly aftermath, but it does so in a matter-of-fact manner; to the Barksdale gang, and to the Baltimore PD, Brandon's mangled body is just another statistic. The true impact of this brutality, however, is the way it impacts Wallace and turns him spiritually inside out, starting with a creeping, suffocating zoom into his nauseated expression when he discovers Brandon's corpse.

The young drug runner shows the most intellectual and emotional promise amongst his peers, but when he eventually falls victim to them— their boss Bell, having grown more paranoid, orders Wallace's execution— he becomes yet another statistic to the gang, and to the city. Of course,

"... to the Barksdale gang, and to the Baltimore PD, Brandon's mangled body is just another statistic."

Wallace also functions as an exception to this status quo; prior to his death, he crosses paths with several members of the police unit, including Lt. Cedric Daniels (Lance Reddick), who spend enough time with D'Angelo that they begin to see his potential, too—and therein lies the tragedy. They mourn not only his loss, but the casualness with which "the game" chews him up and spits him out, turning him into yet another body on the pile. So when D'Angelo famously asks Bell, "Where's Wallace?" and the camera pushes in on D'Angelo's anguish, what he's really asking for isn't a factual answer: He knows that Wallace is dead. What he seems to demand from Bell is acknowledgment. Acknowledgment that a life—a dynamic person, with heart and promise, like any one of the Terrace's children—has been cruelly snuffed out. By the end of the season, even the cops and lawyers who pursue justice in Wallace's name turn him into just another bloody photograph on the wall as they build their case; their "game" uses and discards people, too.

*The Wire*'s first season walks a fine line in its exploration of humanity. Its overarching surveillance plot necessitates frequent depictions of the cops' reductive viewpoint, where forward momentum depends heavily on information uncovered from afar—whether that information concerns Wallace, D'Angelo, Bodie, or an entire web of characters bound by poverty, racism, and lack of opportunity. But twenty years on, what stands out about these characters isn't the statistics, the factual tidbits, or the documentation of their movements. Rather, they're defined by the way the surrounding pillars of society influence their actions, and more important, by their playful camaraderie, and by the difficult conversations they have away from prying eyes—conversations in which escaping that influence and aspiring to something greater become unspoken concerns (followed, inevitably, by unspoken disappointment when reality rears its ugly head). The looks on their faces, the silent glances, are unlikely to be found in police logs. And yet, they are what linger most in the mind once each episode comes to a close.

The series, through its visual language, seems to ask: What is truth, if the mechanisms meant to unearth and define it fail to paint the whole picture? Where can the truth be found if records themselves are subject to whims, emotions, and manipulation? Can it be found in the walls, boxes, borders, and documents a society uses to define its people? Or is it found somewhere deep within the self—an intangible that, by its very nature, evades mere factual recording? Whatever the answer, *The Wire*'s camera attempts to capture truth in *all* its forms—a lofty ambition, but one at which it succeeds when its five dynamic seasons are tallied and accounted for.

# ANDRE ROYO

## Interview by Nikki Stafford and Robert Thompson

Playing troubled but kindhearted drug addict Reginald "Bubbles" Cousins across five seasons of *The Wire* gave Andre Royo the opportunity to showcase his remarkably nuanced acting skills. Known for his work in a wide variety of television projects, including roles in everything from *CSI: NY* to *Bob's Burgers*, Royo also appeared in the George Lucas-produced World War II feature *Red Tails* (2012).

**How did you land the role of Bubbles?**

I was born and raised in New York, in the Bronx. I was doing a lot of off, off, off, around the corner Broadway—a lot of theater—and I thought that was going to be the life. For a New Yorker, the idea of just stepping off the Broadway stage, going out the side, signing a couple of *Playbills*, and walking off to the bar—that was the dream.

I had just finished doing this twenty-four-hour celebrity play where I was on stage with Philip Seymour Hoffman, Julianne Moore, Benjamin Bratt . . . I kinda put my name out there and was getting a lot of love, and I was feeling great. The next day, my head was big, and I was like, "Okay, I'm on my way: I'm becoming a Broadway star." My manager, Terry Whatley, called me up and was like, "Listen, you got a baby on the way. I know you want to do theater, but HBO's got a new show coming out, and they want you

to audition." And I was like, "Oh!" HBO at that point was *Six Feet Under*, *The Sopranos, Sex and the City*, and *Oz*, so it was the heat. I was like, "Okay, I could do HBO. HBO is not beneath me." And she said, "Yeah, it's a show called *The Wire*, and it's for a character named Bubbles." And I just got pissed off. I was like, "What the fuck is that? I'm not doing it." I had like a vision of myself walking down the street blowing bubbles with goldfish in my fucking heel. I was like, "No, I'm not doing it. I find it to be disrespectful, blah blah blah." And then she started laughing. She was like, "Oh, you must have misheard me. I didn't say they wanted to give you a part. They want you to audition. They must have heard of you, but they don't know you. How about you go there, book the part, and then tell them you don't want to do it?"

And I took that as a challenge. I was like, "Oh, I'm gonna book the part." The next day I went to casting

director] Alexa Fogel's office. I'm walking in there, and I see a bunch of New York actors sitting there chewing bubble gum. I was like, "Ooh, okay," and went into the bathroom to spit out my bubble gum. It was like, "It's time to go deeper! Let's try to figure this out." And I just went in and auditioned—I think Clark Johnson, Ed Burns, and Alexa Fogel were there. I felt pretty good because I was already like, "I don't get it, I don't want it, and if I get it, I'm gonna turn it down, so this is a win-win." And I got the callback, and then I got another callback, and by the third callback, all of a sudden, I really wanted this part.

Then I got a call from Terry, and she was like, "Listen, they love you. You're the guy." And I'm like, "Yes!" But she continued, "in New York. We have to go to LA [to audition] now." I was like, "What the fuck?" But that mental shift had happened where I was like, "I gotta have this part." My manager's like, "I'll tell them you don't want it." And I was like, "Fuck off. I want this part." Later on, when I got the part and was on set, I met with Ed Burns, and he was like, "You can act, man. You have an essence about you that really reminded me of Bubbles"—and Bubbles was his police informant in real life. Man, Ed also told me that Lance Reddick, who played Lt. Daniels, had been next in line to play Bubbles if I had turned it down. He said, "Well, Lance Reddick looked more like Bubbles. Bubbles was a big guy." And I said, "Why did I get the part?" And he said, "Well, you have more of the essence of Bubbles."

that? How do I get into that level?" If I can't, then what's the point? The two movies that stuck out to me, that I looked at as a framework when beginning to create Bubbles, were *The Panic in Needle Park*, with Al Pacino, and *Lady Sings the Blues*, with Richard Pryor.

The great thing about working for HBO was that we booked the part, but I had about two months before we started shooting. I started trying to understand and to map out addiction. In Manhattan, the funniest thing you used to see was that in the winter, all the people would be outside smoking cigarettes. I was like, "That must be a hell of a fix if you have to go outside in the winter cold." I tried to think about what I did every day that I couldn't live without, and I thought about my TV. As a TV head, if you turn off the TV for a month, that TV becomes the biggest thing in the fucking living room. So I switched my TV off, and there were sporting events and shows I wanted to watch, but I was just looking at a black TV and itching to turn it on for a little bit. That got me the itch I needed. Then I went out to Baltimore, and I met Denise Francine Boyd Andrews, a former addict who they based the lead character of *The Corner* on. She was a dear friend of mine. [Andrews died on May 3, 2022.]

Fran was the reason that Bubbles came to life. Up until then, I was doing the framework. When I got to Baltimore, she took me to the underbellies, and I got to speak with like fifty to seventy-five people who were dealing with addiction. Some were heavy into it and I watched people shoot up, and some were recovering. I was trying to find, for lack of a better word, a stereotype, like, "Oh, that's the junkie in the show!" But I couldn't find it, because everybody was different. Everybody was so happy to talk to me because it was a chance for their story to be heard without judgment, and they were informing me on how to do it right.

That was the moment where I was like, look, the idea of trying to play an addict is ridiculous. Playing a human with an addiction problem is where I have to go, and all praises to Fran for that. That's what stuck in my head, and that's what helped me not fall into some cliché. It enabled me to really give Bubbles certain dimensions that I guess people hadn't seen that much before.

My mother was fucking insulted. She was like, "Why does my son have the essence of a drug dealer? What the fuck? We raised you up right!" And the rest was kind of history, because I got a chance to go down to Baltimore. It was a whole process. Ed Burns gave me his book *The Corner*, and I had to read that. At that point I was a drinker, but I didn't really know about narcotics. I grew up in the Bronx, so I knew of it, but I hadn't partaken in any of it.

**How did you research the role?**
They told me that Bubbles has been a junkie for a long time, and I was scared because all I could see was Chris Rock in *New Jack City* and Sam Jackson in fucking *Jungle Fever*, and I was like, "How do I do

OPPOSITE In the season one episode "The Detail," Bubbles (Andre Royo, *left*) puts hats on D'Angelo (Lawrence Gilliard Jr., *center*) and Poot (Tray Chaney, *right*) as a means of marking them out for the cops surveilling the Pit.

TOP Between takes, Andre Royo (*center*) spends time with Isiah Whitlock Jr. (*left*), who plays shifty Maryland senator Clay Davis, and Sydnor actor Corey Parker Robinson (*right*).

**In some ways, Bubbles ties the whole show together, because he's there the whole five seasons. He has an arc that is constantly changing, but it seems he can never get out of his circumstances, which makes him such a tragic character.**

Yeah. He also transcends all the worlds. He's probably the only character who interacts with everyone—the kids on the corners, the cops—he plays in all those worlds. But how do you evolve a character when you don't really know what the third, fourth, or fifth seasons are going to hold for Bubbles? I mean, they could have had Bubbles die partway through the series—they could have done a lot of things if they wanted to, right? [But from Bubbles' perspective,] he got up every day and wasn't worried about his arc like we were. All he wanted to do was either get high that day or try not to get high that day. That's all I had to worry about. Outside of that, I don't know where I'm going, and I don't know what's going to happen to me—that's all I can do.

After season one, David Simon told Michael K. Williams and me, "Look, you two guys are these outside characters. I'm not sure how long it's gonna last—I don't know if Bubbles and Omar are gonna make it." Michael and I used to call each other every episode, like, "We're coming back!"

And I found out that Bubbles died in real life, so I was just reading every episode waiting for that moment. And when it wasn't happening, I went up to David and Ed and was like, "I don't know if this is right. This sounds like it's a bootleg move." And David was like, "Look I've got this show full of despair, full of grief, with people just giving up. I'm looking at how this world works and how this city is being destroyed from all angles. I gotta have some hope, or nobody gets out of bed. So I think Bubbles is gonna be our light." And it was a small light, but it was [a way of saying], "We have to try our best to live our day the best way we can." So you know, I've got to give all praises and thanks to David Simon. He was real smart.

I remember once we shot a scene where Johnny [Leo Fitzpatrick] and I are stealing copper, and we did the scene perfectly. I was chilling, and then a junkie who was on set came up to me like, "That was dope!" They loved Bubbles—when I was in Bubbles' character, I was a part of the gang. But he said to me, "That was good, but you threw your cigarette butt out. We don't throw away our cigarette butts." So I went to David Simon while the grips were packing everything away and moving to the next location, and I was like, "David, yo, I need to do that scene again, because I threw away the cigarette butt." He was like, "It's probably not even in the shot." And I was like, "I don't know." And he was like, "All right, let's go back, let's shoot it." You don't tell grips and electricians to unload just to see me hold my cigarette, and they were not happy! But that's David setting the tone for all of us in front of and behind the camera. He was like, the details matter, and I'm not letting nothing go; this is about the authenticity of these people's lives. And that really seeped into all our heads.

**The last two seasons are rough for Bubbles, but the very end of the series offers some hope for him. How did you approach the conclusion of his arc?**

The fifth season was probably one of the hardest seasons for me to do because in the story, Bubbles has been clean for a year. I got scared. I was like, I don't even know what that means. Bubbles is never clean. And when I read the script for the finale, with Bubbles walking up the stairs [to be with his sister and niece], I thought it was anticlimactic. But David was like, "No, this ain't Disney, man! This is real life. You walking up the stairs is all people need, because realistically we all just want to have hope." We don't know if Bubbles is going to stay clean. We know he's clean that day. To see him walk up the stairs, that just hit home for the concept of hope, and again just added more weight to the show and to the show's meaning.

It was really great to be a part of a show that was really focused on educating, inspiring, and entertaining at the same time. And I would say I'm chasing the dragon now, looking for that same kind of opportunity.

BOTTOM Bubbles (Andre Royo, *left*) plies his trade with corner boys (*left to right*) Poot (Tray Chaney), Bodie (J. D. Williams), and Little Kevin (Tyrell Baker).

# DEBI YOUNG

## Interview by Chris Prince

Hailed by the cast and crew as the "Godmother of *The Wire*," Debi Young served not only as the show's makeup department head, but as a confidant, mentor, and champion for every person who came through her trailer. After working on the entire series, the Baltimore-raised Young has gone on to amass a remarkable list of screen credits including the acclaimed HBO dramas *Treme*, *True Detective*, and *Mare of Easttown*.

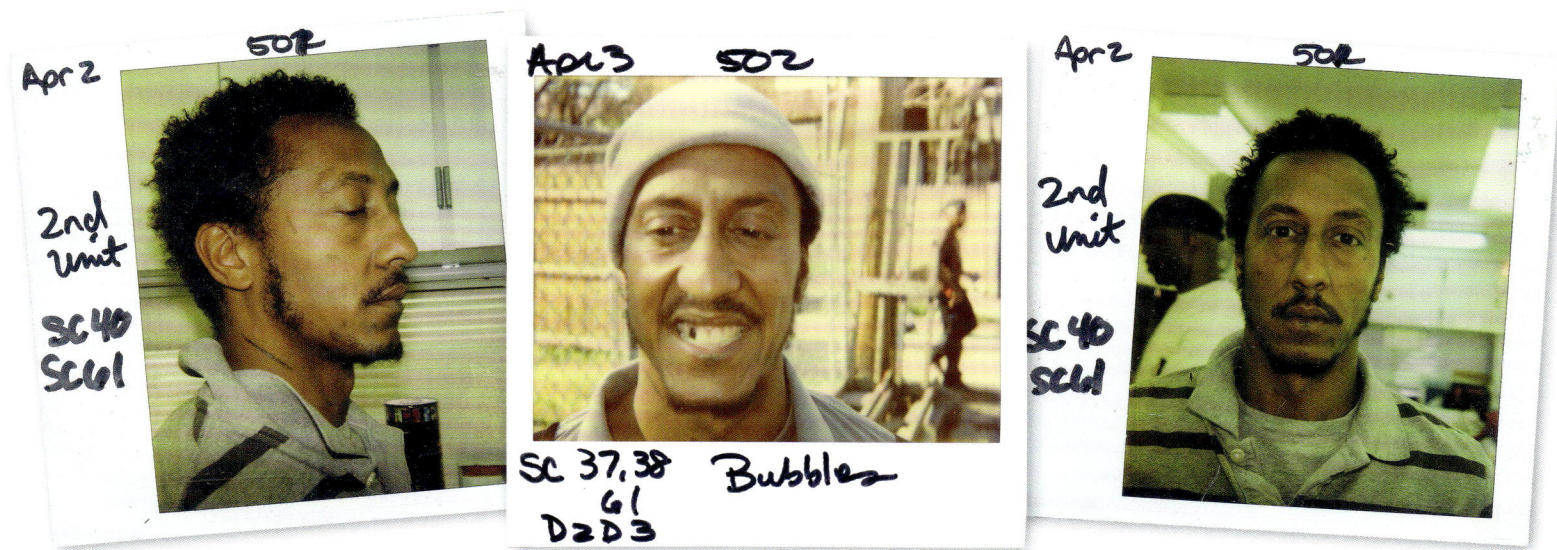

**How did it all begin for you on *The Wire*?**

I was working on NBC's *Homicide: Life on the Street*, and Clark Johnson was an actor on the show. He directed the pilot for *The Wire* and he requested me for that because he knew me from *Homicide*. When they called me, I didn't even know what *The Wire* was and I didn't know he had recommended me, but I am ever so grateful. Because, honestly, I was there from the pilot all the way to the very end. We had the same makeup and hair department all the way through the series.

**What were your first impressions of *The Wire*?**

Baltimore is my hometown. I used to work for the Baltimore Police Department from 1974 to 1979, taking emergency calls. At the time, David Simon was a reporter for the *Baltimore Sun*. He would come in to pick up the police statistics that he would use [so] he could write his column. Little did I know that we would be working together in this capacity some years later. Even though I was working for the police at the time, I'd be doing my colleagues' makeup in the ladies room. I've always done makeup since I was a child. I guess I did it as a hobby. I loved that people would get up out of my makeup chair and feel more confident. I'd do

any kind of makeup job I could find, working behind the counter, promoting [product] lines, going to this place and that place—but I never ever thought about film. One day, one of my clients, a journalist for the *Washington Times*, asked me if I would do her makeup for a local television show. She was hosting it for a week because the regular host was away for a week. She said, "They can't pay you, but they can give you screen credit." I did it, and then, when the regular host came back, he asked me to stay. So, my career in makeup kind of evolved from there.

**When you started on the makeup work for *The Wire*, what was the main challenge that you faced?**

I like gritty. Even though I did beauty before, I like grit—I like authenticity. And David Simon was a reporter and Ed Burns was a homicide detective, so I knew that they knew what it looked like at a crime scene, so we had to be authentic. Sandra Linn was my key makeup artist, and then we had Janice Kinigopoulos, our hairstylist and barber. Because we were required to create the makeup for crime scenes, Sandy got a clinical pathology book which we would use to look up real-life crime scenes. But

OPPOSITE Behind-the-scenes photos from Debi Young's archive: (*clockwise from top left*) Michael K. Williams; Young with Dominic West; Young and Idris Elba; hair department head Janice Kinigopoulos, Tosha actress Edwina Findley, and Young.; Andre Royo and Sonja Sohn; Anwan Glover (*left*), who plays Barksdale associate Slim Charles, and Marlo Stanfield actor Jamie Hector (*right*); Young with actor Robert Wisdom, who plays Howard "Bunny" Colvin; Young and Tristan Wilds, who makes his debut in season four as Michael Lee; Young and her makeup department comrades Sandra Linn and Janice Kinigopoulos.

TOP Continuity Polaroids track the Bubbles makeup that was applied to actor Andre Royo.

PAGES 70–71 Crime scene makeup designs created by Young's team.

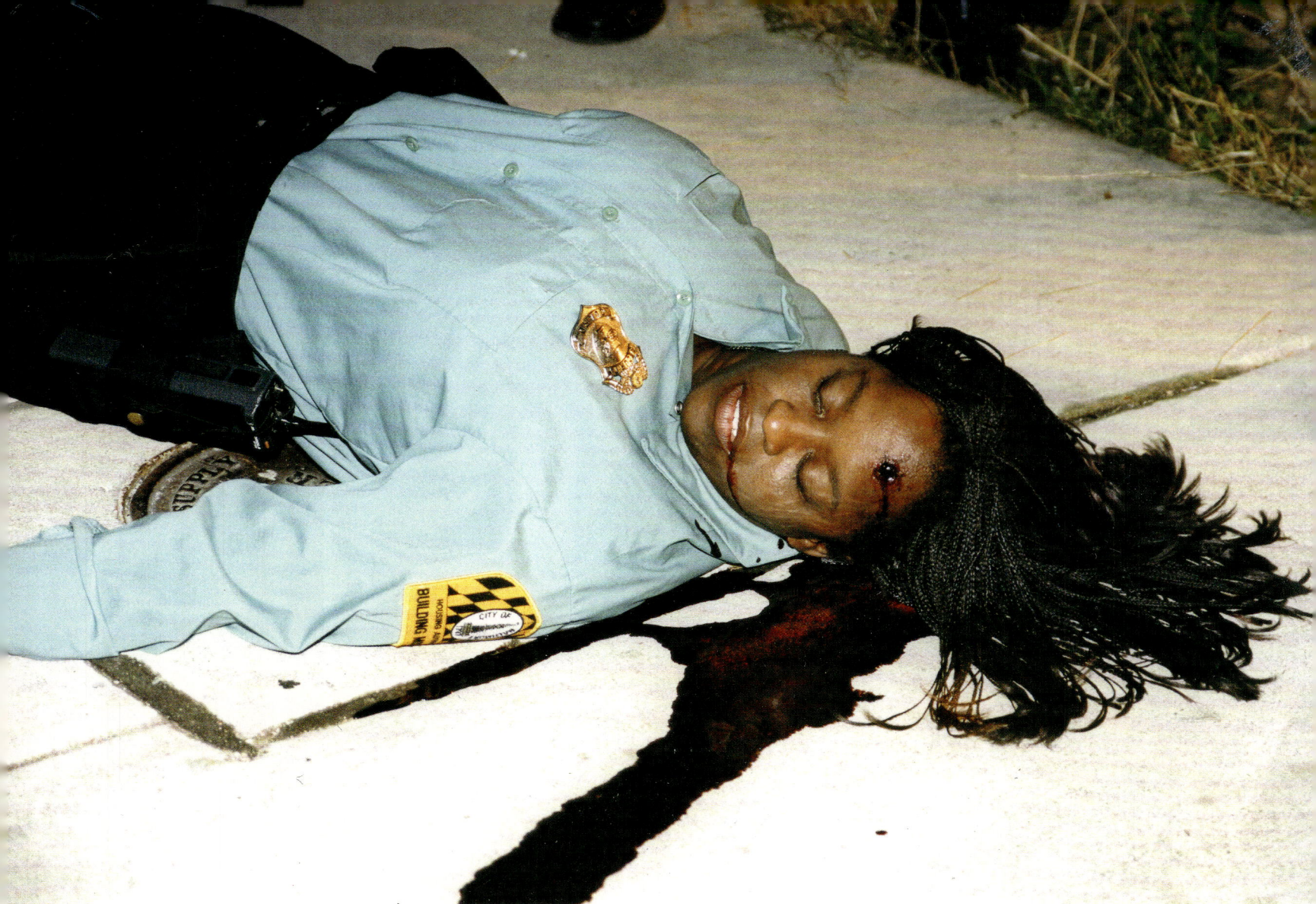

that was tough because they were real dead bodies, even if their faces may have been blacked out. We had a medical examiner consultant on set every day, so I decided that instead of depressing myself flipping through the pages of that book, I would describe to the expert what we were trying to do. I would say, "I have a body that's been floating in Baltimore Harbor for a month, in February. How would he look?" I would have him describe the details to me—February's a cold month so the body's not going to decompose as it would in July. You need all those details in order for it to be authentic. And that's how we started doing it. Sandy and I, we were doing it on the fly. We would go to the craft services table and get noodles and other things we could use to mash up and make brain matter!

There were also more elaborate effects that were done by Matthew Mungle in LA. There was one episode where a character was beaten so badly that the director wanted to have a puppet made so the actors would perform the beatdown on the puppet— the scene would begin with a stuntman being beaten, and then they'd use the puppet. So, I had to describe to Matthew how the puppet should look: "He should

look contorted, have his head this way and his mouth open." That kind of thing. We sent it out to Mathew's studio, and he did a head cast of the actor. When that silicon puppet came back to me and I opened the wooden crate in front of David Simon, I had never seen him smile so big. It was incredible! Every hair, every mole, every blemish, everything was exactly the same. Later, one of the executive producers told me that when they were cutting together the episode, the editors got sick when they saw the puppet getting beaten because it was so realistic. So, we took that as a compliment!

**How much of the job revolved around the more elaborate makeups and how much of it was more subtle things, like the look of Andre Royo's character, Bubbles?**

Sandy created the makeup for Andre, and she just brought so much nuance to it—down to the yellowing and blacking out of the teeth, the track marks in his arms, and the irritations and bruising around the injections. That Bubbles makeup was hers, but we had so many addicts that we had to do makeup for on the show, so we really had to get into how people look when they are in that state. And Andre Royo is such an amazing actor. I remember one time he was dressed as Bubbles and went to the craft services table to get something to eat, and one of the security people pulled up on him—he didn't realize that he was an actor on the show. That makeup was really, really authentic.

**Was it sometimes a challenge to deal with the sheer volume of cast members that needed to go through makeup? Hamsterdam in particular must have been difficult to stage . . .**

Do I have a story about Hamsterdam! My daughter-in-law, Ngozi Olandu Young, is a makeup artist, and she came and joined us the third season. She was brand new at the time. I remember there was a day in Hamsterdam we had so many background performers to work on. We weren't able to hire a whole team for the sequence, we just had Ngozi, so Sandy and I gave her a big bag of special effects makeup and said, "Go over there, break them down, and turn them into crackheads." It was over a hundred people, and I'm telling you, she did a great job. When they got to set, they looked so good, and that's how we broke her in.

**Was it easier to create makeups for the cop characters, like McNulty and Bunk, who were more conventional looking?**

It was easy-peasy. There were some rules and regulations about how the detectives looked undercover, so there were differences between the uniformed patrol men and the undercover police officers. Mostly, a lot of the rules around the police characters were around the shaving. Should they be clean-shaven? Could they have a mustache? Could they have a goatee? That sort of thing. The rules were a little bit relaxed on the Black officers because they had a tendency to get folliculitis, like razor bumps, if they shaved every day. We didn't have them totally clean shaven unless they decided to do so, but for the other officers we always did.

**How did you approach the makeup for the Barksdales and other street gangs?**

Authenticity was the key for me. I didn't want anybody made up as if they were in a soap opera. I like to see sweat. I like to see skin that looks a little glowy. I grew up in East Baltimore and I wanted to see the streets of Baltimore up on the screen. And there are some street guys who are really well put together. The Stringer Bells and Avon Barksdales of that world were making

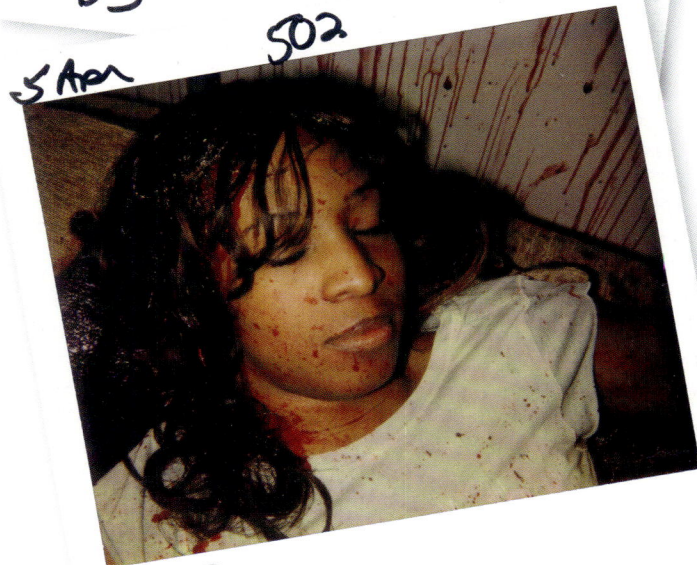

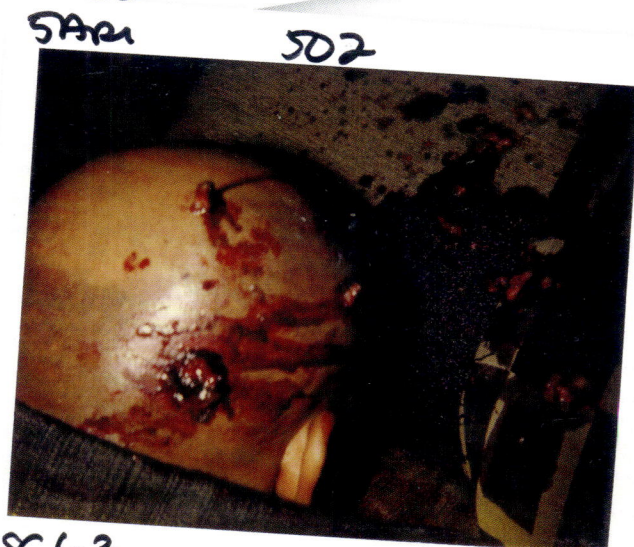

money. They knew how to dress themselves and how to put themselves together. So again, authenticity was key for me.

I remember one time we were shooting a scene with a corpse in a coffin. The director said to me that he wanted the dead person to be paler. I said, "Sir, with all due respect, Black people don't look like that when they die." I just wanted people to watch the show and see things the way they really are, you know?

**How did your role evolve as the seasons progressed?**
I think in the very beginning, it was a little complicated because people didn't know each other. It was an ensemble cast and there were times, I guess, when people felt like, "This person's not giving me enough in this scene" and that sort of thing. I feel that because the makeup trailer is where the actors start the day,

it's my job to make sure they're in a sacred space where they can ready themselves to go out there and do what they have to do. There were times when they might show up in a playful, partying type mood: Okay, they'll probably have a lighter day. But then there'd be times where an actor might be depressed or fearful, so I would let them drive how the energy should be in the trailer, so that we wouldn't disturb it and take them off their game, so to speak. So, it's very important to me to have a peaceful, kind, efficient, supportive makeup and hair department.

I wanted the actors to understand that they were not there by accident; they were there by divine order. I remember when Michael K. Williams came to the series, his character didn't even have a name—he was Watcher Number One. For the longest time I'd see him in silhouette at night, in a vehicle looking out the

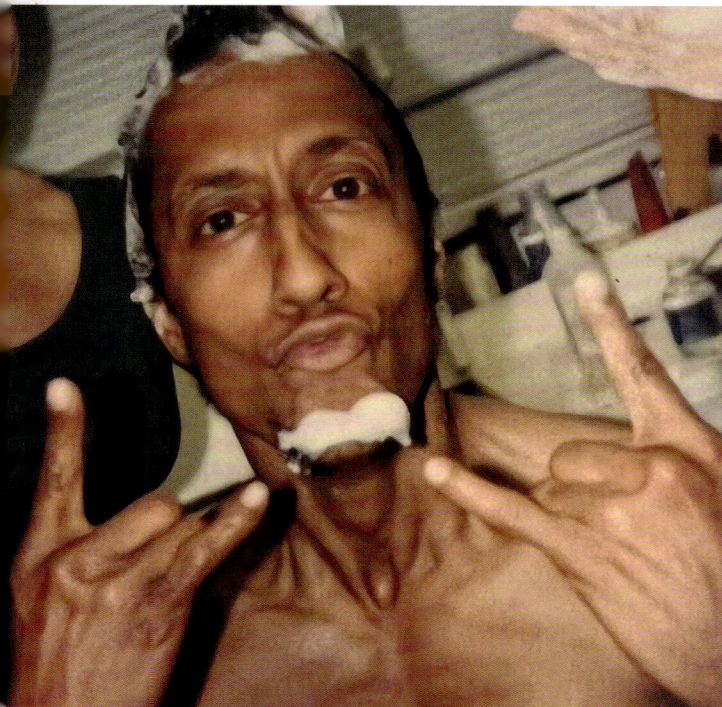

window. I just remember he was so nervous—a sweet, kind, beautiful personality, but he was nervous; I could tell. I just remember putting my hand on his shoulder, and telling him, "You're not here by accident, you're here by divine order. So you get out there and you dance as hard as you can." And I just kind of spoke a little blessing or prayer over him, he gave me a hug, and, I'm telling you, he went out there and the next thing I know we had Omar coming. He was just wonderful. I just loved the fact that over the years we all kind of loved on each other and supported one another. It's a family. For real.

**At what point did you realize *The Wire* was becoming a phenomenon?**

Let me tell you, we heard it from the people on the street. If people in Baltimore knew that you worked on *The Wire* or they thought *The Wire* was shooting somewhere, they would come around. I don't think the show got much recognition from the Emmys and that sort of thing while we were shooting it. I remember there was some disappointment from some of the cast members because of that. I used to tell them, "Listen, you know the job you do, you don't need anybody to give you an award. Don't you dare be down on yourself because you didn't get anything." And, of course, years later it's considered to be the best television show of all time!

**What was it like shooting in the streets of Baltimore?**

I thought it was of utmost importance that because we were shooting in people's communities, we shouldn't just roll up in there like a Hollywood production and start telling them, "You can't go this way." I remember, when we were on location one time, stopping one of the security guys who I felt was being a little bit aggressive in the way that he spoke to someone from the local community. I pulled him to the side and I said, "Listen, we are in their community. We have to treat them with the utmost respect because to treat somebody in that way may instigate something. You don't want somebody coming here shooting up this film set, so you better show respect." We just had an immense respect for the community. Before we even started, our main security team went in to talk to the local drug dealers to let them know that we would be coming in to film in their neighborhood and to ask them if they could refrain from business during the time that we're there. I'm telling you, on many days, there would be kingpins sitting on their stoops watching as we filmed.

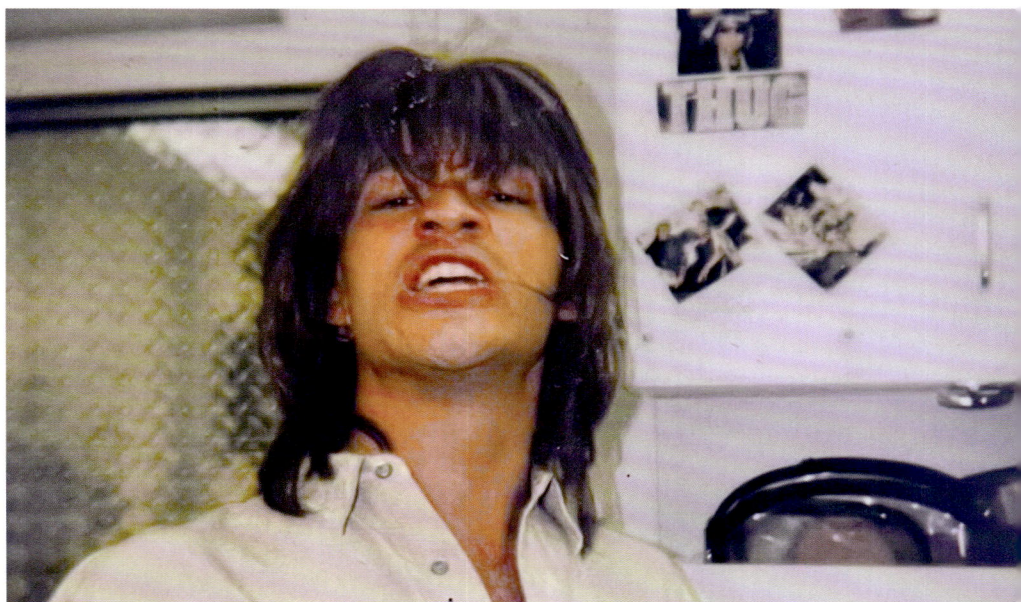

**You've worked on many shows since *The Wire*. How did the experience shooting it compare to your subsequent work in the industry?**

There was something special about *The Wire*. I don't even think we knew how special it was in that moment. But, as the years went on, you could see that the people who worked on it cared about each other. People still supported one another. During the season there would be softball games and things like that, and sometimes people would connect on the weekends.

And at the end of the seasons, we'd have talent shows and we'd all get dressed up and do our thing. The makeup and hair team were The Golddiggers and Wyatt Belton, hair department key and barber, was Ray Charles. Michael K. Williams and Jermaine Crawford were doing Michael Jackson's *Thriller* video with all the dances, and I think they came in second. We won!

# SEASON ONE EPISODES

**S01E01:** The Target

**Written by:** Story by David Simon and Ed Burns; teleplay by David Simon

**Directed by:** Clark Johnson

**Original airdate:** June 2, 2002

**Epigraph:** ". . . when it's not your turn." −McNulty

**Description:** In the pilot episode of this drama series, Baltimore homicide detective Jimmy McNulty gets into hot water and winds up assigned to a detail of narcotics outcasts charged with investigating drug lord Avon Barksdale and his powerful operation.

**S01E02:** The Detail

**Written by:** Story by David Simon and Ed Burns; teleplay by David Simon

**Directed by:** Clark Johnson

**Original airdate:** June 9, 2002

**Epigraph:** "You cannot lose if you do not play."
−Marla Daniels

**Description:** McNulty feels the heat when a witness who testified against D'Angelo is found murdered. Meanwhile, Greggs is given the lay of the land regarding Avon Barksdale's key players, and Herc, Carver, and Prez find big-time trouble at the towers.

**S01E03:** The Buys

**Written by:** Story by David Simon and Ed Burns; teleplay by David Simon

**Directed by:** Peter Medak

**Original airdate:** June 16, 2002

**Epigraph:** "The king stay the king." −D'Angelo

**Description:** The early morning "field interviews" by Herc, Carver, and Prez result in a minor riot, a boy losing an eye, and some bad publicity. On the other side of the law, D'Angelo teaches Wallace and Bodie how to play the game (chess) and later impresses Bell.

**S01E04:** Old Cases

**Written by:** Story by David Simon and Ed Burns; teleplay by David Simon

**Directed by:** Clement Virgo

**Original airdate:** June 23, 2002

**Epigraph:** "It's a thin line 'tween heaven and here." −Bubbles

**Description:** Greggs and McNulty try to get Hardcase to turn informant as arraignment begins for those caught in the raid. Barksdale places a bounty on the head of rival gang leader Omar. Meanwhile, McNulty takes Bubbles on a cultural field trip.

**S01E05:** The Pager

**Written by:** Story by David Simon and Ed Burns; teleplay by Ed Burns

**Directed by:** Clark Johnson

**Original airdate:** June 30, 2002

**Epigraph:** ". . . a little slow, a little late." −Avon Barksdale

**Description:** McNulty's detail finally gets "clone" pagers to track Barksdale and his gang, but nobody can crack the codes used by the callers. Meanwhile, Bell instructs D'Angelo on how to school his lookouts while simultaneously flushing out a possible snitch.

**S01E06:** The Wire

**Written by:** Story by David Simon and Ed Burns; teleplay by David Simon

**Directed by:** Ed Bianchi

**Original airdate:** July 7, 2002

**Epigraph:** ". . . and all the pieces matter." −Freamon

**Description:** When Rawls looks to make a premature arrest for three murders that are linked to D'Angelo and Avon Barksdale, McNulty and Greggs must argue for a delay in order to preserve the valuable wiretap gains they have made.

**S01E07:** One Arrest

**Written by:** Story by David Simon and Ed Burns; teleplay by Rafael Álvarez

**Directed by:** Joe Chappelle

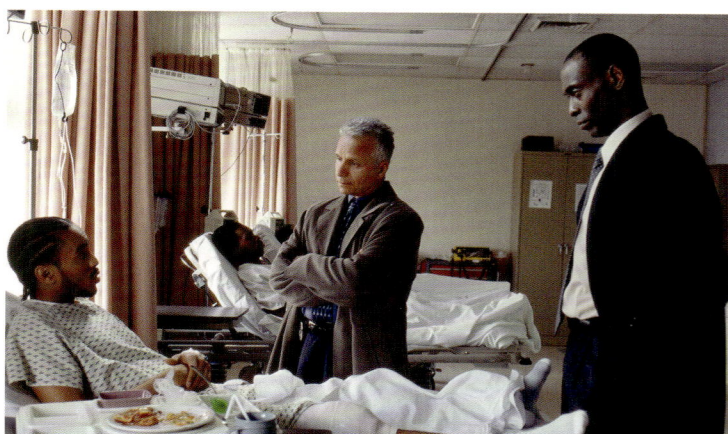

**Original airdate:** July 21, 2002

**Epigraph:** "A man must have a code." –Bunk

**Description:** Tipped off by the wire, Greggs, Herc, Carver, and Freamon make a bust, but the incident makes Avon and Stringer suspicious, leading them to close shop in the Pit. Meanwhile, Bunk and McNulty look for another witness in the Gant slaying.

## SO1EO8: Lessons

**Written by:** Story by David Simon and Ed Burns; teleplay by David Simon

**Directed by:** Gloria Muzio

**Original airdate:** July 28, 2002

**Epigraph:** "Come at the king, you best not miss." –Omar

**Description:** An unlikely source gives McNulty the tag of a car driven by Stringer Bell. Meanwhile, Greggs and Carver bust a congressional aide carrying dirty cash but are forced to let him go. Later, Omar earns his "loose cannon" moniker.

## SO1EO9: Game Day

**Written by:** Story by David Simon and Ed Burns; teleplay by David H. Melnick and Shamit Choksey

**Directed by:** Milčo Mančevski

**Original airdate:** August 4, 2002

**Epigraph:** "Maybe we won." –Herc

**Description:** Barksdale plays an expensive game of one-upmanship with an Eastside rival. Meanwhile, Herc and Carver take some cash off Wee-Bey's hands, and Omar resurfaces with a bang.

## SO1E10: The Cost

**Written by:** Story by David Simon and Ed Burns; teleplay by David Simon

**Directed by:** Brad Anderson

**Original airdate:** August 11, 2002

**Epigraph:** "And then he dropped the bracelets . . ." –Greggs

Description: With Wallace in custody, McNulty and Daniels try to figure out what to do with him in the months before he testifies.

Sydnor and Carver track down one of Barksdale's stash houses, and Prez shows off his "gift for the paper trail."

## SO1E11: The Hunt

**Written by:** Story by David Simon and Ed Burns; teleplay by Joy Lusco

**Directed by:** Steve Shill

**Original airdate:** August 18, 2002

**Epigraph:** "Dope on the damn table." –Daniels

**Description:** The police turn up the heat on tracking down Savino, Wee-Bey, and Little Man. Burrell orders Daniels to hit drug dealers for results that will impress the press. Barksdale sees his ranks thinning after the hit on Orlando.

## SO1E12: Cleaning Up

**Written by:** Story by David Simon and Ed Burns; teleplay by George Pelecanos

**Directed by:** Clement Virgo

**Original airdate:** September 1, 2002

**Epigraph:** "This is me, yo, right here." –Wallace

**Description:** The low-rise pay phones are out of service, so McNulty and Daniels keep pace by tapping Barksdale's office. Bodie gets some new responsibilities from Stringer; Freamon gives Shardene a "new look"; and D'Angelo goes to NYC on an errand for his uncle.

## SO1E13: Sentencing

**Written by:** David Simon and Ed Burns

**Directed by:** Tim Van Patten

**Original airdate:** September 8, 2002

**Epigraph:** "All in the game . . ." –Traditional, West Baltimore

**Description:** Season one finale. Every crew has weak links—including Avon Barksdale's. With the heat turned up in the high-rises, Daniels and McNulty turn to a higher authority in an effort to crack the case wide open.

# THE WIRE

# SEASON

2

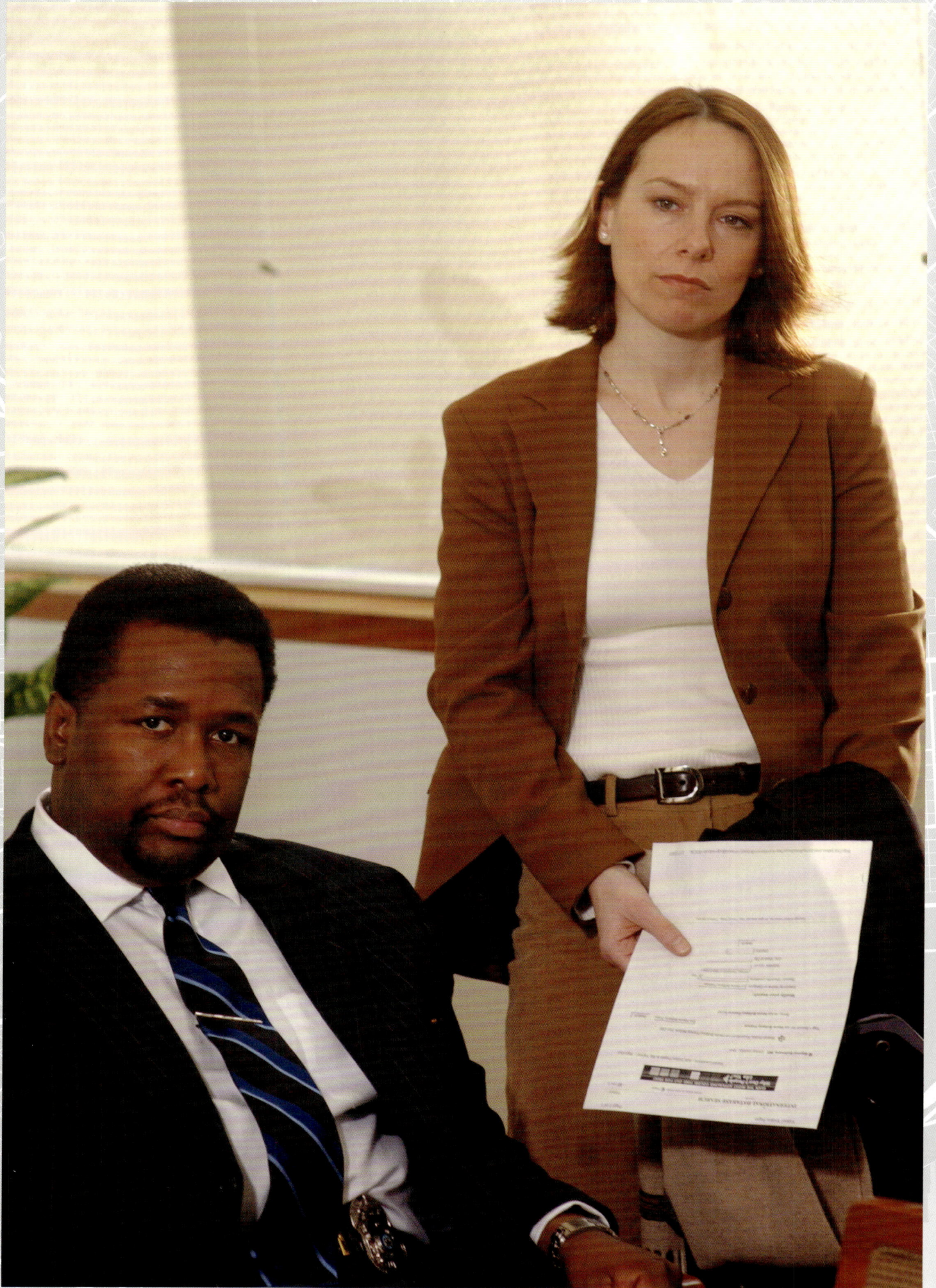

# AN INTRODUCTION TO SEASON TWO

By D. Watkins

**S**eason two is the wild card. Many fans fell in love with the bosses and corner boys that ripped and ran through the streets of West Baltimore. But by the end of season one, Avon Barksdale and D'Angelo Barksdale are both incarcerated, which allowed the creators to start a new conversation: What happens to young men once they enter the system? Some make it through and even excel like Avon, obviously, but D'Angelo's character is not cut out for jail—even though he is smart enough to know the consequences of his actions, even though he committed the crime, even though his uncle is one of the most powerful men behind the wall.

D'Angelo eventually begins to come into himself while in jail, carving out his own identity without using the Barksdale name. But, being

"Some make it through and even excel like Avon, obviously, but D'Angelo's character is not cut out for jail . . ."

OPPOSITE In season two of *The Wire*, Bunk (Wendell Pierce) works with port authority officer Beatrice "Beadie" Russell (Amy Ryan) to solve the deaths of the thirteen women found in a cargo container on the Baltimore docks.

TOP Idris Elba during shooting of D'Angelo's funeral in the season two episode "Backwash."

incarcerated picks at D'Angelo, causing him to commit the number-one offense for any outlaw: He snitches, and you can't come back from that. With Avon behind the wall, Stringer is left to control the operation outside, and this gave us a chance to understand that street politics are not cut and dry. Stringer is forced to have D'Angelo, the nephew of his best friend and business partner, killed to protect their organization, a decision that alters his life and their organization forever.

As the Barksdales deal with their drama, we meet the Sobotkas, a Polish American family from South Baltimore. The family's patriarch, Frank Sobotka (Chris Bauer), is the treasurer for the International Brotherhood of Stevedores at the Baltimore docks—a job wrapped in as many favors and conflicts as both the police department and the streets. Initially, some viewers wanted to dive back into the world of West Baltimore and not take a detour to the docks. But fans quickly became comfortable with the blue-collar relatability of Frank's world and were taken aback by the way the drug trade had a negative impact on white communities as well. The war on drugs is too often written off as a Black issue—and following the media in Baltimore would lead you to believe so. The countless Black stories involving drugs and violence are overreported while the same kinds of stories involving white people slip through the cracks.

Season two showed that our ridiculous war on drugs is more than a Black problem—it's an American problem.

BOTTOM A floor plan for the wiretap detail offices set that was used for seasons two through five.

OPPOSITE TOP LEFT D'Angelo (Lawrence Gilliard Jr.) is strangled to death by Muggs (Dakota Anderson) while serving time, an order given by Stringer Bell.

OPPOSITE TOP RIGHT Avon Barksdale (Wood Harris), also in prison, is unaware of Stringer's plan to kill D'Angelo.

OPPOSITE BOTTOM Treasurer at the International Brotherhood of Stevedores, Frank Sobotka (Chris Bauer) becomes a major figure in season two of *The Wire*.

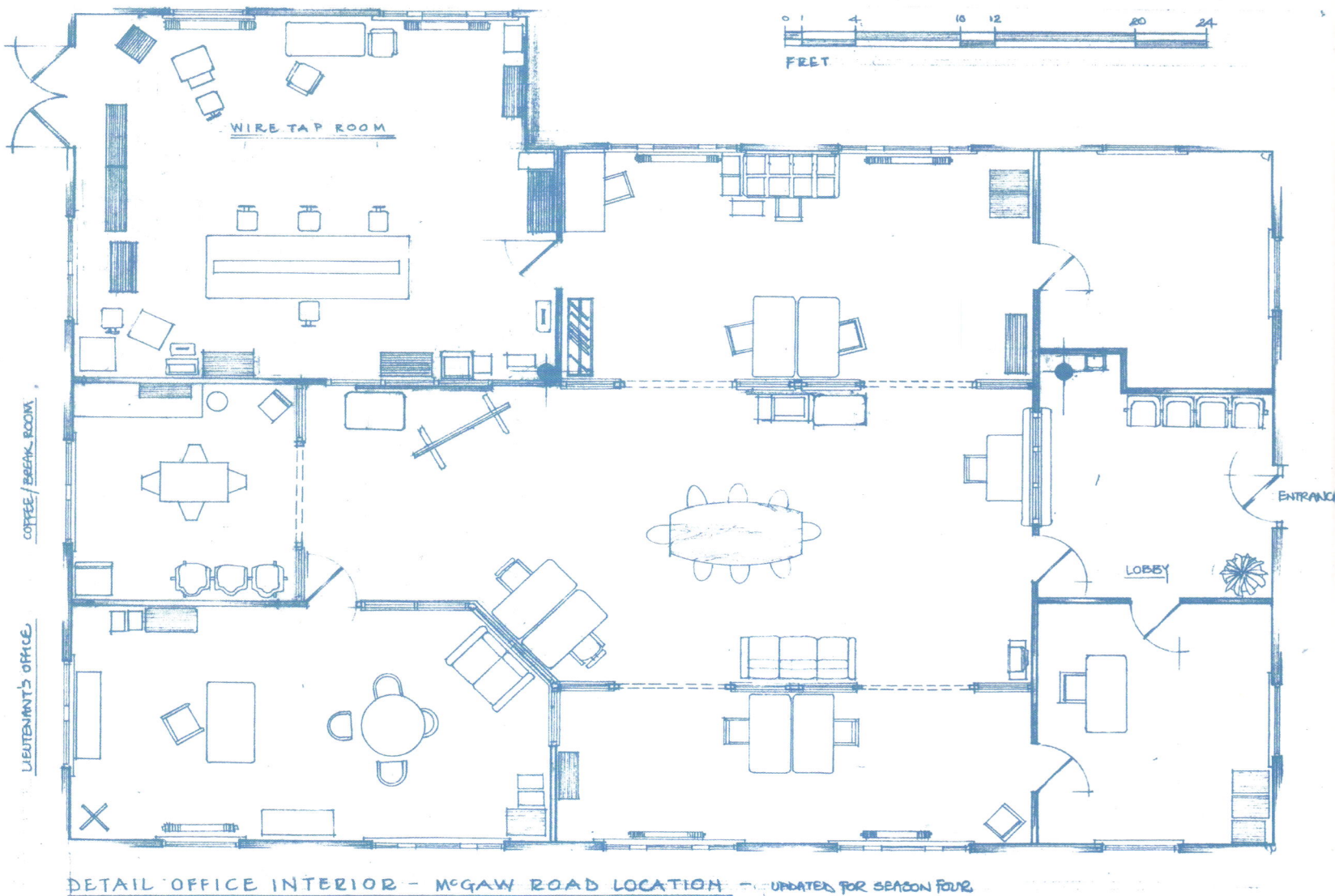

DETAIL OFFICE INTERIOR - McGAW ROAD LOCATION - UPDATED FOR SEASON FOUR

# THE WIRE SEASON TWO: THE GREEK TRAGEDY

by Jesse Einhorn and Nathaniel Friedman

I t's been fourteen years since *The Wire*'s series finale closed out with a shot of the Baltimore skyline and some traffic. And here we are, still asking ourselves the same question we've had from the beginning: What the fuck was that?

> "What *The Wire* is depends on who you're talking to."

What *The Wire* is depends on who you're talking to. It's the single most damning indictment of the war on drugs, and certainly the one most frequently dismissed as copaganda. It's a love letter to Baltimore—Baltimore as a microcosm of American decline, and Baltimore as an allegory for said decline.

Maybe this person will cite the show's majority Black cast as a groundbreaking moment in prestige TV. Or explain to you how serialized novels work. Or quote a bunch of rap lyrics about Marlo Stanfield.

But there's only one right answer, in that it's the only one that allows for all of the above: *The Wire* is a compendium of stories about individuals and systems. Each season is built around a single idealistic character who takes on the system—sometimes unwittingly, sometimes on principle,

OPPOSITE Chris Bauer as Frank Sobotka, a decent man ultimately broken by the system.

TOP Sobotka's offices are raided by the FBI at the end of season two.

TOP McNulty (Dominic West, *left*), who begins season two assigned to the Marine Unit, and Bubbles (Andre Royo, *right*).

ABOVE Frank's son, Chester "Ziggy" Sobotka (James Ransone), is a troubled individual heading for tragedy.

OPPOSITE Continuity Polaroids taken during shooting of scenes set in Clement Street Cafe, the bar frequented by Frank's stevedores in season two. (*Clockwise from top left*) James Ransone; Dominic West and Clarke Peters; unknown (*left*) and Charley Scalies (*right*) as Thomas "Horseface" Pakusa; Jeffery Pratt Gordon as John "Johnny Fifty" Spamanto.

and sometimes in spite of themselves. In season one, Jimmy McNulty's desire to do good, honest police work puts him perpetually at odds with the culture and incentive structure of the Baltimore Police Department. Throughout the first three seasons, Stringer Bell tries to rationalize Baltimore's drug game in the name of efficiency and fairness, albeit only for the people selling the drugs. In seasons three and four, Howard "Bunny" Colvin is a well-meaning disruptor who tries to change things for the better—first by legalizing drugs in Hamsterdam, then by hacking Baltimore's underfunded school system.

And of course, there's season two's Frank Sobotka, the show's single most poignant figure and its most romantic, quixotic idealist. Frank is incredibly likable, which makes his death at the end of the season a gut punch. But what puts him in a class by himself and makes the character such a critical part of *The Wire*'s cosmology is exactly what leads to this untimely demise.

Frank's defining characteristic is that he's a good guy. He's a mensch who can get along with almost anybody and never once balks at helping someone out of a jam. In *The Wire*, morality is at best slippery or murky. Frank's purity is the exception that proves the rule. He's not just a good guy—he's *the* good guy. McNulty is the show's protagonist. But Frank is the closest that we get to a hero in the classic sense.

Frank is also a hero in the classical sense: a tragic one. David Simon once described *The Wire* as "Greek tragedy for the new millennium," which, incidentally, makes the supposed country of origin of The Greek (Bill Raymond), the Mediterranean kingpin who orders Frank's murder, worth noting (even if he's not actually Greek). What makes Frank so unique is also his tragic flaw: his idealism. He gets embroiled in The Greek's smuggling operation only because he wants the members of his union, including his nitwit son, Ziggy (James Ransone), to still have work. When Frank decides to go to the police, it's because he can no longer stomach being mixed up in an obviously destructive and exploitative operation. He's murdered because, like Stringer, he believes in something bigger than himself. Unlike Stringer, his beliefs are rooted in empathy for others.

The takeaway is bleak. In the show's sprawling universe, there's exactly one character for whom idealism itself is a matter of principle, and he's destroyed in a slow, brutal manner that's difficult to watch. To get Greek about it again: In *The Wire*, the Platonic ideal of the Good—and the notion that individuals can shape material reality through their own good intentions—is futile. There's no silver lining or upside to Frank's story. He tried to do the right thing and paid the ultimate price. A "fate worse than death" is supposed to be an open-ended query, but in the case of an idealist like Frank, the death of his ideals, and of the very possibility of ideals in general, is even more grave.

That's why Frank is the real hero of *The Wire*. His character has the most emotional resonance. His moral clarity contrasts starkly with the outright amorality or greatly compromised sense of right and wrong that furnishes much of the show's complexity. And because of the moral stakes involved, his arc has a timeless, transcendent quality in no way particular to time or place.

If Frank is good, then there must be an evil that he opposes. The most obvious candidate for that is The Greek. But Frank is also a hero in the tragic, Greek sense, and in Greek tragedy, there is no such thing as

sc41      201

202

SII7
~~Bank~~ IV·6

Sc 41      201

Sc41      201

TOP Frank Sabotka (Chris Bauer) amongst the shipping crates that will ultimately lead to his demise.

evil. Heroes aren't actually undone by their foes or even the gods. It's all a matter of fate, which is going to happen regardless of the choices that any mortal, or immortal, makes. This worldview is at once demoralizing and oddly neutral. We think of "doom" as bad and "destiny" as good. But they're one and the same. They're both just what's going to happen, *inshallah*, with nobody in the driver's seat. Fate would be the villain. But the Fates are just three ladies with a job to do, and no ability to change the yarns they spin.

That's why the villain of *The Wire* is that there's no villain. Individuals are always foiled by institutions, impersonal historical processes, or, to quote Elizabeth Warren, "big structural change." In season two, Frank is undone by the forces of post-industrial capitalism—the global shift

РУССКАЯ
БЕЛУГ
BELUGA MALOSSOL 000
CASPIAN CAVIAR
УТОНЧЕННЫЙ МАСЛЯНИСТЫЙ ПРИВКУС
ХРАНИТЕ ОХЛАЖДЕННЫМ

in urban economics from cities that build and ship things to cities that speculate and consume, the so-called FIRE sectors (finance, insurance, and real estate) that have come to dominate America's urban centers. Real estate is Frank's primary foe, as personified by the shadowy Andy Krawczyk (Michael Willis), the developer who wants to turn the grain pier into a condominium complex.

Far more than the international drug lords and local cops, Krawczyk is the real antagonist for Frank and IBS Local 1514—or not so much Krawczyk himself but the forces he represents. (Krawczyk barely appears on screen, though he pops up again in future seasons, most notably as the witness to Stringer's final showdown with Omar.) Frank needs to dredge the canal and restore the grain pier so that ships, and work, will return to the port: All his political machinations, legitimate and corrupt, are in furtherance of this end. Krawczyk has a different plan—he wants to transform Baltimore's manufacturing infrastructure into an object of bourgeois consumption and line his pockets in the process—and in the end, his plan wins.

Krawczyk doesn't succeed in the way that most antagonists do; he doesn't outsmart, or double-cross, or triumph through some dastardly deed. Krawczyk wins for one cold and simple fact: The port is worth more for its real estate than its output. Transforming the land into fancy condos generates more economic value—if not social or community value—than the toiling of honest labor. And as hard as Frank tries, no amount of conniving can change that iron calculus. The logic of the market is the hand of fate. In this way, season two differs from other popular portrayals of union woe: Local 1514 isn't broken by evil strike-breaking bosses

TOP Ziggy (James Ransone, *center*) gets into hot water with Cheese (Clifford Smith Jr., *right*) when a drug deal goes wrong.

CENTER A caviar shipping label used by The Greek's crew as cover when smuggling contraband.

LAW ENFORCEMENT SENSITIVE - DO NOT SHARE

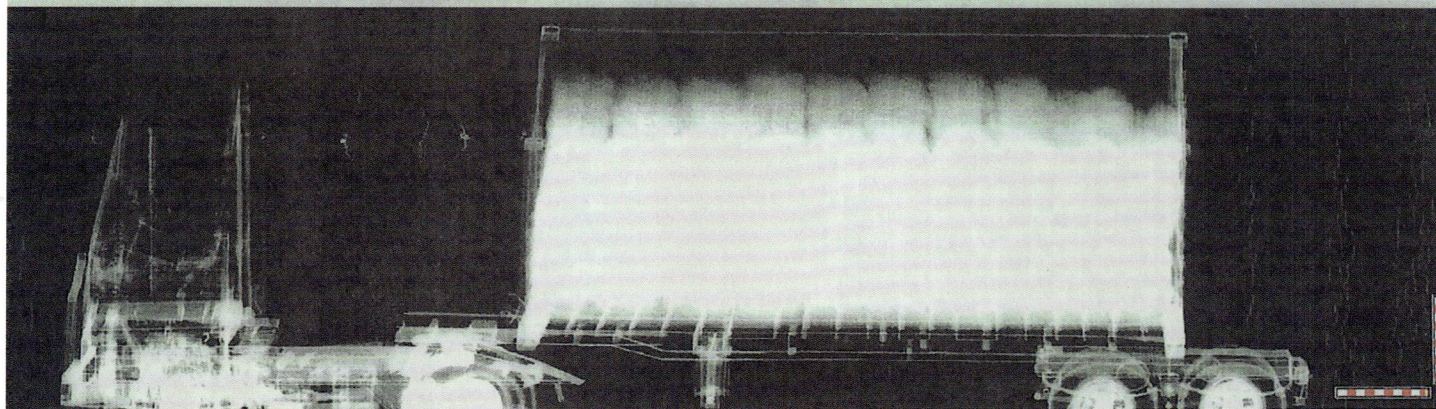

PATAPSCO CARGO TERMINAL    CONTAINER NO: GCCJ 986438 1    DATE: 2003/5/23 TIME:10.12 pm

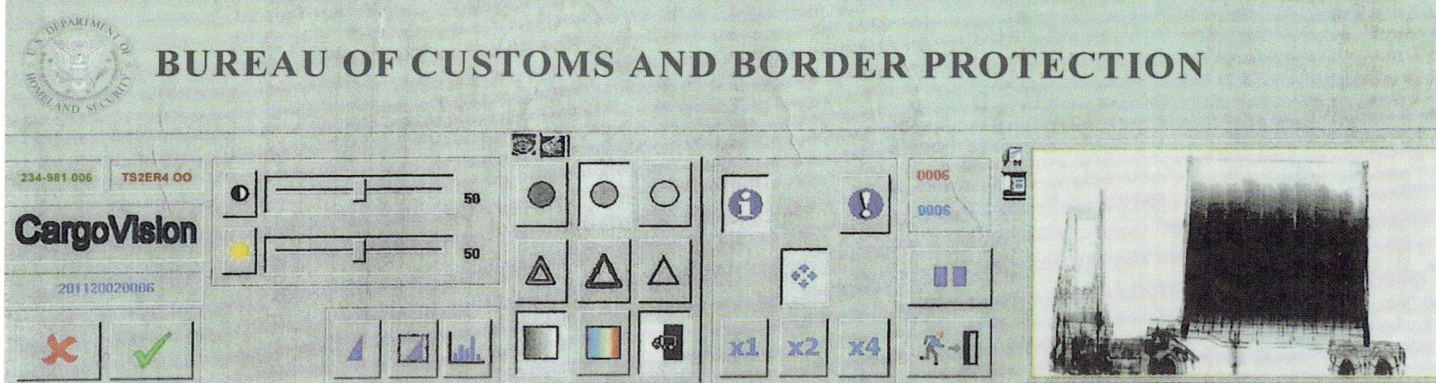

BUREAU OF CUSTOMS AND BORDER PROTECTION

TOP A truck X-ray graphic created by *The Wire*'s art department for a scene in season two in which Beadie Russell investigates the port's container-traffic computer system.

OPPOSITE TOP With backup from Puddin (De'Rodd Hearns, *left*), Bodie (J. D. Williams, *right*) gets into a gunfight with another crew, resulting in a tragic civilian casualty.

OPPOSITE BOTTOM Horseface (Charley Scalies), one of Frank Sobotka's trusted allies.

(*Justified*; *Matewan*) or its own internal corruption (*On the Waterfront*; *Blue Collar*). The union is broken by housing prices.

Real estate, and the twin forces of gentrification and deindustrialization, make themselves felt in other ways, too. When Frank's nephew Nick (Pablo Schreiber) and his girlfriend, Aimee (Kristin Proctor), go house-hunting in episode five, they quickly learn that Nick's union salary isn't enough to buy a modest home and raise a family in Baltimore's red-hot real estate market. They visit a house that used to belong to Nick's aunt, which has been fixed up and refurbished and now costs more than a working stevedore can afford. The real estate agent, Elena McNulty (Jimmy McNulty's ex-wife, played by Callie Thorne), explains that the neighborhood has a new name—and a new living standard. The impossibility of living a middle-class life on a working-class income is what ultimately pushes Nick deeper into the drug game.

Of course, it's not quite as simple as that. "People deal drugs because there aren't enough jobs" is the kind of pat moral sermonizing that gives liberals a bad name. The same could be said of every other character in *The Wire*—surely D'Angelo or Wallace would have been spared their fates as well, had gainful employment been a viable option. But that's not the point Simon is trying to make. After all, when Stringer goes legit, what does he do? He becomes a real estate developer and partners up with Andy Krawczyk! Even by going legit, Stringer's energies are channeled

toward the same rotten system and institutions that destroyed Frank one season earlier. And this is the deeper point that Simon is making: It isn't about good or bad options, much less right versus wrong choices. It's about the iron cage we all find ourselves trapped in—the structures none of us can escape.

Simon once told an interviewer that the show was about the "triumph of capitalism over human value," and really that's the only explanation that makes sense. Global capitalism is our era's answer to the Fates. Blaming individuals for capitalism or describing capital as evil is the lingua franca of online Marxism. But it has very little to do with Marx. When we talk about the System in twenty-first-century America, what we mean is capitalism, and every institution the world over ultimately falls under this umbrella. That's why Simon's quote is also the ultimate answer to the question "What was *The Wire?*" Because it's not just about people being destroyed. It's about how individuals, and communities, come to sacrifice their humanity at the altar of market forces.

The dehumanizing effect of capitalism is a specter that haunts season two from beginning to end. The very first scene features McNulty, having been unceremoniously dispatched from the Major Crimes Unit to the Marine Unit, driving his boat past the old Bethlehem Steel shipyard— once the crown jewel of Baltimore's mid-century manufacturing economy, now a monument to industrial decline. "My father used to work there," he says with a certain wistful pride.

In episode five, Frank and The Greek's right-hand man, Spiros Vondopoulos (Paul Ben-Victor), have a tense meeting on the shore of the Patapsco River. Frank says he wants out of the smuggling game, and, for a brief moment, it seems that our hero might choose a different path. Spiros, in a faux-plaintive tone, gestures across the river: "They used to make steel there, no?" The two men stare at the zombie factory. "Smoke from stacks. But inside . . ." The message is clear: The die of history is already cast, and Frank's fate, like the fate of Baltimore's manufacturing economy, is already set. In 2018, a decade after *The Wire* ended, Amazon opened one of its massive fulfillment centers in Sparrows Point—the same location that used to house the old Bethlehem Steel plant. The prospect of America's largest and most notoriously anti-union corporation setting up shop in the ashes of Jimmy's father's steel mill is a metaphor Simon would likely scorn for its obviousness.

Despite its dreary conclusion, and despite the fatalistic rendering of our hero's doomed ideals, season two doesn't leave us completely hopeless. Frank's story ends in tragic failure, but the labor union he gave his life for is still on its feet when the credits roll. Institutions are usually the bad guy in *The Wire,* whether it's stat-obsessed police departments or test-obsessed school systems. But just as Frank comes across as the show's singular good guy, his union is the one institution in Simon's universe that is both morally righteous and functionally sound.

Within the International Brotherhood of Stevedores, class solidarity goes hand-in-hand with multiethnic, multiracial solidarity. And this is another thing that makes the union, and season two itself, so unique. Throughout its five seasons, *The Wire* portrays a city and a society that are deeply unequal and intractably segregated. Race, and racial inequality, isn't something the show often tackles head-on, but it's the subtext of every storyline and scene—from the Westside housing projects

"Throughout its five seasons, *The Wire* portrays a city and society that are deeply unequal and intractably segregated."

to the all-Black classrooms at Tilghman Middle School. But on the docks of season two, we find something different—a sometimes fraught but otherwise harmonious multiracial coalition. Both the fragility and the power of this coalition are evident in the very first words we hear Frank speak in episode one: "If the canal gets dredged, it means we all work—your people, my people," he says to Nathaniel "Nat" Coxson (Luray Cooper), his Black counterpart in Local 47. The Black and Polish workers may be united by little more than shared economic self-interest, but they're united—and that's the most important thing.

The possibility of a multiethnic, multiracial workers' democracy offers hope—the only hope we have in *The Wire*. It may be battered and strained by the counterforces of global capitalism, but it's still alive at the end of season two. In episode thirteen, the denouement of the IBS storyline shows Vernon "Ott" Motley (Bus Howard), Frank's Black political rival in the treasurer's race, defying the FBI and declaring his support for Frank's re-election (and his plans for the port). "One man, one vote," he says, then exits the union hall. Individuals, no matter how clever or well meaning, have little hope of changing things on their own. Simon shows us that much. But perhaps, if workers can awaken the sleeping giant of their collective power, heroic triumph is still possible.

OPPOSITE BOTTOM LEFT A packing box graphic created by Halina Gebarowicz's art department that bears her surname.

OPPOSITE BOTTOM RIGHT The packing box as seen in the final show in a scene featuring Amy Ryan and Pablo Schreiber.

TOP The Baltimore and Ohio Locust Point Grain Terminal Elevator, which, as in the show, has since been demolished.

INSET A logo for the cargo terminal from season two created by the art department.

# PABLO SCHREIBER

## Interview by Nikki Stafford and Robert Thompson

Recently cast as iconic video game hero Master Chief in the Paramount+ TV series *Halo*, Pablo Schreiber has built an acting career that's a testament to his range, with key roles in projects including Netflix's prison comedy *Orange Is the New Black*, Starz's adaptation of Neil Gaiman's *American Gods*, and the action film *Skyscraper* (2018), in which he starred alongside Dwayne Johnson. Appearing primarily in season two of *The Wire*, with a brief cameo in season five, Schreiber brings real power and pathos to Nick Sobotka's tragic arc.

**How did you get the role of Nick Sobotka?**

I was pretty fresh out of college. I had done a tiny little ridiculous movie called *Bubble Boy*, as well as a Hallmark TV movie called *A Painted House*, and I think I may have done one play by then. I may have done *The Manchurian Candidate* (2004) by that time, but that was a tiny little role. I had done a small independent movie called *The Mudge Boy*, in which Emile Hirsch played the Mudge Boy. I had a supporting part of a bully, like a small-town local kid, and the movie went to Sundance.

So *The Wire* was real early in my career, and it was obviously a big audition. I was at Sundance when I found out I got the gig. My agents had found out there was an opening, it seemed like it notched my type or whatever, and they sent me for the audition. At this point, I don't remember how many times I had gone in to audition for Alexa Fogel, the casting director, but I had seen her at least once or twice, and she had not cast me. But, as an actor, that's like the most common thing, right? We go to so many auditions, especially early in our career,

OPPOSITE Pablo Schreiber as Nick Sobotka.

TOP Nick (Schreiber, *left*) and his uncle Frank (Chris Bauer, *right*), partners in crime.

and just hope that if [you don't get the part] these casting directors maybe remember you and bring you in for something else. And that was the case here: She'd seen me for something else, and she decided to bring me again. For this, I made a tape with her, and I think it went to David Simon and Robert F. Colesberry—from what I could tell, the second season was his baby.

So I had a callback with Robert and David, and we made a tape. They taped the audition [with me] doing it a couple of different ways with suggestions from Robert and David, and then that tape got sent to the network. Two or three other guys were put against each other via tape, and I ended up getting the job.

**Were you familiar with the show by that point?**

I wasn't at all familiar when I got the audition. By the time I was doing the auditions and doing the test, I had watched the first season. It was out already. But to be honest, my impression of the first season was, "Okay, it's an interesting premise, I'm curious to see where it goes." But my sort of takeaway was that the production value was pretty low. What I thought was, they're trying something interesting, but it doesn't look all that rich or expensive or whatever. What has now become clear in retrospect is that there was

obviously this amazing tapestry that was going to be woven over time. But not a lot of that was clear when watching the first season.

**Interestingly, because season two was so different from season one, watching the first season probably didn't give you much insight into how season two would unfold.**

I mean, 100 percent. I love that I'm a part of the second season because of how integral I think it is to teaching you how to watch the show. It was a complete 180 from where they were going in the first season—it was about the drug dealers and the cops, and we all kinda thought that was what the show was going to be about. All of a sudden there was this other element brought in. It was that detour that sort of taught you not to hold anything too closely, that there would be all kinds of zigs and zags and that this thing would expand and expand and go all over the place. So for that reason, I love that we were sort of the first strange detour.

**Nick Sobotka is a complicated character—he's neither a good guy nor a bad guy. He's caught between different worlds. Given that David Simon and the other creators often didn't give the cast**

TOP Nick (Pablo Schreiber, *right*) and Frank (Chris Bauer, *left*) discuss an uncertain future.

access to information about upcoming scripts, how did you decide how to play Nick not knowing how his whole arc goes?

Trust. Just trust. You know, obviously we were so lucky that we were being shepherded by David, and he knew what he wanted to do, even if he wasn't telling any of us. He was just writing beautiful words that were eminently and obviously playable. The beauty of the show was that the writing was so simple and honest and true that you didn't have to do very much to bring it alive—you just had to be honest, you know?

And even looking back on it, I still think that that's the beauty of it, top to bottom: It's an amazing cast that was just staying out of the way of the material. Nobody was trying too hard to steal focus; nobody was trying to do their own thing. It was a whole bunch of people who just showed up and did their job, and to this day, it's still kind of the best experience I've had in that regard.

What was your take on Nick's arc throughout the season? A lot of the characters on *The Wire* don't end up in better spots than where they started, and your character is a prime example of that.

Yeah. I mean with a show like this, I don't think you want them to, right? To me—and I've never heard David say this, so I'm just giving you my own

take—the beauty of *The Wire* is that it's always been an exploration of the root causes of poverty in America, looked at through the lens of one individual city, looked at deeply in all directions of what creates poverty and why our system is stuck in this cycle. So, to that end, I think that's why you had that sort of detour in the second season. It's not a show about race, although race is hugely important in the story. It's a show about poverty, and when you're in Baltimore, you see poverty in all different corners of that city.

INTERNATIONAL BROTHERHOOD OF STEVEDORES
LOCAL 1514
I.B.S.
BALTIMORE, MARYLAND

BELOW An International Brotherhood of Stevedores logo created by the art department.

BOTTOM In season two, Nick (Pablo Schreiber) is driven to crime because the cost of living in Baltimore has become untenable for working-class people.

So how does Nick fit in? He is kind of parallel to Larry Gilliard Jr.'s character on the first season. He's sort of the white D'Angelo. Although Nick doesn't die, he's essentially sentenced to death, given the trade he's decided to sit with. So obviously it's a tragic story about jobs going away and our economy moving and shifting and going in different directions, and what that does to certain demographics. Nick is the victim of a system. And if the story is looking at the root causes of poverty in America and why the system functions as it does, you have to have victims of the system. If you had a happy ending for that character, it would spoil sort of the whole premise of the show.

**Nick makes a cameo in season five, heckling Mayor Tommy Carcetti at a ribbon-cutting ceremony for the condos that are going to replace the grain pier. Were you surprised to get called back for just that last bit?**

Yeah, I was surprised. I thought it was funny. I loved it. I loved that it was not anything that was hung on or made too much of a big deal. It was like if you blinked you would miss it. Like, who's that guy yelling at Carcetti? Given the way that Nick was such a prominent part of the second season, it was great to have this background moment, like, "Oh fuck, are you kidding me?" Back in the same fucking position, you know? That, to me, just established the impossibility of his situation. And the fact that it's not getting better, you know? That it's only getting worse.

**What impact did *The Wire* have on your career trajectory?**

It was huge, and for me it jump-started a whole process that is still going. I'm twenty-five years into this amazing journey and career that I feel so lucky to get to do. And *The Wire* is one of the big reasons that

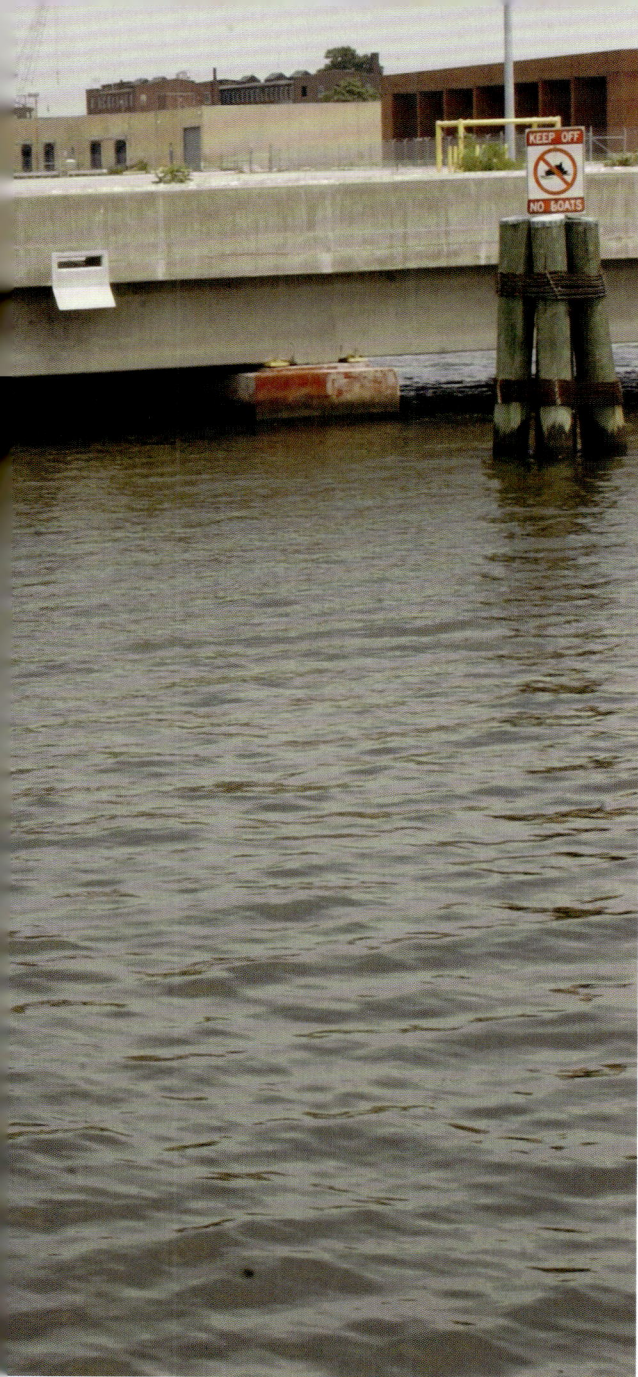

I get to do that. When I go into meetings, especially with writers and directors, everybody still knows that show and blows it up. So it's a touchstone and will be for the rest of my life. I also think it's a big legacy for my career and me; it made me really respect and honor great writing, and to this day, I keep that a priority. And if it's not great, I'll fight for it—[I believe in] starting with great material and advocating for writers. Just knowing that the material and writing is paramount, which in Hollywood tends to get forgotten quite often—that for me has been what's left the biggest mark on my career and on me.

As far as legacy of the show, it was such a unique time, because it was the early days of HBO, and it just seemed like they didn't quite know what their sweet spot was going to be. They were experimenting and looking for those things, and it's so hard to imagine another show like *The Wire* being made just because of the time we're at now. The good news is that now

there are so many different outlets and so much content being made that it probably does provide another opportunity for somebody to throw some money at something that might not be a huge audience hit. That's part of the legacy of *The Wire*—it was never a hit or a highly watched TV show; it's hugely critically acclaimed, but it never had that moment where everyone was watching it at the same time. That's its legacy, too: that one of the greatest shows of our time wasn't a hit. It's like, how do you make something as brilliant and genius as what David put together if you're just trying to give a studio or a network what they want or trying to make money and score points with audiences? You probably wouldn't make a show like that, you know? So there's that legacy too.

OPPOSITE Nick (Pablo Schreiber) at the docks where he makes a living working for his uncle.

TOP RIGHT Nick (Schreiber, *left*) with fellow stevedore Vernon "Ott" Motley (Bus Howard, *right*).

# PAUL BEN-VICTOR

## Interview by Nikki Stafford and Robert Thompson

An accomplished character actor who has appeared in a wide range of film and TV roles, Paul Ben-Victor made his mark on *The Wire* as Spiros Vondopoulos, the right-hand man of The Greek. Although Spiros and his clan are ruthless, Ben-Victor brought a surprising level of likability and integrity to his character, making him far more nuanced than the typical TV show mobster.

**When you were cast in *The Wire*, were you familiar with the show?**

Not at all. I wasn't a big television watcher until the pandemic happened and everybody stayed home and watched all these great shows.

And I still didn't know [how popular the show was] until after it had been on for at least a season or two, when the fans started really approaching me and saying, "God, this is the greatest thing." And then there was a book that was sent to us from the show, like a magazine-size booklet, thick with rave reviews about the show from across the country.

**You were a veteran actor by the time you did *The Wire*; did the show strike you as different from other television you'd done before? What did you make of it?**

Just really good scripts. Great writers. I thought, "Wow, this is good. This is great writing; this is wonderful." But, you know, at the time I was busy. It was an exciting time for me because I was doing a lot of things at the same time. I thought to myself, "This is really great writing, so don't mess with it. Just hang in there and do the best you can." And I think I was focusing more on trying to get the guy, you know? All these years later, I'll see a scene here and there, and I'll think, "I could have done better." But I guess I did okay. My focus was getting this guy to be grounded and real.

There were these two wonderful, wonderful guys who helped me shape the character—there was an MMA-type guy, and I'd go see him at this club, and he would just say to me, "Oh, I took this guy out! I choked him out, I took him down, I killed him—he's dead!" [That line] became my hook into the character, and I'd always say, "I took him out, I took him out." And there was this Greek guy who would come over to my mom's apartment in the

OPPOSITE Paul Ben-Victor as Spiros "Vondas" Vondopoulos, The Greek's right-hand man.

TOP Business meeting: (*left to right*) The Greek (Bill Raymond), Spiros (Ben-Victor), Frank (Chris Bauer), and Nick (Pablo Schreiber).

TOP Spiros (Paul Ben-Victor, *left*) and The Greek (Bill Raymond, *right*) run their business operation from a nondescript café.

OPPOSITE Frank (Chris Bauer, *left*) and Spiros (Ben-Victor, *right*) discuss their plans on the waterfront.

Village, and I would turn the tape recorder on, and I think I made him say my lines. So that was the big thing: The hook for me was the Greekness, trying to sound like these guys with a subtle accent, maybe not as strong as their accents were.

**What did you make of Spiros? There are subtleties to the character that you maybe don't traditionally see in these types of shows.**
Absolutely. In as many episodes as I was in, I don't think I ever went, "Listen to me!" Usually with these bad guy characters, there's some level of explosion, but in this show, it was tender. The writing was poetic. And that's, I think, what made for me my character. And with Spiros, I think what I connected with was that he seemed very understated, which made him very powerful. The writing just had a softness to it, a very tender quality. That's what I connected with—the beauty, the poetry of the writing. It was nice.

**They brought you back a couple of seasons later to reprise your character briefly. When you come back to a role, do you approach it any differently than you would have when you started?**
No. You just dive in and go to work. I'm a very guttural actor: I work from instinct, from the music of it and how things feel. It's about how the shoes feel, how the cloth feels, how a cigarette might feel. I'm not cerebral; I don't work like that. It's more about how

it feels in my gut. It's the movement, the walk—it's a very instinctual thing for me, and so when I come back, whether it be a year or two or three, I've got the words, I've got the character—and I just go to work like time hasn't passed at all.

**Your character is so understated. Do you think he's a character who is sort of ever-present in the show, like he's still there in that world, unseen?**
I like your interpretation. It's obviously very subjective, but that's the wonderful thing about being a viewer of a show like *The Wire*. You might have the sense that he's maybe a little bit ethereal, just sort of lurking around any corner and watching. He's so quiet and sort of under the radar, so perhaps he's one of those guys who could stick around forever and just sort of reappear—and that's in the writing. It'd be nice if they did a movie one day, wouldn't it?

**It would be interesting, because some of the characters would obviously not be with us, and it would be fascinating to see who would re-emerge.**
Yeah, I could see Spiros being alive and well and doing wheelings and dealings on some massive level.

**Yeah, but very quietly, right?**
Very quietly.

# ALEXA L. FOGEL

## Interview by Nikki Stafford and Robert Thompson

Casting director Alexa L. Fogel was vital in assembling *The Wire*'s remarkable ensemble cast, bringing together Baltimorean actors, performers from across the US, and some key players from the UK. Across an extremely distinguished career, Fogel has cast a huge range of projects, including HBO's *Oz*, *Generation Kill*, and *True Detective*, plus Netflix's *Ozark* and FX's *Atlanta*.

**How do you begin assembling the cast for a show like *The Wire*?**

We sort of have a general approach. We know the difference between a character who needs to carry a story arc and characters who really can just help to create a realistic and authentic [atmosphere]—you know, bringing to life whatever the world is that we're building.

**You pushed hard for Idris Elba and Dominic West, despite their British accents. How did you know they were going to be the perfect fit for the show?**

It's a hard question to ask a casting director, because it's what we do.

Speaking the language of acting is my job, and some of it is instinctual. I think in Dom's case, he was very different from what we were initially looking for in terms of physicality and what was on the page. He was younger, he was less physically over the hill, but the essence of McNulty, where he was in his life and the way he always got in his own way—Dom understood it. I think that's what you're really looking for. You're looking for the essence of the character. Sometimes it comes in a different package than what you initially thought it will be. And I really felt like he intrinsically understood it—sometimes it's just in the bones. I think Dom would be the first person to say this: He had to work pretty hard on his American accent, because he got the job so close to when we started shooting.

Idris was a different situation. I had asked him to put himself on tape once we were at a kind of critical point, but Idris had recently read for me for a different project that he had not gotten, so he was very fresh in my mind. Many of the actors in *The Wire* read for multiple roles, because the process is very important. Trying to figure out who these characters were, and which actors really were bringing them to life best, was a process. It was the same thing with Idris. He essentially brought that character to life, he understood it, and he had a command of it. I don't

think too much about where people are from. I think that if you have a good ear, you can tell whether people will be able to overcome accent issues with some professional help. Particularly people who have grown up listening to American television.

**Were there any moments in the auditions when somebody completely took you off guard? Were there memorable auditions where you at first thought someone might not be right and then they completely blew you away?**

It doesn't really work like that. Lightning doesn't really strike: It really is a process. And then it coalesces, and then it really all starts to make sense. I will say that when Wendell [Pierce] and Dom were together, that was thrilling. I'm not a big believer in chemistry reads per se, but I think as people they just got each other so completely. There's such an enormous friendship between those two guys.

TOP A continuity Polaroid featuring Wendell Pierce.

OPPOSITE Continuity Polaroids: (*clockwise from top right*) Sonja Sohn, Clarke Peters, Delaney Williams, who plays acerbic supervising detective sergeant Jay Landsman, and Dominic West.

30 Mar 502

SC B354 Westie
D3          McNultys

30 Mar    502

SC 354 Greggs
D3

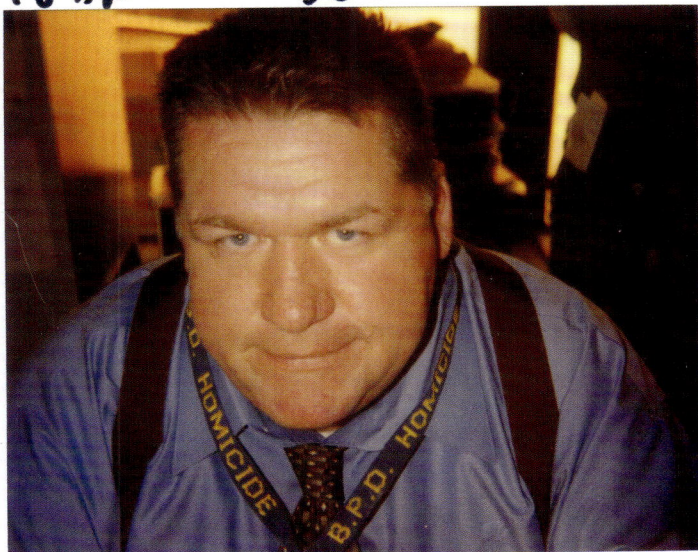

18 Apr    503

SC45      Landsman
D4

E503    2nd ce    8/17

Clark                SC.70

4 May     504

SC51
N2     Snoop

4 May     504

SC51
N2     Chris

4 May     504

SC51
N2     Cheese

E501     2nd Unit     4/2

Rae     SC 40
D1

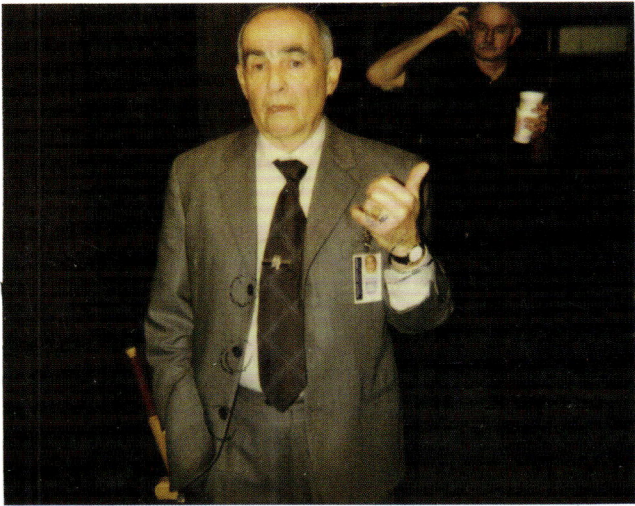

FOERSTER
SC 25-27

Lobby/Elevator/Lobby
D3

206

S·58

D·5

**The Wire was one of those shows that seemed to be on the verge of being canceled after every single season. Did that mean that you weren't given a lot of prep time?**

That's what television is. Particularly in a time when you really are doing everything week to week. You're always trying to catch up. Schedules change. I knew that there was a long-term plan and what it was in terms of certain different institutions, but beyond that, it would be once we knew that we were going, then I would get more detailed about where we were actually going. The hardest part of that was casting kids, because you need more time for that, and we just didn't have it.

**And in season four, you've got the four kids carrying an entire season . . .**

And we didn't have any of the material. I knew where the arcs were going, but we didn't actually have that material for them to audition with. So we had to do a lot of improv and just try to mix and match them and hope they'd be able to emotionally act it later.

**What do you think is the legacy of The Wire?**

You know, it's hard because I think the legacy of it changes over time as more and more people find it. It's really difficult to think about when you're inside it. The fact that it has endured and has had an impact so far beyond what it did when it was airing is fascinating. Has it had any actual effect in terms of creating change? No. But it does point out some systemic problems through real storytelling. What it did and continues to do is point things out by showing real people in a real way.

OPPOSITE Continuity Polaroids: (*clockwise from top right*) Gbenga Akinnagbe, who plays Marlo Stanfield's enforcer Chris Partlow; Eisa Davis in costume as Rae, Bubbles's long-suffering sister; Clifford Smith Jr., who portrays Cheese; Felicia Pearson and Akinnagbe (Pearson plays Snoop, Chris Partlow's partner in crime).

TOP Continuity Polaroids: Raymond Foerster (*left*), who plays the commander of the Criminal Investigation Division (CID), and Susan Rome (*right*) as Ilene Nathan, deputy state's attorney of the Major Crimes Division.

# SEASON TWO EPISODE

**S02E01:** Ebb Tide

**Written by:** Story by David Simon and Ed Burns; teleplay by David Simon

**Directed by:** Ed Bianchi

**Original airdate:** June 1, 2003

**Epigraph:** "Ain't never gonna be what it was." –Little Big Roy

**Description:** In the season two premiere, Det. Jimmy McNulty–exiled to police boat duty–finds the body of a woman floating in the Baltimore harbor. Meanwhile, Bodie drives to Philly to make a connection for the Barksdale crew.

**S02E02:** Collateral Damage

**Written by:** Story by David Simon and Ed Burns; teleplay by David Simon

**Directed by:** Ed Bianchi

**Original airdate:** June 8, 2003

**Epigraph:** "They can chew you up, but they gotta spit you out." –McNulty

**Description:** Major Valchek gets back at Sobotka for the church gift fiasco and a feud begins; Avon Barksdale continues to run his empire from a prison cell; on the waterfront, port cop Beatrice Russell investigates the contraband found in The Greek's container.

**S02E03:** Hot Shots

**Written by:** Story by David Simon and Ed Burns; teleplay by David Simon

**Directed by:** Elodie Keene

**Original airdate:** June 15, 2003

**Epigraph:** "What they need is a union." –Russell

**Description:** Bunk and Freamon chase their crime scene, a container ship, to Philly, where none of the crew finds it useful to speak English. Lt. Cedric Daniels–disgusted with his exile to the evidence control unit–lets it be known he's going to leave.

**S02E04:** Hard Cases

**Written by:** Story by David Simon and Joy Lusco; teleplay by Joy Lusco

**Directed by:** Elodie Keene

**Original airdate:** June 22, 2003

**Epigraph:** "If I hear the music, I'm gonna dance." –Greggs

**Description:** Sobotka reprimands his nephew Nick for stealing the cameras and orders him to bring the cargo back–too late. McNulty is on a self-assigned moral mission to identify his floater, but his old partner, Bunk, says they have a more pressing matter.

**S02E05:** Undertow

**Written by:** Story by David Simon and Ed Burns; teleplay by Ed Burns

**Directed by:** Steve Shill

**Original airdate:** June 29, 2003

**Epigraph:** "They used to make steel there, no?" –Spiros Vondas

**Description:** Ziggy loses his prized Camaro to drug dealers who aren't buying his alibis about not paying up. Unable to dump the homicide investigation on other police agencies, Col. Rawls measures Bunk for the blame, if the cases go unsolved.

**S02E06:** All Prologue

**Written by:** Story by David Simon and Ed Burns; teleplay by David Simon

**Directed by:** Steve Shill

**Original airdate:** July 6, 2003

**Epigraph:** "It don't matter that some fool say he different . . ." –D'Angelo

**Description:** Trying to let go of work and return to his marriage, McNulty gives up on identifying his Jane Doe. In their investigation of Sobotka, the detectives discover a pattern and explain the connection to Daniels, but he still won't take on the murder cases.

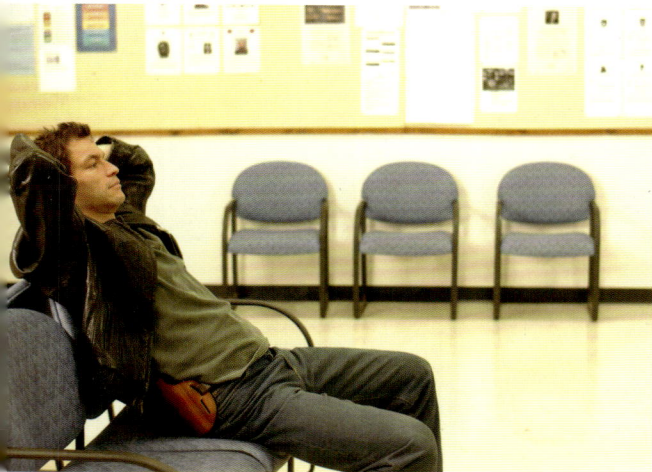

**S02E07:** Backwash

**Written by:** Story by David Simon and Rafael Álvarez; teleplay by Rafael Álvarez

**Directed by:** Thomas J. Wright

**Original airdate:** July 13, 2003

**Epigraph:** "Don't worry, kid. You're still on the clock." −Horseface

**Description:** Sobotka gives his lobbyist grief over the status of port legislation. Russell tells Sobotka the investigation is over, but a port computer is cloned, and when a container goes missing, the detectives follow.

**S02E08:** Duck and Cover

**Written by:** Story by David Simon and George Pelecanos; teleplay by George Pelecanos

**Directed by:** Dan Attias

**Original airdate:** July 27, 2003

**Epigraph:** "How come they don't fly away?" −Ziggy

**Description:** McNulty is back to his old self, on a drunken binge. Urged by fellow stevedores to fight Maui, Ziggy is again humiliated, but has a moment later at the bar. Worried about McNulty, Bunk tries to get Daniels, and Rawls, to take him on.

**S02E09:** Stray Rounds

**Written by:** Story by David Simon and Ed Burns; teleplay by David Simon

**Directed by:** Tim Van Patten

**Original airdate:** August 3, 2003

**Epigraph:** "The world is a smaller place now." −The Greek

**Description:** Bodie's effort to improve sales ends disastrously, forcing Bell to rethink his strategy. Ziggy, duck in tow, pulls Johnny Fifty into a new caper that should have the Greeks paying off big. McNulty, undercover and outnumbered, awaits "rescue."

**S02E10:** Storm Warnings

**Written by:** Story by David Simon and Ed Burns; teleplay by Ed Burns

**Directed by:** Rob Bailey

**Original airdate:** August 10, 2003

**Epigraph:** "It pays to go with the union card every time." −Ziggy

**Description:** The detail uses satellite technology to its advantage. Bodie is unhappy that Proposition Joe's people are slinging on his turf, but business flows−until a new face from New York arrives. Stringer Bell looks to an unlikely solution to the problem.

**S02E11:** Bad Dreams

**Written by:** Story by David Simon and George Pelecanos; teleplay by George Pelecanos

**Directed by:** Ernest R. Dickerson

**Original airdate:** August 17, 2003

**Epigraph:** "I need to get clean." −Sobotka

**Description:** With the clock ticking, the Detail makes a desperate move, and Daniels reams out Landsman for dropping the ball. Nick's deceit is in the open as Sobotka is overwhelmed by bad news.

**S02E12:** Port in a Storm

**Written by:** Story by David Simon and Ed Burns; teleplay by David Simon

**Directed by:** Robert F. Colesberry

**Original airdate:** August 24, 2003

**Epigraph:** "Business. Always business." −The Greek

**Description:** In the season two finale, the detail has a setback, and needs a new cooperator, while Russell and Bunk visit Philly, looking for evidence. Brother Mouzone talks with Stringer Bell regarding their agreement, leaving Bell to deal with Avon Barksdale.

# SEASON

3

# AN INTRODUCTION TO SEASON THREE

By D. Watkins

**B**altimore has become the home of indicted public officials—within the last decade we saw a collection of mayors, senators, and even a police commissioner get sent to federal prison.

Season three of *The Wire* introduces us to the wild machine politics of Baltimore City. We learn about the arrogance and dealmaking it takes to be a successful mayor in a major metropolitan city and how hard it is to keep that position.

Baltimore's fragile legal system is also on full display in season three. After all the strategy, planning, overtime, and manpower needed to bring down Avon Barksdale, he is quickly released. Many of the police officers who worked that case are just as furious with the system as the Black residents they police every day. In the meantime, Stringer Bell has been making wonderful strides on the surface: organizing all the drug dealers in Baltimore to work together, compiling their money and

"Season three introduced us to the wild machine politics of Baltimore City."

OPPOSITE Avon Barksdale (Wood Harris) returns home from prison in season three to discover that Stringer Bell has been making some moves of his own.

TOP Herc (Domenick Lombardozzi, *left*) and Kima (Sonja Sohn, *center*) take part in a raid on a Barksdale organization safe house in the final episode of season three, "Mission Accomplished." On his knees is Barksdale enforcer Perry, played by Perry Blackmon, the production's real-life security supervisor.

## Vision • Leadership • Integrity

# WATKINS

*"Building now for Baltimore's future...."*

# Del. Odell Watkins

**Maryland House of Delegates 40th District**

Tony

# GRAY

# FOR MAYOR

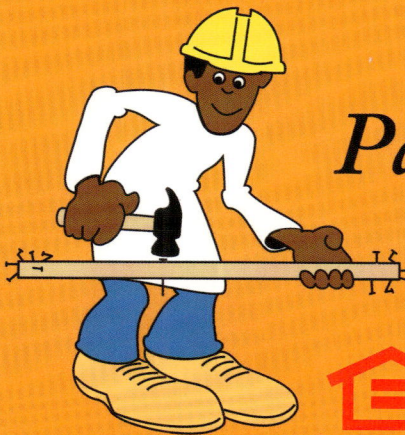

**Mayor Clarence V. Royce**
**and the citizens of Baltimore**

*Pardon our dust......*
*We're building a new future*
*for West Baltimore*

HOUSING AUTHORITY OF BALTIMORE CITY (HABC)
U.S. DEPARTMENT OF URBAN HOUSING AND DEVELOPMENT

TOP Two political posters created by *The Wire*'s art department featuring Frederick Strother as House of Delegates representative Odell Watkins and Christopher Mann as mayoral candidate Tony Gray.

ABOVE A piece of art-department-created signage heralding Mayor Clarence Royce's urban development plans.

OPPOSITE TOP Shooting scenes at Amsterdam, the drug-dealing amnesty zone set up by Bunny Colvin.

OPPOSITE BOTTOM Filming a scene from season three episode "All Due Respect," in which Omar Little poses as an elderly man to gain entry to a stash house. The two guards at far right are played by real-life brothers Joshua and Ethan Dixon.

purchasing larger quantities of a purer product—something that Avon would never do. Bell finds a better way to play the drug game. He flips the organization's drug money, then invests it all into legal businesses that pay taxes and issue paychecks. Now, the Barksdale organization is making as much legal money as street money, giving them the opportunity to live like productive citizens with a valuable stake in society. Stringer then tries his hand at real estate, only to be ripped off by Clay Davis (Isiah Whitlock Jr.), a slippery politician with a fondness for the word "Sheeeeeeeee-it!"

The idea of legalizing drugs, which is something that this country surely needs to consider, was also introduced in this season. Major Howard "Bunny" Colvin (Robert Widsom) is so sick of the way drugs are destroying his West Baltimore community that he legalizes them in three separate zones within his district, an area that the street kids name Hamsterdam (*Ham*, because it's slang for money in Baltimore, and *Amsterdam* because of that European city's drug laws). The idea is brilliant and the city quickly sees crime go down, but in Baltimore, the stigma of drug use is more important than a strategy that works—so here we are.

Major Colvin, like Bell, finds a better way to play the game—and in the end that creativity costs Colvin his job. But it could have been worse: Bell's creativity costs him his life.

OPPOSITE Isiah Whitlock Jr. as duplicitous senator Clay Davis, famed for his catchphrase "Sheeeeeeeeee-it . . ."

TOP RIGHT A political campaign poster created for Whitlock's character.

BOTTOM Stringer Bell (Idris Elba, *left*) meets with Davis (Whitlock, *right*), unaware that the wily politician plans to rip him off.

Sen. R. Clayton "Clay"

# DAVIS

## for Senate ★ 39th District

"Your unbought, unbossed representation in Annapolis..."

Authority: Clay Davis for Senate, L. Mambo Payne, Treasurer

# GEORGE PELECANOS

## Interview by Nikki Stafford and Robert Thompson

An accomplished crime fiction author, George Pelecanos was brought on to *The Wire*'s writing team by David Simon, who admired his work. After penning the penultimate episode of season one, Pelecanos became a producer on *The Wire*, writing multiple episodes and becoming an important creative voice on the show.

**When David Simon approached you to write for *The Wire*, did you get a sense of what your role was going to be?**

It was vague. I agreed to write one script in the first season, and people liked what I did. It was a sort of notorious script because it included the death of Wallace at the hands of his friends. And from then on, David and I had sort of an unofficial handshake saying that I would get the penultimate script every year, which is when a lot of things happened. I think in the back of David's mind, he thought, *Well, this guy's a crime novelist, so he knows how to make the engine go.* So it worked out. And by season three I had become a producer. I learned how to write for television through David, and I learned how to produce through Nina K. Noble and the late Robert F. Colesberry, so I had a lot of great teachers.

***The Wire*—with its vast number of characters, storylines, and complexities—bucked the trends of regular television. As a writer, how did you approach the series?**

Not to speak for David, but I think that he wanted me because I hadn't written for television yet, so I hadn't learned any bad habits. He never hired network screenwriters—not because there aren't any good ones, but because they've learned a lot of things that are very hard to unlearn. This includes the idea that everybody has to be redeemable and that there has to be redemption in the end.

David read one of my books, *The Sweet Forever*, and it happened to be a deep urban novel that I wrote here in DC. It was very similar to what he was doing, and I think that's what got him interested.

OPPOSITE Author George Pelecanos, who wrote several key episodes of *The Wire*.

TOP (*Left to right*) Ayesha Chaney with husband Tray Chaney (*both seated*), Robert F. Chew (*standing*), Pelecanos (*seated*), Donnie Andrews, the real-life inspiration for character Omar Little, and his wife, Denise Francine Boyd Andrews (*both standing*), and Jamie Hector (*seated*).

TOP Stringer Bell (Idris Elba, *left*) meets with Clay Davis (Isiah Whitlock Jr., *right*) in the George Pelecanos-penned season three episode "Slapstick."

OPPOSITE BOTTOM A floor plan for the Barksdale gang's safehouse set.

## What interested you in *The Wire*?

I had seen *The Corner*, and I thought it was different from anything I had ever seen before, and it lined up with my politics. One thing that was attractive to me about television was that I could reach three million readers a week, instead of the 20,000 or 30,000 readers who buy my hardcover books. So it was an opportunity for me to put these ideas out into the world that I was behind, and that David was behind.

## *The Wire* wasn't afraid to kill some of the characters that were most integral to the show: Nobody was really safe. How significant do you think it was for you to nail that in a way that still resonates with people?

For me, the secret to writing is that you don't think of these people as characters; you think of them as people. Wallace's death scene, for example, is less about what Wallace is going through than what his friends are going through. Because they're all kids, and that's their boy, that's their friend, and they're put in an awful position. So I tried to empathize with all of them. Those guys, to me, weren't cold-blooded killers—they were three friends who were going to go through something that was emotionally wrenching, and one of them was going to die.

And Snoop was very pretty and had beautiful eyes, so I thought that she would probably care about the way she looked and the way she would be found. And so [in her death scene], she says to [her killer],

"How my hair look, Mike?" And he says, "You look good, girl." And then he kills her. When David got the script, he called me up and said, "Help me understand this." But there are some things you really can't explain: It's intuitive. I just thought it was right. If you remember the way it was shot, the camera pulls back, it's a wide shot, and you just see the flash of the muzzle. I said to David, "Do me a favor: Let's just shoot it the way I wrote it. If it doesn't work, you don't have to use it, but I feel strongly that it will work." To his credit, that's what he did.

## Which scene that you wrote for *The Wire* is your favorite?

Probably the best scene I ever wrote in *The Wire* is the one where Stringer Bell and Avon Barksdale are on the roof, and they talk about their childhoods and their dreams and everything, and they're both about to betray each other. Stringer thinks he's going to get the upper hand, but Avon set him up for his death. And then they give each other a hug.

## Was Omar a favorite to write for from the beginning?

It was a combination of the fact that he was a cool character and also that the actor [Michael K. Williams] was bringing something to it that was just extraordinary and larger than life. The reason that Omar's death was sort of anticlimactic was that he had become this larger-than-life character, and the interesting thing about the way we wrote it—I think

Dennis Lehane wrote his death—is the scene in the newsroom where they get the news of it, and it's just another dead guy. In other words, Omar was a big deal in his world, but in the larger white world of Baltimore, he's disposable.

**He must have been an interesting character to write for.**
Well, I have to give credit to the crew; his iconic shotgun and black coat was all them. Once Mike held that gun, I think it changed him. I remember the very first day that he had the gun, he didn't know how to load it. And I remember seeing Ed Burns step out into the street and show him how to rack a shotgun. And that's a lot. A gun in your hand changes you in a lot of ways. And Mike was a gentle guy.

There's that scene in the park between Omar and Bunk, which I wrote. I was listening to Wendell talking to the crew one day, and he was saying that the guys in his school called him Schoolboy because they knew that he was smarter than everybody else, but he didn't puff up or anything. They actually encouraged him and protected him. I asked Wendell if I could use his story for the scene between him and Omar, because I wanted to take a little bit of the wind out of Omar,

because the character was getting too mythological in a sense. I needed somebody to dress him down. And it was just an opportune thing, something that I overheard on the set that spurred it on.

**As the characters evolve, you start to get a sense of their popularity, so the notion of sort of putting the character in his place every so often makes sense.**
Another example of that is in season two. I felt like the longshoreman characters, especially the peripheral guys, were being put up on this pedestal of the noble working class. Dave and I had a discussion one day where I said that I grew up in a working-class neighborhood, and many of these guys would get drunk every night and smack their wives, etc. And David listened to me. If you look at the montage at the end of season two, you see some of these hale and hearty guys that we've been seeing all season, and we find out that they're punks. We were always having these kinds of discussions; Let's tell the truth, because we're getting too close to elevating these characters when they shouldn't be elevated.

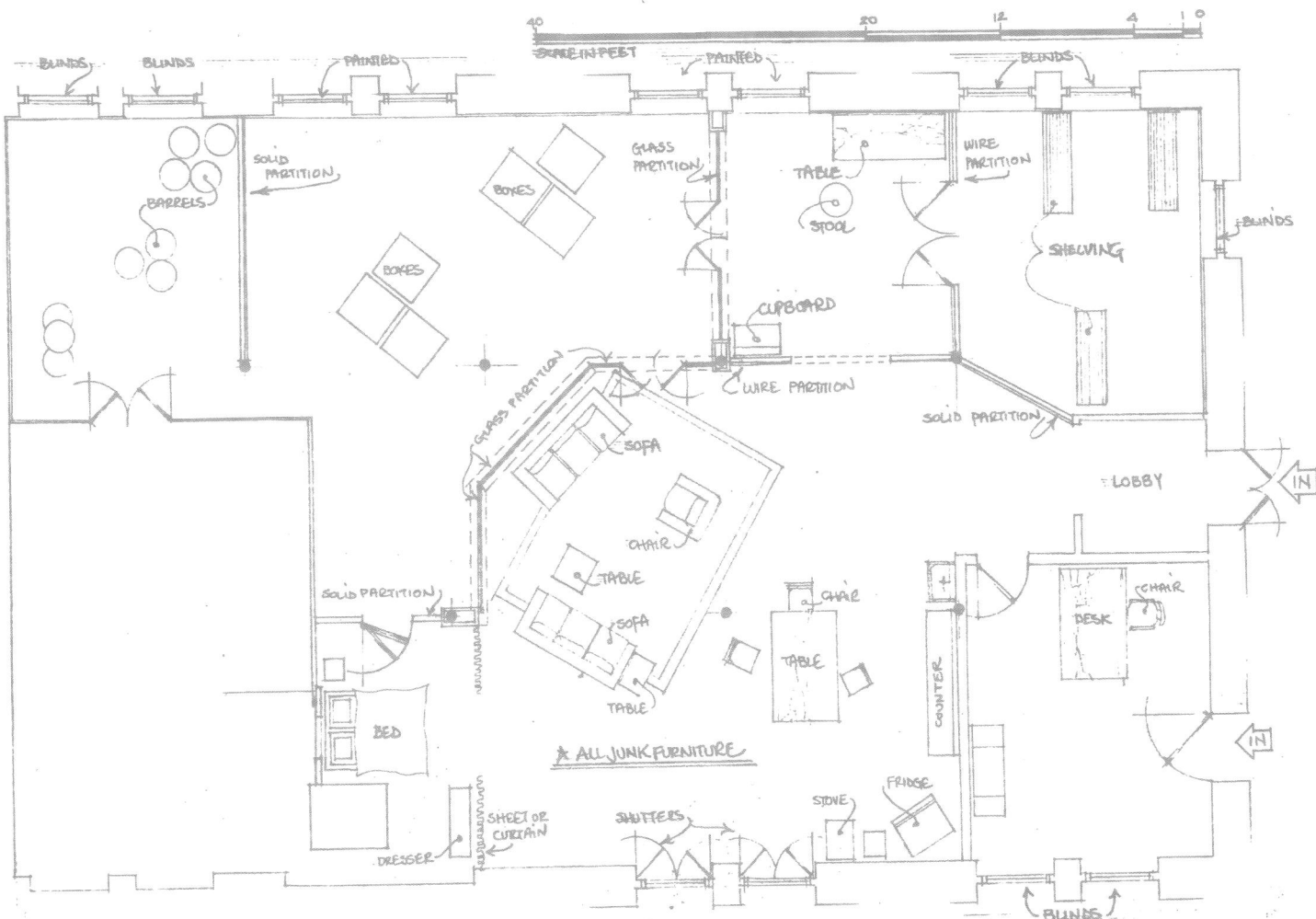

BARKSDALE GANG SAFEHOUSE - STREET LIGHTING DEPOT - OLIVER & WOLFE

# IDRIS ELBA

## Interview by Natalia Winkelman

Stringer Bell, Avon Barksdale's partner in crime, quickly became a key figure in *The Wire* before his shocking death at the end of season three. A breakout role for Idris Elba, the London-born actor has gone on to appear in a remarkable array of film projects including *Prometheus* (2012), *Pacific Rim* (2013), *Thor: Ragnarok* (2017), and *The Suicide Squad* (2021). He also starred in the BBC's long-running crime thriller *Luther* and made a memorable guest appearance in the US version of *The Office*.

**What did you think of Stringer Bell when you first got the role?**

Initially it was just a small part—it wasn't significant because Stringer was obviously [Avon Barksdale's] number two. It wasn't written with lots of direction in terms of how Stringer sounds or what he looks like. He was just Stringer Bell, the number two: sort of a solid dude, basically.

I think that Stringer became popular with audiences, and I guess all of the characters within the drug dealer storyline became more popular, and I think the writers sort of reacted to that popularity—people wanted to see more of these characters. And, of course, that gave the writers a chance to really sort of stretch out these characters, so the audience

got to know them a bit more. So, for me, yeah, it was exciting to watch the evolution because what essentially was one season's work became three seasons. That was obviously exciting to me as an actor on an HBO show, but it was also great because you get to really unpack these characters and their complexities. And it's a testament to David Simon and HBO that they went with what the audience wanted to see, and so for me it was a blessing. I don't think the ambition was to create three seasons of the Barksdale legacy, but essentially that's what it ended up becoming.

**How did you feel when found out that Avon and Stringer were going to betray each other?**

OPPOSITE Idris Elba as Stringer Bell, whose story ends in season three of *The Wire*.

TOP Stringer (Elba, *right*) hosts a meeting at the Barksdale organization's funeral parlor headquarters. Seated is Shaun "Shamrock" McGinty (Richard Burton), Stringer's second-in-command.

Personally, I felt it was inevitable that they were going to fall out. Stringer and Avon wanted different things or approached things differently, and it was just obvious to me that one was going to go one way and the other was going to go the other. I felt that dramatically it made sense for the writers to try and pull these two apart because that's the last thing [the audience] thought was going to happen. I think the audience was sitting on the edge of their seats because here were essentially two brothers suddenly becoming enemies, and that's always compelling to watch. It goes back to some of the oldest stories that we've ever been told—Cain and Abel, you know? And even though I knew it was inevitable, I guess I was saddened by the way that it happened: saddened that there wasn't another way for these characters to evolve.

**Have you rewatched the show recently?**

I've never seen *The Wire*. I find it difficult to watch myself, so I've just never really seen the five seasons. A lot of people will always be like, "You haven't seen *The Wire*?" And I'm like, "I haven't. I don't like to watch myself because if I can avoid it, I try not to watch it." There are films that I've been in that I haven't seen, there's TV shows that I've been in that I haven't seen, and *The Wire* is one of those. I think some actors find it a little bit hard to watch themselves and then continue working because you start to overly criticize yourself or analyze yourself in a way that's not natural.

**Although the show is very serious, there are also moments of levity. How would you describe the tone of *The Wire*?**

Well, from the inside out, the scenes weren't always designed to be funny; they were designed to be real, and we didn't play them for the laughs. That's something that people have always said to me: "If you watched *The Wire* you'd be cracking up." I'm like, "What are you laughing at, though?" And they'll mention Stringer's 40-degree-day speech or some of the D'Angelo scenes with the boys. I always feel like they weren't written to be funny, but the performances are so rich that it comes across as funny. But I don't think it was designed to be that way. I think the balance, though, is healthy for a show like that in terms of the sort of drama/humor ratio.

I think the show is realistic, and *pessimistic* is a good word [to describe it] probably, but I found it raw. Having lived in Baltimore for three years and having been a part of that community while filming

a show about it, there was a lot of symmetry there that was uncomfortable. Baltimore at one juncture of its existence was very much like [its portrayal in the show], and sometimes it was sort of hard to differentiate between drama and reality. There were plenty of scenes where we'd be shooting and either the real 12 O'Clock Boys [street gang] would come through with their motorbikes and just roll through or some beef would spill out, and the producers would be like, "Yo, we need to get off the streets." That was just sort of part of the filming experience, let alone the life experience of the people that lived in those communities. But I felt that people in those communities were optimistic, weirdly enough. They were like, "Oh, these guys out here are making a movie about us? That's great. Now people are gonna see who we are." There was this underlying optimism that things were going to get better. It's not like, "Woe is us."

**Why do you think that the show has continued to be relevant?**

It feels great that *The Wire* has achieved that. It's a surprise in the sense that when we were making the show, I don't think anybody anticipated its power and the impact it would have. The way the show was pitched to me was that it was about wiretapping and these guys that listen to people's conversations, but it turned out to be a lot more than that. That was a massive surprise to all of us, but I'm really proud that people took the time to appreciate how well it was written and how well-observed it was.

It's about a community that has not been given support and the way people choose to live, survive, and make money. It's about how the community pulls together, whether good or bad—gangs, family, whatever. That's not unique to Baltimore, and we've seen stories like this all over the world. I remember going to Baltimore for the first time and saying, "This reminds me of Manchester in the UK." There's a very similar community there in Moss Side, an [inner-city area] where the police couldn't even go in. That community sort of survived on its own rules, and there are gods and heroes in those places, and there are demons and devils in those places, you know? Go to Africa, Brazil or certain parts of Eastern Europe and France—that encasement is real.

It highlighted an underbelly of America which for a long time had a certain outward-facing [ideal that the] American Dream is amazing and you can come here and do what you want. I dined on that dream too, living in East London and thinking about what I

could achieve in America as an actor. But Baltimore offered a different outward facing reality and it was 100 percent a wake-up for me.

I don't think Baltimoreans felt like *The Wire* was new news. They've gone through generations of living like that—not only Baltimore, but Philly, Chicago, Detroit. It's cyclical, and it has been like that for centuries. When we made [the Netflix Western] *The Harder They Fall* (2021), we tried to talk about how there were once more towns that were Black towns, and it wasn't until those towns became successful that people started to tear them down. This has been going on and on and on in Black communities for a very, very long time.

### What impact did *The Wire* have on your career?

*The Wire* came at a juncture where it was make-or-break for me as an actor in the States. I moved out there about five years prior to getting it. My wife at the time was pregnant with my daughter—she was due in January, and I was auditioning all through November and December.

And if I didn't get that job, I would have to pick up sticks and get back to the UK, where there was a little more of a support system and maybe more work, so I could feed my kid. So, this show really changed the trajectory of my life beyond anyone's comprehension.

And subsequently, I was allowed to create a character that still resonates and informs how people see me as an actor. For a long time people wouldn't accept me as any other character apart from Stringer Bell. When I spoke in my native tongue as an Englishman, people thought I was taking the piss. They'd be like, "Nah, dawg, come on, knock that off." So, it really did change my life 100 percent for the better, and it became one of the characters that people most recognize me for to this day. I've managed to keep my career going for about twenty years now since *The Wire*, and some people still only have ever seen me in *The Wire* and only want to see me in that show. So, that's fascinating to me.

I think it was just last week someone told me that *The Wire* is like the number one TV show or the most respected TV show in the last two decades, and I was like, "Really? Wow." I don't watch that much TV, but I know that there's lots of great shows that have come since *The Wire* , but we still hold the crown, so to speak. So yeah, I'm feeling the effects of *The Wire* to this day. I'm super proud of it and thankful that I got an opportunity as a young actor in New York to audition for it. Shoutout to Alexa Fogel. I'm really thankful that I got that opportunity.

TOP Stringer (Elba) tries to win the drug game with his wits rather than muscle but finds himself outmatched when he becomes involved with Baltimore's political class.

# BALTIMORE COMSTAT

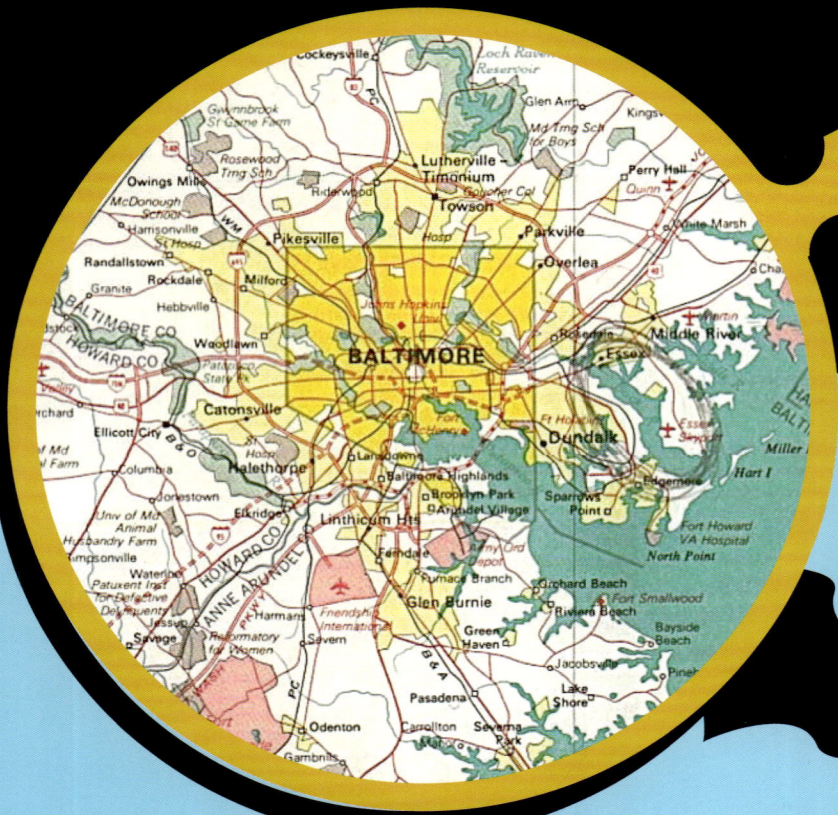

MAYOR
CLARENCE V. ROYCE

# THE WIRE SEASON THREE: TRYING TO MAKE SENSE OF THE GAME

by Justine Elias

I thought Stringer Bell was the hero. But that's what I get for coming late to the party.

My first experience of *The Wire* wasn't just mid-series or mid-season. I walked in on *The Wire* mid-episode: season three, episode eleven, "Middle Ground," just as Bell, the drug dealer with MBA ideas, sees all his big plans fall apart. He's betrayed and murdered by his childhood friend.

When I jumped into *The Wire*, I did so to quiet hectoring from friends, acquaintances, and random taxi drivers who said: "What? You're not watching *The Wire*?" So judgmental. As though we all had HBO, or DVD box sets of *The Wire*, and time to start watching from the beginning. When I did finally get my act together, I realized one thing for certain: *The Wire* was not a series with traditional rooting interests. Viewers couldn't be wholeheartedly Team Cop, not when the season opener features narcotics detectives tearing into a multiple-vehicle high-speed chase, narrowly missing a jogger and children at play. (The suspect, an unarmed teenager who might be carrying a bag of drugs, gets away.)

In the war on drugs, the police have turned into warriors. One

OPPOSITE A poster created for scenes in *The Wire* in which William Rawls berates his subordinates over the latest crime statistics; Comstat is short for computer statistics.

TOP At a party to celebrate Avon Barksdale's release from prison, Stringer Bell (Idris Elba) raises a toast.

ABOVE Stringer (Elba, *left*) and Avon (Wood Harris, *right*) find themselves at odds over the running of their organization.

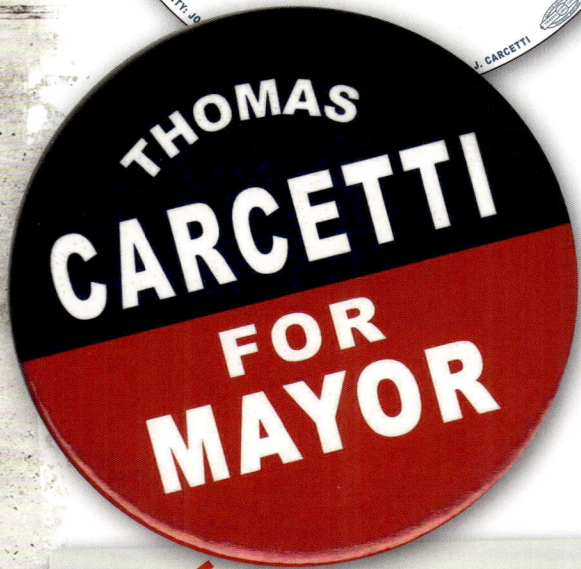

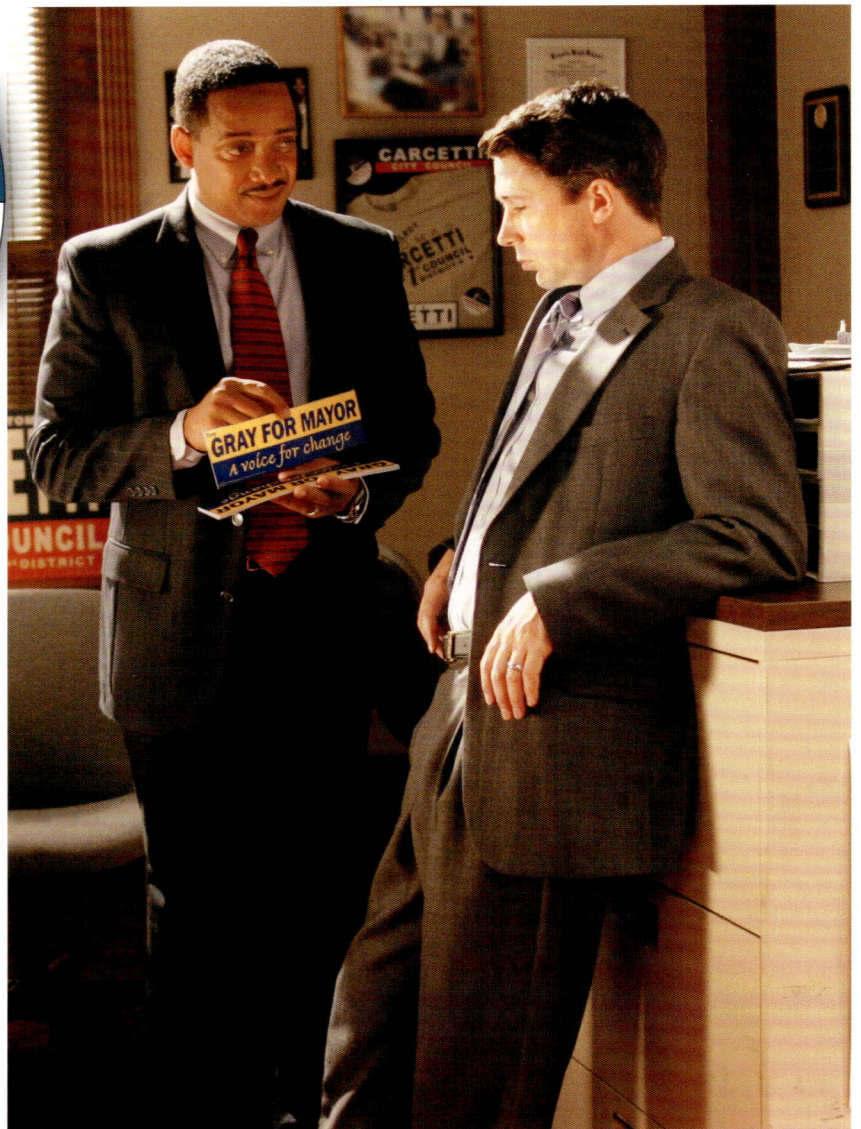

LEFT Political campaign materials created for ambitious Baltimore politician Tommy Carcetti (Aidan Gillen).

TOP RIGHT Carcetti (Gillen, *right*) with his comrade, mayoral candidate Tony Gray (Christopher Mann, *left*). Carcetti ultimately betrays Gray and pursues the role of mayor himself.

undercover cop, maddened with frustration, climbs atop a car and yells at the long-gone drug runner: "We do not lose. And we do not forget. And we do not give up." Like an angry, abusive parent, he carries on, shouting, "If you march yourself out here right now and put the bracelets on, we will not kick the shit out of you. But if you make us go into the weeds for you, or if you make us come back out here tomorrow night and catch you on the corner, I swear to Christ we will beat you longer and harder than you beat your dick."

But the *Wire* could never lure anybody onto Team Criminal either: Despite endless attempts at enterprise (rival dealers banding together to nail down better wholesale prices; an endearing junkie who hawks scrap metal, T-shirts, and information)—there is no honor among these thieves. Family and friends die just as easily as drug soldiers.

Nor are there any heroes to be found in politics, either.

As on-the-make City Councilman Tommy Carcetti, actor Aidan Gillen flexed his Machiavellian muscles long before he perfected the art of the backstab as Littlefinger in *Game of Thrones*. Carcetti snakes his way toward higher office by urging the city police chief, at a diner meeting, to trust in him rather than the mayor. ("You come to me. I can give you what you need," he says.) Rewind the scene, and you realize that Carcetti appears to switch seats mid-pitch, from the right to left and back again. The effect is deeply unnerving: Carcetti's a schemer too quick to catch in real time. The police chief turns him down, but Carcetti finds a new stratagem: leaking damaging information to the press about the mayor and the police.

I fancied myself a battle-tested TV watcher. I thought I knew how it would all unspool. The special investigation team, Detective Jimmy McNulty, Detective Kima Greggs, Detective Lester Freamon, holed up in an old building with outdated equipment, find themselves outgunned and out-tech'd by criminals, who toss old phones like cigarette butts. Meanwhile Stringer Bell would try to move his business into a new era where drugs are just another commodity, and there's plenty of money to go around. Detective McNulty, imagining himself a knight errant, would try to paint Bell as old-fashioned gangster, a pure and simple Bad Guy. This was all unfolding in the autumn of 2004, when we were in the middle of a presidential election that felt very much like the same old game, with the same terrifyingly high stakes. Maybe Stringer Bell really could forge a way forward. Maybe *The Wire* is more than a television show about all the ways our society is irredeemably messed up. Maybe Stringer could show us a way to break the machine.

But like the Franklin Terrace housing projects, demolished as part of a high-minded city plan to improve Baltimore life, Bell wasn't a harbinger of the future. He was a relic of the past, doomed to destruction. When the Terrace towers came down at the beginning of season three, a cloud of dust choked former residents and neighbors. That cloud seemed to be *The Wire*'s

TOP Drug dealers and addicts in Bunny Colvin's drug amnesty zone, nicknamed Hamsterdam by the locals.

BOTTOM McNulty (Dominic West, *right*) confronts Stringer (Idris Elba, *left*) at the gangster's print shop in the season three episode "Straight and True."

warning to viewers: Superficial attempts to fix our cities are, in many ways, worse than doing nothing at all—exercises in toxic obfuscation.

Season three dug deep into political corruption, of elected officials, yes, but also of every organization covered by the show. The Greek word *politika* means "affairs of the cities," and on *The Wire*, those affairs are not limited to the mayor's office or city council chambers: There are politics—and bureaucracy—at work in every institution or business shown on *The Wire*. (Given a twenty-two-episode season, I'm sure the show could have sniffed out crooked dealings in the Baltimore Symphony Orchestra. How *does* first chair violin get the position anyway?)

Inside the Barksdale-Bell drug gang, disagreement between the boss (Avon Barksdale) and the money man (Stringer Bell) grows as territory shrinks. Barksdale values honor, reputation, and family, while Bell, a student of economic theory, motivates his street drug dealers with patter that wouldn't sound out of place at a pharmaceutical sales conference. Sometimes his Robert's Rules of Order approach works, and sometimes his rigidity gets hilariously out of hand: "You're taking minutes? During a criminal conspiracy?" Bell asks, when he catches a dutiful underling scribbling away. Inevitably, Bell's so caught up in his own methods that he offhandedly orders a hit on a rival while the other man is at church with his grandmother. Sunday is a day of truce, which Bell should know. (Even worse, Bell's gunmen wound the rival's grandmother, which sets off even more violence.)

Within the city police department, the police commissioner demands statistics that will make the city appear less crime-ridden, regardless of whether the streets are actually becoming safer. In Baltimore's Western

District, the top cop, Major Bunny Colvin, wants to retire knowing he's made a difference. He's tired of grieving with the families of officers killed and injured in the field. Seeing the futility of endless "buy-and-bust" arrests that catch only low-level offenders, Colvin comes up with a radical plan to deal with what is becoming an unwinnable war. He recalls that the city once forbade alcohol consumption in public, but the street corner, he says, is "the poor man's lounge." If cops arrested everyone who drank a beer in public, there would be no time for any other kind of police work: "If they look the other way, they open themselves up to all kinds of flaunting, all kinds of disrespect." The compromise was letting people hide their booze in paper bags.

Instead of fighting the war on drugs, Colvin squeezes the problem into three "free zones," a few derelict blocks where drug dealing is de facto legal. Into the free zones come dealers, followed by their now-unemployed legmen—most of whom look to be middle school or high school age—and drug users, along with their children.

Social services arrive next: needle exchanges, condom distribution, sex worker outreach. But this one-to-one harm reduction is donated by a local university, not the city. At night, though, the free zones have no electricity, no water, no rules. In one remarkable sequence, Bubbles, whose struggles with addiction stretch back well before he was introduced in *The Wire*'s first

TOP Wood Harris shoots a scene as Avon Barksdale in season three of *The Wire*.

TOP Avon (Wood Harris, *left*) and Slim Charles (Anwan Glover, *center*) meet with Stringer (Idris Elba, *right*), who advocates a more cerebral approach to the drug trade, which is at odds with that of his hot-headed partner.

ABOVE Amsterdam at night, a vision of hell that even Bubbles finds difficult to stomach.

episode, wanders the blocks at night, cringing in recognition at the misery around him. When word of the free zones reaches the media and city hall, the search is on for someone, anyone, to blame. Who let this happen?

A better question might be: Did any aspect of the free zones work better than the previous approach, which wasn't working at all? Residents outside the Western District's free zones would probably say yes, since crime on their blocks is down. The police made to guard the edges of such a place might find it disgusting and frustrating: They're powerless to intervene or aid. But Colvin's stated mission—in addition to protecting his colleagues from harm—is to allow them to do real policing: "The kind of police work that's actually worth the effort, that's actually worth taking a bullet for." It's a stirring speech, but so often in *The Wire*, you have to rewatch and wonder: Who is the character talking to? What does he want? What do those words even mean?

When Bunny is called to account before the mayor and city council, Carcetti makes a show of defending him, then launches his mayoral campaign: "Enough to the despair that makes policemen think about surrender. Enough to the fact that these neighborhoods are beyond saving. Enough to this administration's indecisiveness and lethargy, to the garbage that goes uncollected, the lots and row houses which stay untreated, the working men and women who every day are denied a chance at economic freedom. Enough to the crime which every day chokes more life from our city."

Listen carefully, though, to what he says next: "If we don't have the courage and the conviction to fight this war the way it should and needs to be fought, using every weapon that we can possibly muster—if that

doesn't happen, well, we are staring at defeat. And that defeat should not and cannot and will not be forgiven." That language echoes the frustrated shouts of the narcotics cop standing atop a squad car, demanding that a drug dealer turn himself in. (It didn't work.)

Carcetti is using the language of war. The war on drugs. The war on terrorism. He's got a great voice and a smooth presence. He might even mean what he says and truly care about the people he hopes to represent. But if I hear right, he's calling for more of the same.

What do we want from our entertainment? Inspiration. Do we want to see the harsh realities of life artfully displayed? Or escapism, the poetic justice that is mostly missing in life? Bertolt Brecht wrote that "art is not a mirror held up to reality but a hammer with which to shape it." *The Wire*'s hammer blows fixed nothing, changed nothing. But looking back at it now, with facts still on the endangered species list, there is something bracing about *The Wire*'s clear-eyed pessimism. Change doesn't come from electing any one politician. The system, any system, absorbs threats to its existence like the Blob. Agents for change are true heroes because they are fighting for a hopeless cause.

Of course, I was wrong about Stringer Bell being the hero of *The Wire*. But his downfall was even more affecting the second time around. His dream of turning drug cash into tangible real estate wealth was dragged down because of betrayal by old associates and by new ones in city and in state politics.

As episode eleven begins, Stringer's scheme of peaceful drug lord cooperation is ruined by his close friend Avon Barksdale's old-school approach, and the new technology of burner phones.

To quickly recap: Stringer cannot get Avon to call off his war with rival gangster Marlo Stanfield, so that revenue stream is in serious danger. And his real estate business is in tatters after he paid $250,000 in cash bribes to a state senator, which the politician simply pocketed without helping Stringer. When Avon refuses to sign off on the politician's assassination, Stringer rats out Avon to Bunny. What Stringer doesn't know is that Avon has done the same to him, giving him up to enforcer Brother Mouzone (Michael Potts), whom Stringer had betrayed the previous season. Again, just business.

> "... Stringer's scheme of peaceful drug lord cooperation is ruined by his close friend Avon Barksdale's old-school approach ..."

TOP LEFT Avon (Wood Harris, *seated*) is treated for a gunshot wound after being outplayed by Marlo Stanfield's crew.

TOP RIGHT Tensions boil over between Stringer (Idris Elba, *top*) and Avon (Harris, *bottom*), leading to a physical altercation that marks the beginning of the end for their partnership.

TOP Stringer (Idris Elba) runs for his life after being cornered by Omar Little and Brother Mouzone in season three's penultimate episode, "Middle Ground."

ABOVE Omar (Michael K. Williams) fires a shotgun blast at his nemesis.

If that isn't *Godfather* enough for you, there's also a salute to poor Fredo Corleone. Stringer and Avon have a remarkable farewell scene on a rooftop overlooking Baltimore Harbor. With a smear of colored lights behind them, a backdrop fit for a Meg Ryan–Tom Hanks romantic comedy, Avon advises Stringer to "kick back and enjoy the view," as if he's trying to have one last special night with his best guy.

Stringer gets into the spirit, at first, as they drink and laugh about their exploits as kids. Stringer stole a badminton set when he had no grassy backyard in which to set it up—Avon laughs that the toy shop nabbed him while Stringer ran off, badminton set in hand. And that's Stringer in a nutshell: Even as a kid, he had fancy dreams. (Did he also leave Avon to get caught?) Stringer looks out at the glittering cityscape and regrets that he didn't have his drug money back when harbor real estate was cheap. Avon doesn't want to talk business, because he's chosen business over friendship, and he doesn't want to admit it, not quite yet. And then it happens, the *Godfather Part II* kiss of death. Avon asks Stringer what time he'll be on the building site tomorrow. Stringer is no Fredo: He immediately senses danger, yet he gives Avon the details, perhaps because his guilty conscience drives him to it. Or maybe because he is bone-tired of playing a losing game. With a salute of "To us, motherfucker," they embrace for the last time, a double-barreled betrayal that cuts them both deeply. Neither man looks the other in the eye. Avon will end up back in prison, but Stringer's end comes sooner.

Despite that ominous discussion that plays like a breakup scene, Stringer goes ahead with his meeting. (He's there to berate his contractor:

Nothing more bourgeois than that.) That's when Omar Little strides through the door with his signature shotgun and kills Stringer's bodyguard.

Omar. How have I said so much about a season of *The Wire* and not yet mentioned the series' most indelible character? Mostly because if you have begged, bought, or stolen a copy of a book about *The Wire*, then you already know all about Omar. If Stringer's story is straight out of Mario Puzo, Omar is a scion of Shakespeare. His motto is always: To his own self, be true. This man who owns his sexuality, his violence, his desires, is the perfect Angel of Death for Stringer: a man both too smart and not crafty enough for his own good, a man who craved legitimacy but disdained rules. A man who does not truly know himself and who has run out of time to solve that particular puzzle.

Stringer makes a run for it, the shaky handheld camera following him through a building with no exits (there's a reason why we need safety inspectors and OSHA, Stringer). He runs out of floors and into the implacable Brother Mouzone, and at this point the camerawork grows very still. Stringer freezes, backlit in front of a large bright window, the sort of feature a realtor would emphasize in a future ad for B&B luxury lofts.

Omar cruelly tells Stringer that it was his best friend, Avon, who gave him up. Well, who else could it be? Elba underplays this final moment. Stringer was never sentimental. "Get on with it, motherfuckers," he says, and they do. In the background, we see the banner for his real estate company:

BOTTOM "This ain't about your money, bro . . .": Omar Little (Michael K. Williams) prepares to kill Stringer Bell.

> "Why did Stringer
> Bell's death strike
> me so hard the first
> time around? Maybe
> because the best
> television, the best
> popular art, pulls
> you toward
> characters who
> aren't necessarily
> good, or even doing
> good things."

TOP Brother Mouzone (Michael Potts) fires a shot at Stringer.

OPPOSITE TOP In the final episode of season three, "Mission Accomplished," McNulty (Dominic West, *left*) and Kima (Sonja Sohn, *right*) attend the scene of Stringer Bell's murder. A real estate sign, created by the art department, can be seen in the background.

OPPOSITE BOTTOM Omar (Michael K. Williams, *left*) and Brother Mouzone (Michael Potts, *right*) leave the scene of the crime.

Coming Soon Residential/Retail Opportunities from B&B Enterprises. A touch heavy-handed, but if any character rates that kind of a send-off, it's Stringer Bell.

Bunny Colvin also pays the price for daring to think outside the box. Hamsterdam becomes a political hot potato, and he takes the fall. It was his idea, but he didn't create the free zones alone. He's demoted to lieutenant, losing his full pension, and sees his project destroyed. In 2022, as we creep toward federal decriminalization of marijuana, the speech Bunny makes to a doubting subordinate about the destructive foolhardiness of the war on drugs is even more poignant today than when it first aired: "You call something a war and pretty soon everyone's running around like warriors. When you're at war, you need a fucking enemy. And pretty soon, damn near everybody on every corner is your fucking enemy."

Unlike Stringer, Bunny wanted to help others, even at the risk of ruining his life. But both men were visionaries. Or, as Stringer said to Bunny when he gave up Avon, "You and me both trying to make sense of this game." Bunny, who implored his young beat cops to know where they were in Baltimore at all times, who even handed out compasses to help them find their way around, forgot where he was in the end. He was mired in a system that he could not change.

Why did Stringer Bell's death strike me so hard the first time around? Maybe because the best television, the best popular art, pulls you toward characters who aren't necessarily good, or even doing good things. But he and Colvin reached further than anyone else I can think of on *The Wire*. And when they lost, they knew it was coming. They fell silently and alone—no musical score, nothing. I can't think of anything that hurts more than that.

# MICHAEL POTTS

## Interview by Nikki Stafford and Robert Thompson

A working actor for three decades, Michael Potts has a huge range of credits to his name, including roles in *True Detective*, *The Blacklist*, *Gotham*, and David Simon's *Show Me a Hero*. For fans of *The Wire*, he is warmly remembered as Brother Mouzone, the enigmatic enforcer who, with the help of Omar Little, finally gives Stringer Bell his comeuppance.

**When you were cast in season two, how defined was the Brother Mouzone character? What did you bring to it?**

There was only what was on the page. I hadn't had any discussion with David or any of the other writers prior to shooting. I had no idea what they were looking for. That first episode, I had one word: "Officer." That's as much as I had to go on. A man of few words. By the second episode, he was a man of many more words. But they were well and deliberately chosen words. Brother was concise, articulate, and well read. Well mannered. Well dressed. I went from there. David and the other writers and producers gave me all the freedom and space I needed to create Brother as I saw him.

**The character himself is interesting—always reading, very defined in the way he speaks. In many ways, it's a quiet, understated role with big implications for the plot. How did you see the multifaceted elements of the character?**

I loved his complexity. I remember walking in NYC sometime after some of my episodes had aired, and a young brother stopped me to talk about Brother. As I was walking away, he shouted to me, "He's anything but a thug." I took that to mean that he appreciated that this character was so out of character for that world. He fit and didn't make sense at the same time. He's this oddity. I gravitate to and appreciate these multilayered personality types, their ambiguities. They're always way more interesting to explore as

OPPOSITE Strange bedfellows: Omar (Michael K. Williams, *left*) and Brother Mouzone (Michael Potts, *right*) on a mission to bring down Stringer Bell for good.

TOP Brother Mouzone (Potts, *left*) pays a visit to Avon Barksdale (Wood Harris, *seated*).

an actor. But let's not forget that this is how he was written for me. It was an equal partnership. I fed off what the writers put on the page, and they fed off how I interpreted what they wrote.

**Brother Mouzone is also a pragmatist and willing to work with whomever, like Omar. How did you see Brother's worldview?**

He tells us in his second episode: "The game is the game." The game has rules. There is a code. We live or die by that code. I think that's why Brother and Omar are mirror images of each other. The difference is, for Brother, it's rarely, if ever, personal. It's business.

**The scenes featuring Michael K. Williams, who played Omar, are very powerful. What was it like to act alongside him?**

Michael was great to work with. He was so completely, thoroughly invested in the narrative. It wasn't just about Omar. It was about this world of *The Wire* that all these

characters inhabited. We had a great time playing off each other. There was a genuine, mutual respect.

The killing of Stringer was a very, very emotional day for everyone. I remember how ominously quiet it was on set the entire time. No one talked, even between takes. I think we were already grieving Stringer's death before we even shot it. I think it was incredibly painful for Idris, of course. He was deeply saddened. Everyone wanted to make sure we got it right. It was a *huge* event in the narrative. I couldn't

believe that the character I was playing was getting to kill a major character in the story.

**What do you think happens to Brother Mouzone after he exits the show? It's implied that he's killed a lot of people—is that what the rest of his life entails? Do you see him as an assassin or an enforcer?**

The Brother returns to NYC. He returns to his family. There were other jobs, of course. Again, just business. But I don't think that was the entirety of his existence. As you might have noticed, particularly in his scenes with Lamar [DeAndre McCullough], Brother has a sense of humor. I think he enjoys having a good time. He goes to cookouts and throws them, does picnicking. I think aside from his vocation, he goes about his life in much the same way everyone does. When he gets too old and slow, he retires.

When he's hired to take out a major figure or player in the game, he's an assassin. When he's hired to hold territory, he's an enforcer.

OPPOSITE Michael K. Williams (*left*) and Michael Potts (*right*) pose for a publicity shot as Omar and Brother Mouzone.

BOTTOM RIGHT The effortlessly dapper Brother Mouzone (Potts).

# CHAD L. COLEMAN

## Interview by Nikki Stafford and Robert Thompson

Actor Chad L. Coleman brings a deep nobility to Dennis "Cutty" Wise, a character inspired by Baltimore's Calvin Ford, a real-life former drug trade soldier who found redemption teaching street kids to box. After playing Cutty in three seasons of *The Wire*, Coleman went on to land an impressive number of roles in film, television and video games, notably playing Tyreese Williams in AMC's *The Walking Dead*.

**Your character Dennis "Cutty" Wise is one of the few that evolves to a better place within the series. Although the writers didn't share much advance knowledge of the story plots, did you have a sense of where your character was going?**

Well, Calvin Ford was the blueprint, and it was his life that they were using. I had conversations with Calvin, and [the character's] trajectory was staring me in the face. He made a successful transition to becoming a boxing trainer in the hood. They wouldn't tell me specifically how many stones I had to hop and skip across, but I knew that it was going to be a favorable landing for him.

**Your character is interesting because at first he's trying to return to a life that clearly is behind him.**

Yeah. That was the first thing they said. So, it was a matter of giving a transitional vulnerability to Cutty. There was an inner vulnerability to him. He knew that he was making a transition and that he couldn't show full faith or play his hand clearly, because that's just the precarious nature of trying to change your life. Your leverage is based on the experiences you had, and Cutty's leverage was based on his relationship with Avon Barksdale. I didn't know how to articulate Cutty's vulnerability at first, but you could feel it through his awkwardness. He was not the same

TOP Cutty (Chad L. Coleman, *left*) turns to Avon Barksdale (Wood Harris) for work before later deciding to quit the game for good.

gun-toting, whip-your-ass, take-you-out dude, even though he appeared to be, and he understood that. The result of that internal conflict made everything he did seem like it was not on sure footing. And that was what I had to be able to communicate.

**Is it difficult for an actor to portray a character with such a level of complexity?**

I come from the theater and am familiar with character development. I can tell you that [the characters] Harold Loomis from *Joe Turner's Come and Gone* and Caleb Humphries from *Miss Evers' Boys* are ten times more complex. So, I had already played complex characters in the theater and was used to having more say in character development, nuances, and knowing their story from beginning to end. But the writers have every right to play everything close to their vests. For me, I was absolutely the right dude to do it because I was used to doing character work.

**From your perspective, Cutty obviously has a natural arc, but as he evolves he's also connected to the kids and to Avon Barksdale—while trying to escape that life. Do you feel that Cutty's**

**progression ended where it should, and did you enjoy the fact that Cutty is one of the characters that connects many storylines?**

The show was very, very honest, and Cutty almost got taken out as much as he believed in the young men. There is an aggressive homicidal nature if you try to step outside your boundaries, which is shown in the kids, the drug game, and the actions the characters take by any means necessary to make it out. Dukie (Jermaine Crawford) is a kid with so much smarts and agency about him, but Cutty doesn't have that kind of wherewithal to guide him. Cutty's thinking is that "if you're willing to come to this gym, I can help you. But I can't help you outside that." I thought the writers did a great job of not making us appear to walk on water, and that's what I loved most about the series. You wouldn't expect a guy like Cutty to be any kind of moral compass, but he was! He really was. Cutty believed you could change, but he didn't dwell on what that change was. Whatever Cutty's inner moral compass is for him, he's true to it, and he's earnest about it.

I think Cutty is a man looking in the mirror and saying, "I want to be who I believe I can be.

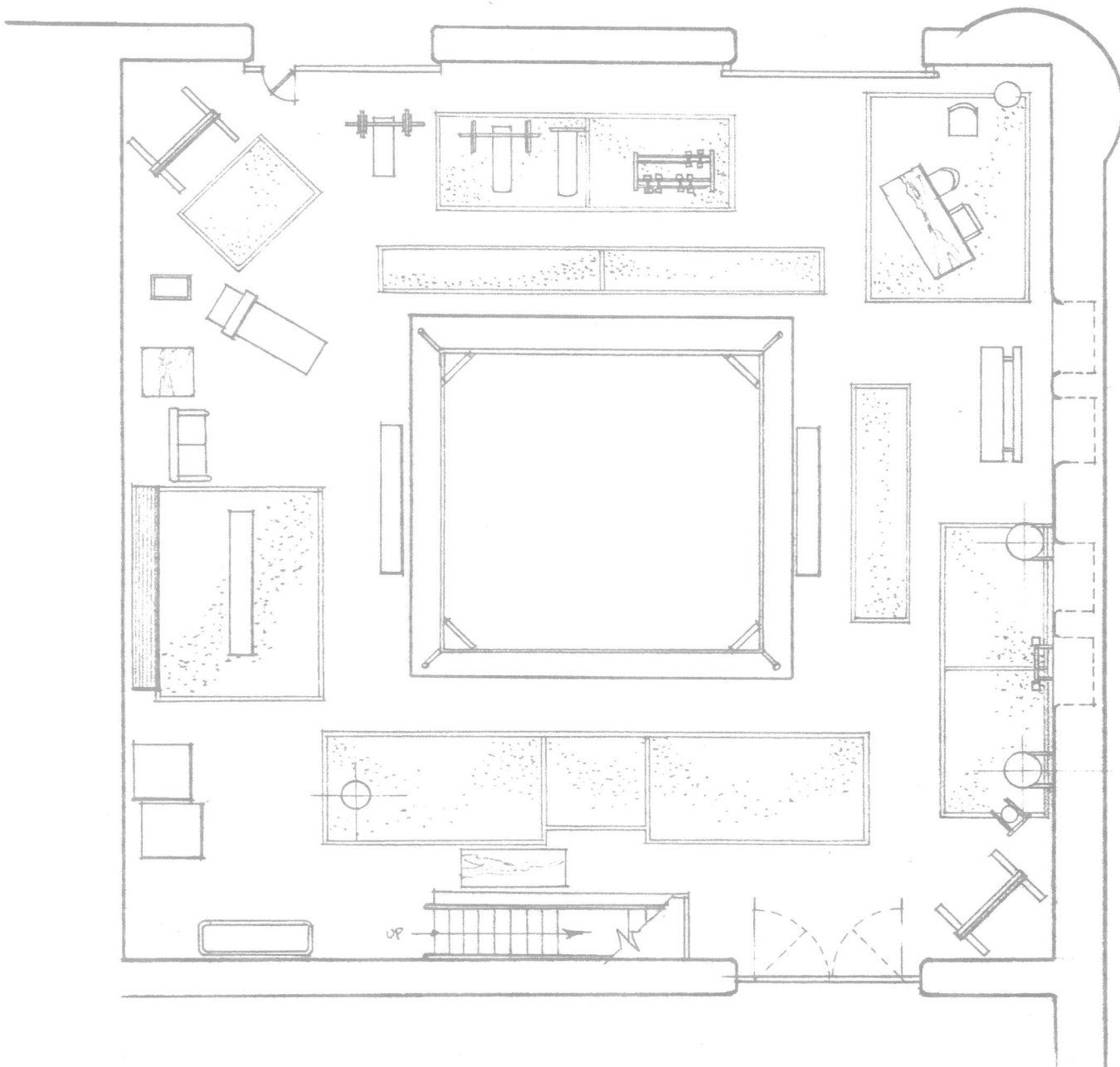

CUTTY'S GYM
STREET LIGHTING DEPOT- WOLFE & GAY STREET

That matters to me. It's important to me that my words and actions match up." And that kind of self-realization is what I think had to do with why he was so adamant. He had missteps all the way, and he didn't understand the nuances of leadership. He was new to leadership and even his sexual prurience got in the way. He had to learn from that, but he said, "Goddamn it, no! I need to be a stand-up man now, and I mean to do right. It matters to me to do right, now." I think he had a spiritual conversion, not a religious one. And that's Calvin, because Calvin is not no Bible-thumpin' dude. He just knew that there was a man inside him that never was given a chance to live, and the pain of that shit was very real. He needed who he *thought* he was to line up with who he *chose* to be—and he did it.

## What do you think is the legacy of *The Wire*?

We ended up with far more rich and substantive story narratives from other producers that it birthed. Whether it is *The Walking Dead* or any number of shows, young producers watched *The Wire* and said, "Oh, shit, we can tell stories like this no matter what the subject matter is. I want to go at it like this. I want it to be rich and layered, and I want to be able to take our time." The series changed the whole course of fast-food television, which is why the streaming world we have today pays homage to *The Wire*. I know this might sound lofty, but I believe it. I think [the young producers today] are "*Wire* babies."

TOP A floor plan for the Cutty's gym set.

# ROBERT WISDOM

## Interview by Nikki Stafford and Robert Thompson

As Major Howard "Bunny" Colvin, Robert Wisdom made a huge impact on *The Wire*, particularly in seasons three and four, in which Bunny takes direct action to try to bring about change in the streets of Baltimore. Across a three-decade career, Wisdom has brought his talent to a vast range of projects, including Christopher Nolan's *The Dark Knight Rises* (2012), the Ed Norton-directed *Motherless Brooklyn* (2019), and HBO's hit series *Barry*.

**Bunny first appeared in season two in a relatively small role. Did you have a sense of how important your character was going to be to the next two seasons?**

I imagine they had the arc for the third season developed, and I'm pretty sure the fourth season came out of my involvement in the show. At the end of season two, Bob [Robert F. Colesberry] and David Simon came into my trailer, and we just talked about who Bunny was. They didn't indicate to me at all what was going to happen to him—we never had advance stories, so we only knew what was happening as we got a script. So we played it in real time, and that was it. But as I look back, all the bones of my character were laid out in those scenes when I

was introduced at the end of season two. The things that Bunny was observing and all that stuff that was building up, it was all laid out in those episodes at the end of season two. So they had a sense of what the character would be taking on and the fork in the road that he was facing. And they laid it out in silence without any words at this stage—it was just the looks Bunny gave, and you just saw the kind of fire building. But I only saw that in retrospect as the years passed and I realized they had a real strong idea of what that character was going to be.

**Bunny is often perceived as an idealist, but in fact he's a realist dealing with a situation in the only way he can, given the hand he's been**

OPPOSITE Robert Wisdom as Bunny Colvin, a man determined to do some good in Baltimore, even at the expense of his police career.

TOP Bunny (Wisdom, *left*) and Western District officer Dennis Mello (Jay Landsman, *right*) check out the area that will become Amsterdam. Landsman is a real-life police officer who inspired the character played by Delaney Williams.

dealt. **In setting up Hamsterdam, he takes on what is perceived to be maybe an idealistic or an extreme perspective, but really it's just being pragmatic in some ways.**

Well, that's the strange thing about the bureaucracy. You know a reformer is going to look like a radical for just moving an inch. There was so much built-in stagnation in that bureaucracy, and the way of doing police business was frozen. Because of his impending retirement and all his years of seeing nothing really getting done—just people shifting chairs on the deck of the *Titanic*—he was at that point where he had nothing to lose. He was forced into moving to what seemed to be an idealistic and commonsense solution, to just give it a try, only because he saw real people. The bureaucrats and the chiefs never saw real people. Bunny saw the old lady who refused to move out of Hamsterdam—she was imprisoned in this neighborhood. He saw bullets flying and killing innocent people. And he saw very little getting done. So it was basically a "Why not?" It was a Hail Mary, and it became, "I can do this." But he also knew that there was a big cost if he ever got found out.

And there did end up being a huge cost. But I think toward the end of season three, he started to just say, "So what?" He realized, what can they do? So he said, "Fuck it, let's go for it."

Then he saw flowers start to blossom on some of the blocks. He saw all the guys on the corner just kind of moving away and people being able to sit out on their stoops again. That was all he wanted. He just wanted livable circumstances for the people who lived in his area. And to maybe inspire some change. I think he thought that the bosses would see the light and say, "All right, let's do an experiment. Let's try it." But that would never be.

**Bunny thinks that because he's retiring, there's not much that his superiors can do to hurt him, but they actually take away part of his pension. Do you think Bunny saw that coming?**

No, he didn't see it coming. But one of the choices I made when I was playing Bunny is that he wasn't a born hero. He was a worker, and he took his job totally seriously. He didn't bend the rules for his own gain and he wasn't seeking power—he was just trying to

BOTTOM Bunny (Robert Wisdom) returns to civilian life in season four of *The Wire*.

OPPOSITE TOP Unlike many on the force, Bunny (Wisdom, *right*) has a cordial relationship with McNulty (Dominic West, *left*), who started his career as a beat cop under Bunny's command.

OPPOSITE BOTTOM A business card prop created for the Bunny character.

administrate fairness within his troops and on behalf of the neighborhood, the community. That's where he was. It was only when he saw the bullets started to stray and hit innocent people—that lit something in him, but it would never really take on full blaze until he decided to stand in front of the guys and just decide to legalize drugs. I think his superiors kind of saw something spectacular there, too. But I think because they were so entrenched in their old ways that they had to shoot somebody, they had to knock him down. And so I think my role in the fourth season was created because it just sort of occurred to David and Ed to see what else happens with Bunny.

**Bunny's role in season four is interesting because it recalls Ed Burns's real-life experience of being a Baltimore cop and then ending up in education.** Yeah. He was caught between worlds. Bunny's first job after leaving the police force is as head of security at a hotel. He had become a new man with experience on the force. He wasn't a cop by nature; he was somebody who burned for people. When he ran up against another old system at the hotel, which just wanted him to kind of play by their dirty rules, he ran out of gas. And he found himself in a place where his ideals could really take off in this crazy kind of quasi-teaching role—working with young people and trying to inspire them and trying to come to terms with his own new idealistic view of the world, which was in its infancy. We just see him grow as he's confronted by larger and larger things.

He was a man of smaller ideals in the third season, but in the fourth season, those ideals have grown. He doesn't know how to actually carry them out with another high-risk group, these young people, so that is a new frontier for him. And we watch him stumble through that.

## BALTIMORE POLICE DEPARTMENT

### MAJOR HOWARD COLVIN

**DISTRICT COMMANDER**
**WESTERN DISTRICT**

OFFICE 410-396-1212                CELL 410-276-6260

## Crime Comparisons
### Post 733
#### Cloverdale Community Association

| Crime | July-Aug | Sept-Oct |
|---|---|---|
| Homicide | 11 | 8 |
| Drug Arrest | 131 | 22 |
| Forcible Rape | 5 | 1 |
| Robbery | 35 | 7 |
| Aggravated Assault | 14 | 3 |
| Burglary | 28 | 4 |
| Larceny | 35 | 5 |
| Auto Theft | 14 | 2 |

Month by month arrests derived from ComStat figures
*includes all dispatched, administrative, and on-view calls.

Twenty years later, do you think much has changed in regard to the issues Bunny was trying to tackle? And what's your perception of the legacy of the show all these years later?

We looked at these problems through the prism of Baltimore. You could have gone to Camden, New Jersey, or Oakland, California—you could go to any growing urban city, and twenty years later, nothing will have changed. We haven't moved an inch. We've legalized marijuana because finally there was a lobby that said, "There's money to be made." So that loosened things up. But there's no money to be made on the side of protecting people from guns. We see all the guns that are flooding neighborhoods, so that just means the situation is doubly out of hand. So we see the growth and entrenchment of gang culture, and whoever is running them, and that's become even more endemic. We are deeper in those issues. But *The Wire* team was able to map out those schematics because of David's experience writing about urban crime for the *Baltimore Sun*. He looked at the police force and education: Those are the two most popular tributaries in a culture, in a society. Looking at that, we saw the blueprint that will always be the map for how to look at urban growth and urban change down the line. So it wasn't just about Baltimore—you can look at any city in the country and you will see just two- or three-tier justice. You will see at the bottom uneducated or badly educated groups, disenfranchised groups, and you will see those who concentrate power at the top. And what *The Wire* did was take individuals and follow them moving through this maze, trying to figure out, "What tiny lines can I straighten out?"

And that's all we can do. We move tiny inches, but *The Wire* made them feel like big, big successes. Even from the side of Stringer trying to reform the drug trade. And Omar's choice to bring a kind of humanity to his world. Those are the ironies and contradictions that make the characters so potent. And the beauty of Bubs, who was just a magician in terms of how he made it through his own addiction—there was a shining character inside him, and the audience got us to see that. *The Wire* had a thousand-mile view of the city, but it also took us right into the heart, and I think that is why the show has lasted twenty years—and in thirty, forty years, we will still be talking about it. I see young people today who are just finding it, and they get it as well. The good stuff is built in, and that's what makes it a genius show. I think *The Wire* really brought all the forces together in a way that we can use, which is why it's being taught in schools everywhere, at Harvard and in Chicago and Oakland and at Berkeley.

Schools use it as a case study for all kinds of laws, and that's why David Simon did it. I think it's brilliant.

**What is your favorite episode?**
I can't say that I could single out an entire episode, no, but I can pull out a few favorite parts of the whole.

If I had to pick a single scene as my favorite, I would say it's the "king stay the king" scene in episode three of season one, where D'Angelo explains the game of chess to Bodie and Wallace, who are playing checkers with chess pieces on a chessboard.

I'd also like to mention a favorite line or two of dialogue, specifically in episode seven of season one, where Bunk tells Omar, "A man must have a code." To which Omar replies characteristically, "No doubt." The line is reprised in season three, episode six, when the roles are somewhat reversed, and Omar underscores a point by reminding Bunk, "A man got to have a code." Bunk just stares at him.

Lastly, I am sort of partial to a line offered by an ill-tempered, foul-mouthed reporter character in season five, when, suggesting he was overworked, the newspaperman tells his editor, Augustus "Gus" Haynes, "Why doncha just shove the broom up my ass, and I'll sweep the floor while I'm at it?"

OPPOSITE TOP In season four, Bunny (Robert Wisdom, *left*) becomes a field researcher for education sociologist David Parenti (Dan De Luca, *right*), working with him to help prevent pupils at Edward J. Tilghman Middle School from turning to a life of crime.

OPPOSITE BOTTOM A table of crime statistics created by *The Wire*'s art department.

BOTTOM A floor plan for the Western District police station set.

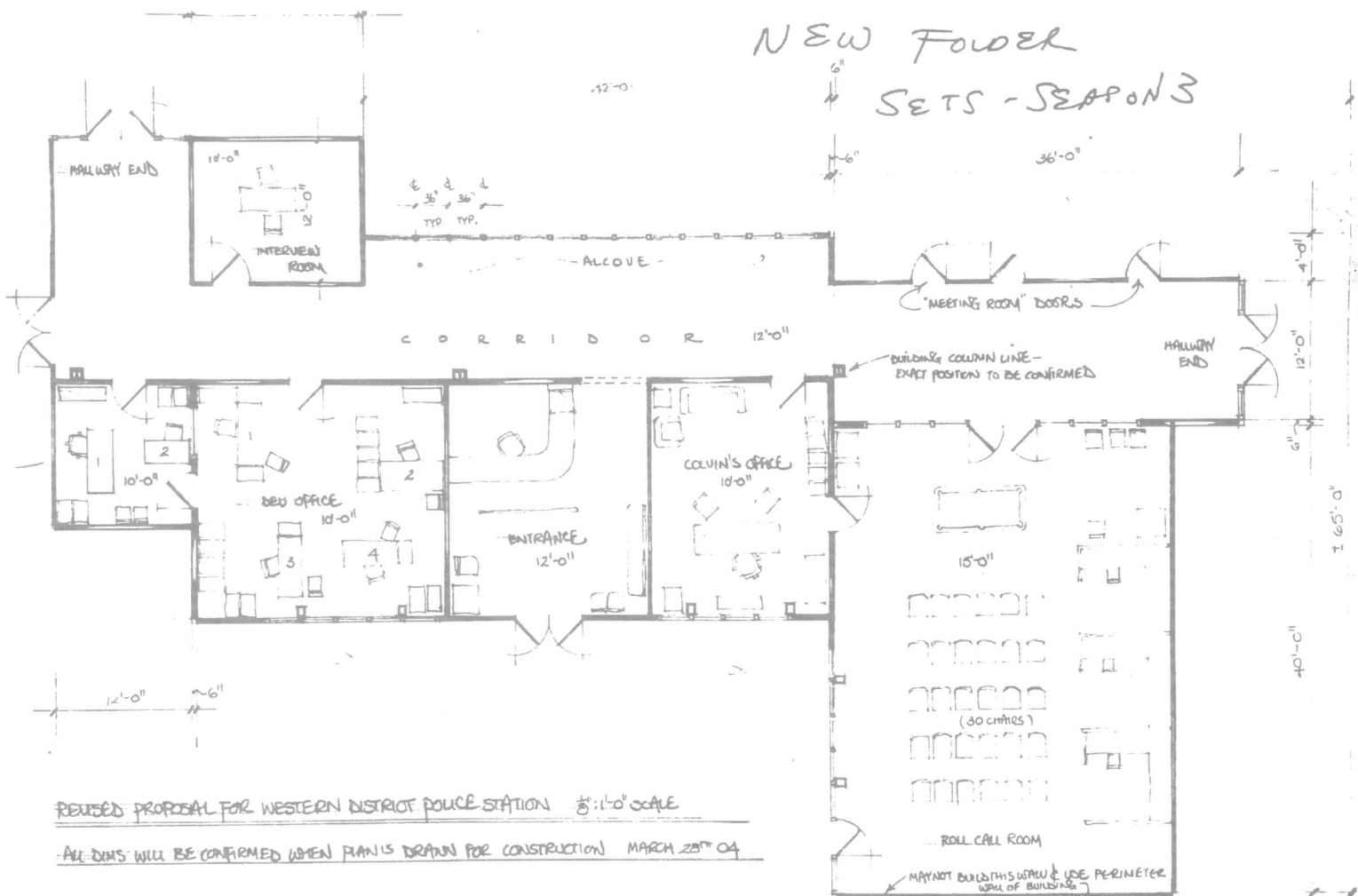

# JOHN DOMAN

## Interview by Chris Prince

After spending almost twenty years in the advertising industry, John Doman started acting professionally at the age of forty-six. Following early work in TV shows including *Law & Order*, *NYPD Blue*, and *The Sopranos*, Doman landed the key role of William Rawls, the commanding officer of Baltimore's Homicide Unit, in *The Wire*. Ruthlessly ambitious and brutally acerbic, Rawls would rise through the ranks across the series' five seasons, eventually becoming superintendent of the Maryland State Police.

**What was the audition process like for you on *The Wire*?**

It wasn't very complicated for me. I know a lot of guys went back a few times and read for different characters, and sometimes even for different characters than those for which they were ultimately cast. My process was pretty simple. I went in to see Alexa Fogel at her studio. The scene I read for her was from the first episode. It's kind of a classic scene, where I give the double bird to McNulty over the desk. "This is for you, McNulty: This one's going into your left eye and this one's going up your narrow Irish ass." I did it once. And she said, "Okay, that's fine." That was it. It was a very simple process—so simple, I thought, "Well, I'm probably not going to get that job."

**What was your initial perception of Rawls?**

My initial perception of Rawls, right off the bat, he's a prick with a capital P. All I knew about him was what was in the first episode, because that's all I saw.

**Were you able to find any positive sides to the character?**

Oh yeah, absolutely. I think when you take on one of these kinds of characters, you have to find things to like about them. As far as he's concerned, he's doing the right thing. He's a very ambitious character—ruthlessly ambitious in the context of the system. He really knew how to play the game, and he wanted to get to the top. He demanded loyalty from the people under him, and if you crossed him, you better watch your shit. It started in season one when McNulty went off and talked to the judge about cases that aren't being followed up on and are being shuffled to the side. And that brought a lot of pressure onto Rawls when the judge started raising hell.

OPPPOSITE The notoriously sharp-tongued Williams Rawls, played by John Doman.

TOP Rawls (Doman, *right*) meets with Ervin Burrell (Frankie Faison, *left*) and Cedric Daniels (Lance Reddick).

**What was it like working with Dominic West? There are so many classic moments where Rawls rips McNulty to pieces.**

Dominic's a great guy and a lot of fun to work with. And he's a terrific actor. What more could you ask for?

**Rawls was said to be inspired by real-life Baltimore CID commander Joe Cooke. Did you get to meet him?**

You know, I never did get to meet him. They told me Rawls wasn't based on one person—he was kind of an amalgam of a couple of different people.

**Did you get much input into the Rawls character and his storyline?**

No. In fact, we never even talked about the arc. I never knew where this was going. I didn't get multiple scripts in advance—I would just get one script for the next episode. You just had to play it as it laid. But the basis of the character was there on the page.

**As an actor, does it help to know the full arc of a character?**

I don't think it matters because you don't know what's going to happen in real life. I certainly didn't know what was coming up when Rawls wound up in a gay bar in season three! That came out of the blue. I hadn't seen the script and I showed up on the set one morning.

The second AD came running over with this big shit-eating grin on his face. He said, "Have you seen the script for the next episode?" Ed Burns was sitting there, and I saw his head pop up and he said, "Oh, John, I need to talk to you about something." We went off to one of the side offices on the set, and he told me there was going to be a scene where you see Rawls in a gay bar. He said, "We want to know how you feel about it." I thought to myself, "It ain't going to make a bit of difference what I think about this—if they want to use it, they're going to use it." So, I said, "Yeah, sure, why not? It adds another element to the character." I never expected it and I'm sure nobody else expects it, so it could be very interesting.

We shot it, and they used it, and I'm thinking to myself, "Okay, now where could this possibly go?" The next episode comes out and it's not mentioned, so my head's going through all the possible scenarios. And then next episode comes out and it's still not mentioned—nothing's happening. So I went to see David Simon and I said, "This gay thing with Rawls, I don't know what you've got planned, but I'm up for anything you want to do!" And he looked at me with this "Are you crazy?" look and just kind of walked off. He never touched it again, and it was absolutely brilliant.

BOTTOM A *Wire* family gathering: (*left to right*) John Doman, Domenick Lombardozzi, Sonja Sohn, Deirdre Lovejoy, Michael K. Williams, and Seth Gilliam.

## Two decades on, what do you think is the legacy of The Wire?

It's taken on a life of its own. It's kind of amazing because when we were shooting it, not that many people were paying attention. We were getting good critical reviews, but we had an audience of only about a million who were regularly watching the show. And HBO wasn't promoting it very much—they were putting most of their money behind *The Sopranos*, which was, you know, the big show back then. It wasn't until the DVDs came out that people started watching it, and the word of mouth really was what drove it, and now it's become a worldwide phenomenon. I was working in Europe, and people would come up to me on the street and say, "Oh, *The Wire*!" I was once in the Grand Bazaar in Istanbul, and it's just packed with people. This guy grabs me by the arm and he's [talking to me in Turkish] and the only thing I could understand was "*The Wire*." And he grabbed his son, and they had a camera and they wanted to take a picture. Yeah, that kind of thing happens. I mean, it's just incredible.

TOP Rawls (John Doman) claws his way to the rank of superintendent over the course of *The Wire*'s five seasons.

BOTTOM An ID badge prop created for the Rawls character.

# SEASON THREE EPISODES

**S03E01:** Time After Time

**Written by:** Story by David Simon and Ed Burns; teleplay by David Simon

**Directed by:** Ed Bianchi

**Original airdate:** September 19, 2004

**Epigraph:** "Don't matter how many times you get burnt, you just keep doin' the same." –Bodie

**Description:** In the season three premiere, a wave of urban reform brings down the notorious Franklin Terrace public housing towers, forcing the Barksdale drug crew to find a new home on the streets of West Baltimore.

**S03E02:** All Due Respect

**Written by:** Story by David Simon and Richard Price; teleplay by Richard Price

**Directed by:** Steve Shill

**Original airdate:** September 26, 2004

**Epigraph:** "There's never been a paper bag." –Colvin

**Description:** Omar continues his strikes on Barksdale stash houses; Bodie faces a critical test against Marlo. As the wire on Proposition Joe continues to yield little, a restless McNulty launches his own reinvestigation of the suicide of D'Angelo Barksdale.

**S03E03:** Dead Soldiers

**Written by:** Story by David Simon and Dennis Lehane; teleplay by Dennis Lehane

**Directed by:** Rob Bailey

**Original airdate:** October 3, 2004

**Epigraph:** "The gods will not save you." –Burrell

**Description:** Colvin feels the sting of Burrell and Rawls during a Comstat assessment of his district's felony numbers; a blown wiretap forces Daniels's detail to turn to a new target; Proposition Joe warns Stringer Bell that the police have been tapping phones.

**S03E04:** Amsterdam

**Written by:** Story by David Simon and George Pelecanos; teleplay by George Pelecanos

**Directed by:** Ernest R. Dickerson

**Original airdate:** October 10, 2004

**Epigraph:** "Why you got to go and fuck with the program?" –Fruit

**Description:** West Baltimore residents get some straight talk from Major Colvin at a community meeting. Bubbles finds gainful employment; Stringer lunches uptown; and Bunk dangles the promise of immunity to a group of corner boys, in exchange for some help.

**S03E05:** Straight and True

**Written by:** Story by David Simon and Ed Burns; teleplay by Ed Burns

**Directed by:** Dan Attias

**Original airdate:** October 17, 2004

**Epigraph:** "I had such fuckin' hopes for us." –McNulty

**Description:** Frustrated in his reform efforts, Colvin arms himself with intelligence and delivers a message to the next level of corner management. McNulty sees Stringer Bell's legitimate business dealings as a sign that he is now unreachable as a drug target.

**S03E06:** Homecoming

**Written by:** Story by David Simon and Rafael Álvarez; teleplay by Rafael Álvarez

**Directed by:** Leslie Libman

**Original airdate:** October 31, 2004

**Epigraph:** "Just a gangster, I suppose." –Avon Barksdale

**Description:** Stringer Bell gets an education in construction management; Bunk uses shoe leather to catch up with Omar and deliver a message; Colvin unleashes the troops on the corner boys ignoring his new edict; Avon sends Cutty and Slim Charles against Marlo.

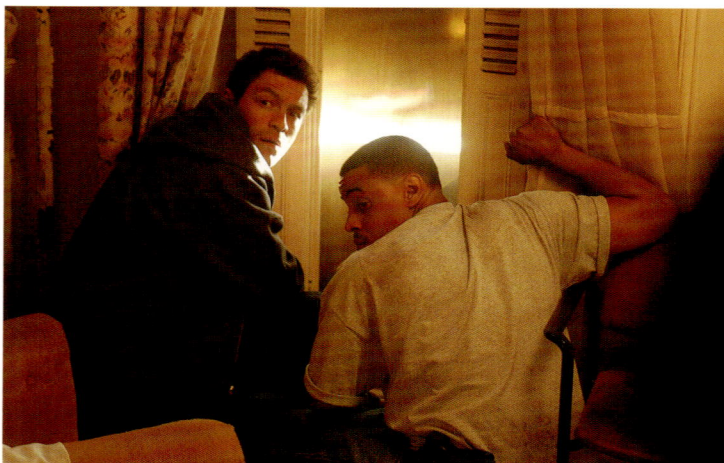

**S03E07:** Back Burners

**Written by:** Story by David Simon and Joy Lusco; teleplay by Joy Lusco

**Directed by:** Tim Van Patten

**Original airdate:** November 7, 2004

**Epigraph:** "Conscience do cost." –Butchie

**Description:** Herc discovers a blast from the past. Daniels blows up over the real reason the detail was reassigned to the Western District. Stringer Bell learns from Donette that she's told Brianna about McNulty's visit and that Brianna is likely to talk to him.

**S03E08:** Moral Midgetry

**Written by:** Story by David Simon and Richard Price; teleplay by Richard Price

**Directed by:** Agnieszka Holland

**Original airdate:** November 14, 2004

**Epigraph:** "Crawl, walk, and then run." –Clay Davis

**Description:** With Hamsterdam running full-tilt, Carver and Truck discover there really is no honor among thieves. Prez impresses the detail with what he's found out from Bodie's cell phone, information that sends McNulty and Greggs on a road trip.

**S03E09:** Slapstick

**Written by:** Story by David Simon and George Pelecanos; teleplay by David Simon

**Directed by:** Alex Zakrzewski

**Original airdate:** November 21, 2004

**Epigraph:** ". . . while you're waiting for moments that never come." –Freamon

**Description:** Responding to an officer's call for help, McNulty and Prez turn down the wrong alley, with unanticipated results. Under orders, a Barksdale crew violates the unspoken Sunday truce with gunplay, increasing discontent among the New Day Co-Op members.

**S03E10:** Reformation

**Written by:** Story by David Simon and Ed Burns; teleplay by Ed Burns

**Directed by:** Christine Moore

**Original airdate:** November 28, 2004

**Epigraph:** "Call it a crisis of leadership." –Proposition Joe

**Description:** Brother Mouzone returns to Baltimore on a mission of revenge and casts a wide net in his search for Omar, who has his own plan for vengeance. Colvin puts off a reporter inquiring about Hamsterdam, while Burrell delivers news to city hall.

**S03E11:** Middle Ground

**Written by:** Story by David Simon and George Pelecanos; teleplay by George Pelecanos

**Directed by:** Joe Chappelle

**Original airdate:** December 12, 2004

**Epigraph:** "We ain't gotta dream no more, man." –Stringer Bell

**Description:** The wire begins to yield information about the Barksdale organization, though finding links to the top proves elusive. Stringer and Avon reminisce about how far they've come, with each harboring plans for the future.

**S03E12:** Mission Accomplished

**Written by:** Story by David Simon and Ed Burns; teleplay by David Simon

**Directed by:** Ernest Dickerson

**Original airdate:** December 19, 2004

**Epigraph:** ". . . we fight on that lie." –Slim Charles

**Description:** In the season three finale, a reticent Avon readies his troops for a seemingly endless war against Marlo. Meanwhile, as the detail works toward the top rungs of the Barksdale organization, McNulty reassesses his pursuit of Stringer Bell.

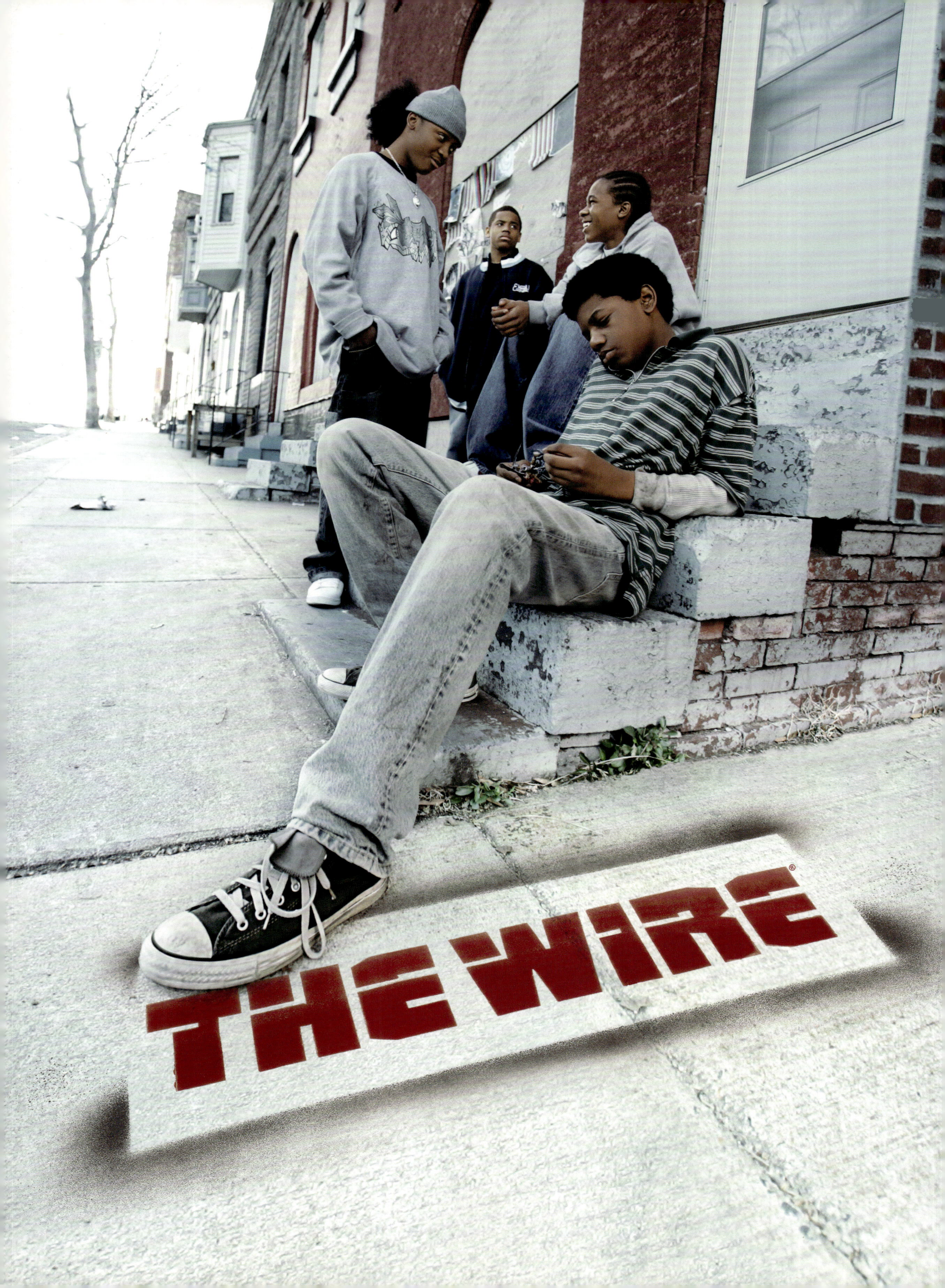
THE WIRE

# SEASON

4

# AN INTRODUCTION TO SEASON FOUR

By D. Watkins

In season four, we dig to the root of two major problems outside of the war on drugs and poor policing: Baltimore's collection of mayors that have consistently failed its residents and our historically underfunded school system.

Former city councilman Tommy Carcetti (Aidan Gillen) is elected mayor, and before he can even understand his role, live up to his campaign promises, and create a safer Baltimore, he sets his sights on being the governor. His political ambitions totally eclipse the reason he wanted the job in the first place, which ultimately leads to nothing getting done, except for his personal advancement, of course.

We are also introduced to a collection of young men in middle school, at the most pivotal point in their lives. In Baltimore, middle school is normally the time when young people decide if they're going to continue their education or try their hand in the streets. Choosing between school and the streets sounds as easy as picking left or right, a 50-50 decision, but in Baltimore it's more like 90-10—the 90 representing the streets. For every good opportunity there is to be educated properly and connect with

"In Baltimore, middle school is normally the time where young people decide if they're going to continue their education or try their hand in the streets."

TOP The four young characters at the heart of season four: (left to right) Duquan "Dukie" Weems (Jermaine Crawford), Randy Wagstaff (Maestro Harrell), Michael Lee (Tristan Wilds), and Namond Brice (Julito McCullum).

OPPOSITE Randy (Harrell, left), Michael (Wilds, center), and Namond (McCullum, right) outside school hours.

some sort of role model outside of the school who can help you realize your dreams, there are about nine opportunities to do the wrong thing. Sure, public figures like professional athletes, TV personalities, and famous rappers are known to make attempts at engaging students; but normally they visit only once a year—with a camera crew—if you are extremely lucky. Dope dealers and gang members are around every single day.

Imagine being bundled up in your underfunded public school where the heat normally doesn't work in the winter, and you freeze while trying to learn Shakespeare. Or where the AC never works in the summer, causing the city to implement early dismissals during every heat wave. The dope dealers normally have more-than-acceptable working conditions and are eager to show you the way.

Season four also touches on the way that drug culture is passed down from generation to generation. This can be seen through the character Dukie (Jermaine Crawford)—a middle school child whose parents are on drugs, so eventually he becomes an addict himself. The reverse effect is seen through Namond Brice (Julito McCullum), who is the same age as Dukie. Namond's father, Wee-Bey, was a notorious gangster, and he dreamed of following in his footsteps to please his mom, but ultimately Namond realizes he doesn't want to be a part of the streets. Luckily Major Colvin saves him from a life of crime, giving viewers another layer to ponder: the idea that the only way a police officer can make a positive difference in a Black kid's life is if they quit the force.

A contrasting reality can be seen in the arc of Michael Lee (Tristan Wilds). Michael loves boxing and is against selling drugs, unless he has to provide for his little brother, Bug, and there is no other way to make money. Michael's mother is an addict whose actions push Michael into the streets, but as soon as he makes enough money on the corner, he instantly quits. But Michael's sexual predator stepfather, Bug's dad, comes home from prison, and attempts to disrupt the small amount of normalcy Michael has created. His arrival forces Michael to make a deal with the Stanfield organization—they will make his stepfather and his abusive ways disappear in exchange for Michael's commitment, his heart, and ultimately his soul.

Places like Baltimore are always critiqued because of the negative actions of adults who often go in and out of the system, but season four offers clear examples of why those same adults end up in bad predicament—including a lack of resources, absence of structure, and the limited opportunities that were available to them as children—clearly defining why only a few lucky ones make it out.

TOP RIGHT In season four, Chris Partlow (Gbenga Akinnagbe, *left*) and Snoop (Felicia Pearson, *right*) try to recruit Michael (Tristan Wilds, *center*) into the Marlo Stanfield crew.

OPPOSITE TOP RIGHT A prone Omar (Michael K. Williams) speaks with McNulty (Dominic West) after being arrested for a crime he didn't commit.

RIGHT During the investigation of the murder of a state's witness, suspect Anthony Wardell (Gordon Timothy, *left*) undergoes a polygraph test. Observing are (*left to right*) Maurice Levy (Michael Kostroff), Ilene Nathan (Susan Rome), Kima (Sonja Sohn), Detective Edward Norris (Ed T. Norris), and unknown.

# THE WIRE SEASON FOUR: THE ONES LEFT BEHIND

by Melanie McFarland

**"As former Baltimore Police Department Detective Howard 'Bunny' Colvin sees it, there are 'stoop kids' and there are 'corner kids.'"**

TOP (*Left to right*) Tristan Wilds, Maestro Harrell, Julito McCullum, and Jermaine Crawford pose for a season four publicity shot.

OPPOSITE Fruit (Brandon Fobbs, *left*), a key player in Marlo Stanfield's crew, and Sherrod (Rashad Orange, *right*), a street kid who Bubbles tries to take under his wing in season four.

PAGES 164-165 (*Foreground, left to right*) Donut (Nathan Corbett), Namond (Julito McCullum), Michael (Tristan Wilds), and Randy (Maestro Harrell) attempt to catch pigeons with an improvised trap.

*I t's not about you, or us, or the test, or the system. It's what they expect of themselves. I mean, every single one of them knows they headed back to the corners. Their brothers and sisters—shit, their parents—they came through these same classrooms, didn't they? We pretended to teach them, they pretended to learn, now where they end up? Same damn corners. I mean, they're not fools, these kids. They don't know our world, but they know their own."* —Bunny Colvin

As former Baltimore Police Department Detective Howard "Bunny" Colvin sees it, there are "stoop kids" and there are "corner kids."

Stoop kids, he explains to a group of educators, are the ones who stay on the front steps when their parents tell them to. They listen to adults and want to stay out of trouble. "The others," Bunny says, "go down to the corners."

As for Duquan Weems, an eighth grader with a bountiful natural intellect and no safe place for him to develop it, where does he fit?

As for Duquan Weems, an eighth grader with a bountiful natural intellect and no safe place for him to develop it, where does he fit?

Duquan should be a stoop kid: He's well-behaved and kind, and he goes out of his way to stay out of trouble. But his mother and father are addicts, and his home hasn't had running water for a year, leaving him unable to shower. His stoop marks the entry to purgatory.

The world beyond isn't kinder. Neighborhood children tease him for stinking, tagging him with the demoralizing moniker "Dukie." The corners claimed his parents, robbing him of his best chance to rise above the morass of low expectations. The corners might be all he has in his future.

But at the end of the summer in 2006, which is when *The Wire* introduces Duquan and his friends Michael Lee, Randy Wagstaff (Maestro Harrell), and Namond Brice, the corner boys don't want Duquan either.

Duquan knows he doesn't fit anywhere. Such a sense of rootlessness might throw any child into a state of rage and despair, and indeed, several of his classmates at Edward J. Tilghman Middle School succumb to acrimony. Incredibly he does not . . . for a time, anyway.

Where previous seasons glide fingers along the threads connecting the machinations of government officials and law agents to the politics of the criminal underworld, illustrating the ramifications borne by the citizens they try (or purport) to serve, the 2006 episodes of *The Wire* are the first to weave in the ways those systems impact Baltimore's ailing public educational system.

Mismanagement has transformed schools serving the poorest neighborhoods into waystations on parallel tracks leading to the local drug trade and/or prison. At Tilghman, kids listlessly page through tattered, outdated excuses for textbooks while boxes of virginal primers sit unopened in a storage room, as forgotten as lifers in a medieval dungeon.

Truancy cops have reached an understanding with dropouts that as long as they attend classes one day a month—enough for a school to maintain its funding—they can wander around for the other twenty-nine or thirty without anybody giving a damn.

Mayors, police chiefs, and governors might as well be giants ruling distant cloud kingdoms, but children like Dukie aren't Davids. They're not even Jack. Think smaller, think. . . very little. That's how the sprawling political system views them.

This makes it even more vital for viewers to meet Namond, Duquan, Michael, and Randy as boys doing what all kids their age are encouraged to do: playing outside and stirring up minor trouble. In the main that involves avoiding beatdowns or violent police harassment. But even in this light, their status as children—not adult-ified minors—is never in question.

Among the principal foursome, Duquan is not the shortest kid. Fundamentally speaking, however, he is the least of them. The other three are louder and shine brighter. The enterprising Randy's smile could power a city block.

None of them are wealthy or even solidly middle class, but Namond enjoys many of the same diversions that better-off kids do. He has dope street fashions and an Xbox he switches on to tune out his mother's pressured demands for him to quit school and start earning in the drug trade.

The protective Michael takes on a single-parent role in place of his drug-consumed mother; he looks out for his little brother and intervenes

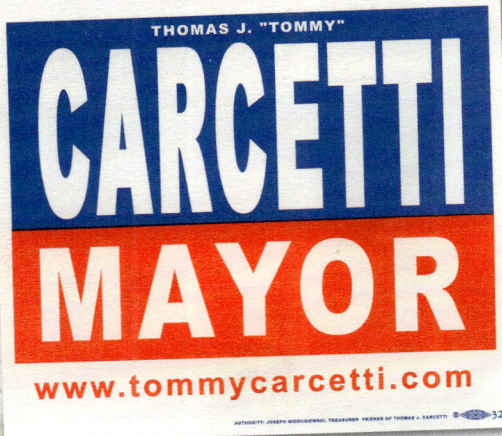

THESE PAGES Various political campaign items created by *The Wire*'s art department.

OPPOSITE TOP Conniving politician Tommy Carcetti (Aidan Gillen, *right*) and his wife, Jennifer (Megan Anderson, *left*).

when Namond picks on Duquan. Michael is tall and athletic, and he works out at a local boxing gym to stay out of trouble. But let's be real, he also wants to learn how to throw a knockout punch, a useful skill on these blocks.

Randy lives with an attentive foster mother called Miss Anna. Having known the bleak life of group homes before coming into her care, he strains to keep his nose clean. Even his entrepreneurial endeavors are legitimate: He buys candy from a local store and sells it to his schoolmates at a modest markup.

Namond flogs the world with braggadocio borrowed from his father's reputation; he's the son of Wee-Bey, one of the dethroned Barksdale crime organization's last men standing, now in prison. He acts like he's ordained by God to run the streets, not simply run in them, and never lets "Dukie" forget his low social standing. He picks on Duquan because he knows he can get away with it. But when anyone else pushes back, Namond folds, just as we'd expect any frightened child to do.

Despite the rejection and abuse, Duquan holds fast to his contemplative nature. Fragile and gangly-limbed, he quietly hangs back, learning the truth about the world around him: who is safe, where predators lurk and what they do to people.

It is no surprise that he excels at school when he's given a real chance to learn; he also demonstrates a practical, self-taught aptitude for repairing things that aren't working. Whether it is fixing his classroom's obsolete computer or reviving a dead handheld fan someone has tossed aside, having been discarded by his parents, the kid knows how to repair broken things. One would think his teachers at Tilghman would seize upon that talent and nurture it.

But the middle school's staff is overwhelmed, their classes overcrowded, their administrators demoralized. Teachers have become classroom stewards more dedicated to survival than to rewarding any single student's achievements; if their kids are literate, they chalk that up as a success.

It's not that they don't want to instill their kids with basic literacy skills or enable them to navigate fractions or remedial arithmetic. Their obstacle is a mismanaged system that evaluates a school's worthiness through standardized testing instead of considering whether its students are learning anything.

Hell, a high percentage of the kids are barely even socialized. Can you blame them? They're simply boys and girls, knocking their heads against stone-hard reality and learning bruising lessons about what it has in store.

Viewing this fourth season from more than a decade and a half hence can be an exercise in constant amazement, in terms of both the storytelling's sensitivity and its depressing prescience.

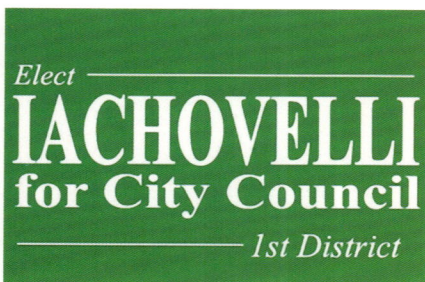

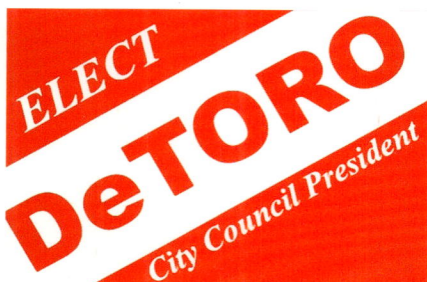

Of course, series creator David Simon and his fellow producer and writing partner Ed Burns are not soothsayers. Mainly what we see throughout the fourth season dramatizes the wreckage left by the No Child Left Behind Act that George W. Bush signed into law in 2002.

Trapped between factions of law enforcement and criminals, and at the mercy of politicians more focused on winning elections than serving their constituents, schoolkids like Duquan are nearly always left behind.

Incumbent Mayor Clarence V. Royce, corrupt as ever, is more focused on defending his office from Councilman Tommy Carcetti, a man selling himself as a reformer and making the necessarily public appearances to persuade Baltimore voters to put him in office.

The election is simply noise to these kids, as one should expect it to be. But to Royce, Carcetti, and other politicians, schoolchildren's needs are a political bargaining chip, some distant concept, not a disaster that continues to generate casualties and is crying out to be ameliorated.

Simon, a former reporter, is an excellent interpreter of institutional

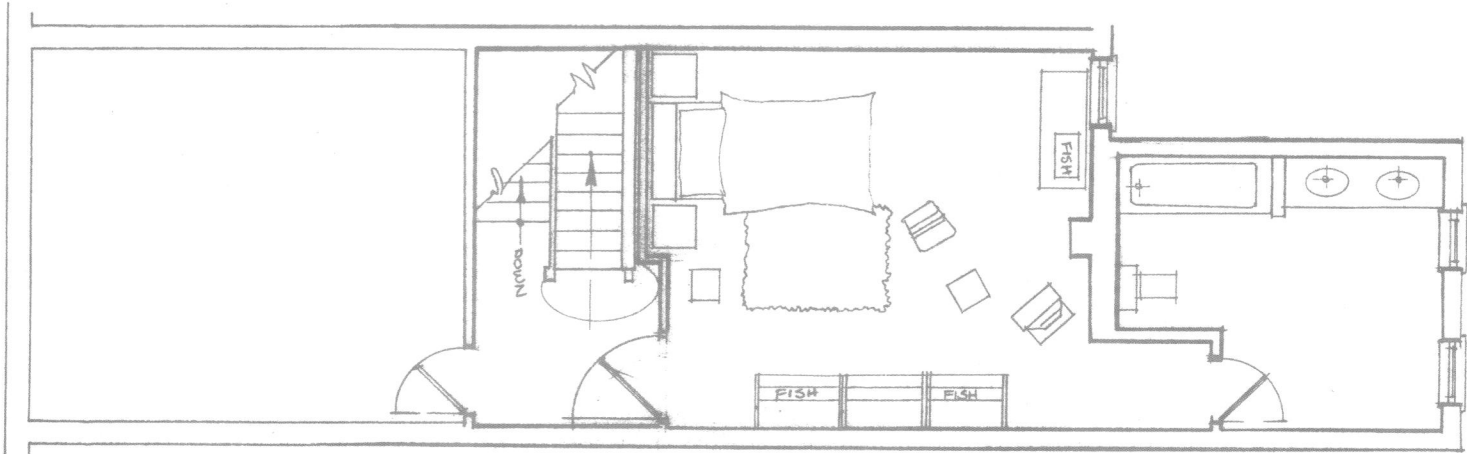

FISH

FISH    FISH

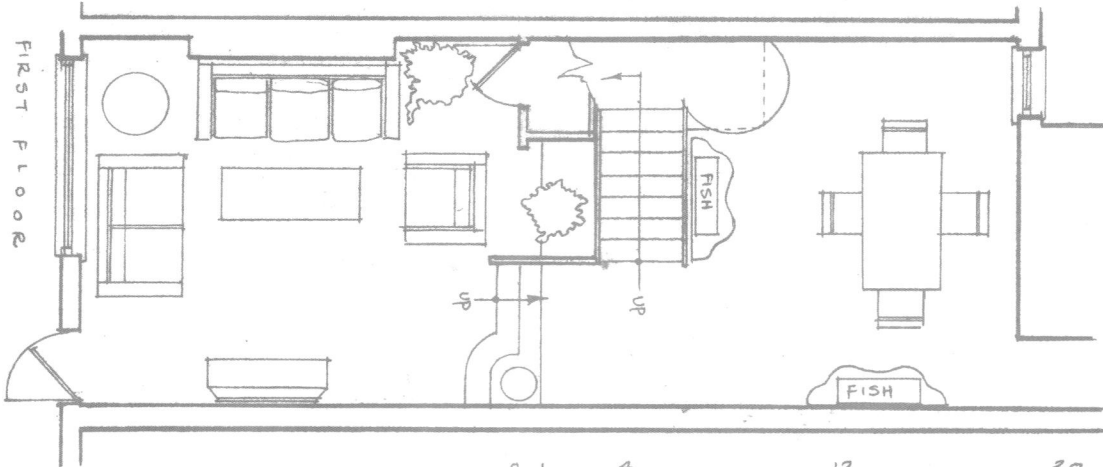

FISH

FISH

0  1        4              12                    20

SCALE IN FEET

TOP A floor plan for the Namond's house set.

failures and the decisions leading to them. But it is Burns's experience with teaching a geography class at Baltimore's Hamilton Elementary/Middle School, his follow-up to twenty years in law enforcement, that fuels the school subplot with vitality, hope, and sorrow.

In a 2008 *New York Times* interview, Burns recalled that 13 of the 220 students in his first class had been shot, two of them twice. "They don't graduate," he told the interviewer.

This season illustrates why that is, and it has nothing to do with a lack of intelligence or other prejudicial bootstrapping myths. Much of the fault lies within a public school system that rewards or punishes schools based on their students' performance undertaking flawed standardized tests that don't consider how different populations learn.

But some of the problem rests with how Americans have been conditioned to view these boys, which is to not see them as boys.

If Duquan, Namond, Michael, and Randy had been born a few years earlier, the cops harassing them might have dropped the term "super-predators," Princeton professor John J. DiIulio Jr.'s alarmist description. Debuting via a 1995 column in the *Weekly Standard*, his warning of a coming epidemic of adolescent "murderers, rapists, and muggers" that would flood America's streets by the year 2000 never materialized. Nevertheless, the phrase proliferated.

That happened after sensationalized coverage of the unjust convictions of Kevin Richardson, Antron McCray, Raymond Santana, Korey Wise, and Yusef Salaam in the 1989 rape of a woman jogging in Central Park seized front page coverage across America. Like the kids in *The Wire*, they

were boys simply hanging out in the wrong place at the wrong time. Local and national media transformed them into a "wilding" wolf pack, and juries found them guilty despite a lack of evidence or witnesses.

*The Wire* doesn't explicitly reference either of these obscene injustices or drop terms like "school-to-prison pipeline"—it doesn't have to. Simon and Burns are acutely aware of how cops and the courts are predisposed to mistreat Black boys. The terrible ends met by Freddie Gray, Trayvon Martin, Michael Brown, and far too many other young Black men prove them right, and keep on proving it.

And in a post-truth world where a distressingly significant portion of the population professes to be sick of hearing about "the system"—or, indeed, refuses to recognize that racist and classist inequities exist at all— this outstanding season remains a pointed curative to such malevolent, willful disbelief.

There are hard, peer-reviewed statistics backing up arguments pointing out the racist bent of systemic inequity in our educational systems, plenty of data derived from studies proving how much more often Black kids are targeted for punishment in educational environments.

Numbers derived from a 2009 report from the National Center for Education Statistics cite that in 2006—the year Duquan, Namond, Michael, and Randy enter eighth grade—more than 3.3 million students were suspended, and over 102,000 were expelled.

The largest percentage of those kids, 15 percent, were Black. At 6.8 percent, Hispanic children were the second most likely to be suspended or expelled, with white kids coming in third at 4.8 percent.

TOP In season four, Prez (Jim True-Frost) embarks on a new career as a math teacher at Edward J. Tilghman Middle School after quitting the police force following an incident in which he accidentally shot and killed another officer.

Racial disparities in school punishment have only yawned wider since then, according to many subsequent studies. We could easily cite them, but that contradicts the central lesson of *The Wire* and its Tilghman arc.

People take comfort in reducing other humans to statistics; stats can be written off. Watching children live the outcome of malicious policy is harder to ignore. That's why what happens to these kids is seared in our consciousness. It never lets us forget how much protection they need and aren't receiving.

Duquan may have basic shelter, but he isn't safe at home. Well-meaning adults try to give him clean clothes, but his parents steal them to sell for drug money. Tilghman becomes his refuge when the school year starts, or it should be. Whenever that proves to be true, it's due to minor decisions such as a teacher sharing a sandwich or providing him access to a shower, enabling him to regain his dignity.

Two men who try to change these kids' lives for the better are former cops. Roland "Prez" Pryzbylewski turns to teaching after he accidentally shoots a fellow officer, a Black man in plainclothes. He comes to Tilghman as the new eighth-grade math teacher and initially struggles, as all green teachers do, before figuring out how to reach the kids using their language.

The other is Bunny, who, when he was a major on the police force, created an unofficial area in West Baltimore where drug sales were unofficially legalized—famously dubbed Hamsterdam. Bunny applies a similarly maverick experiment to targeting disruptive kids at Tilghman for a pilot program he develops alongside University of Maryland Professor David Parenti (Dan DeLuca).

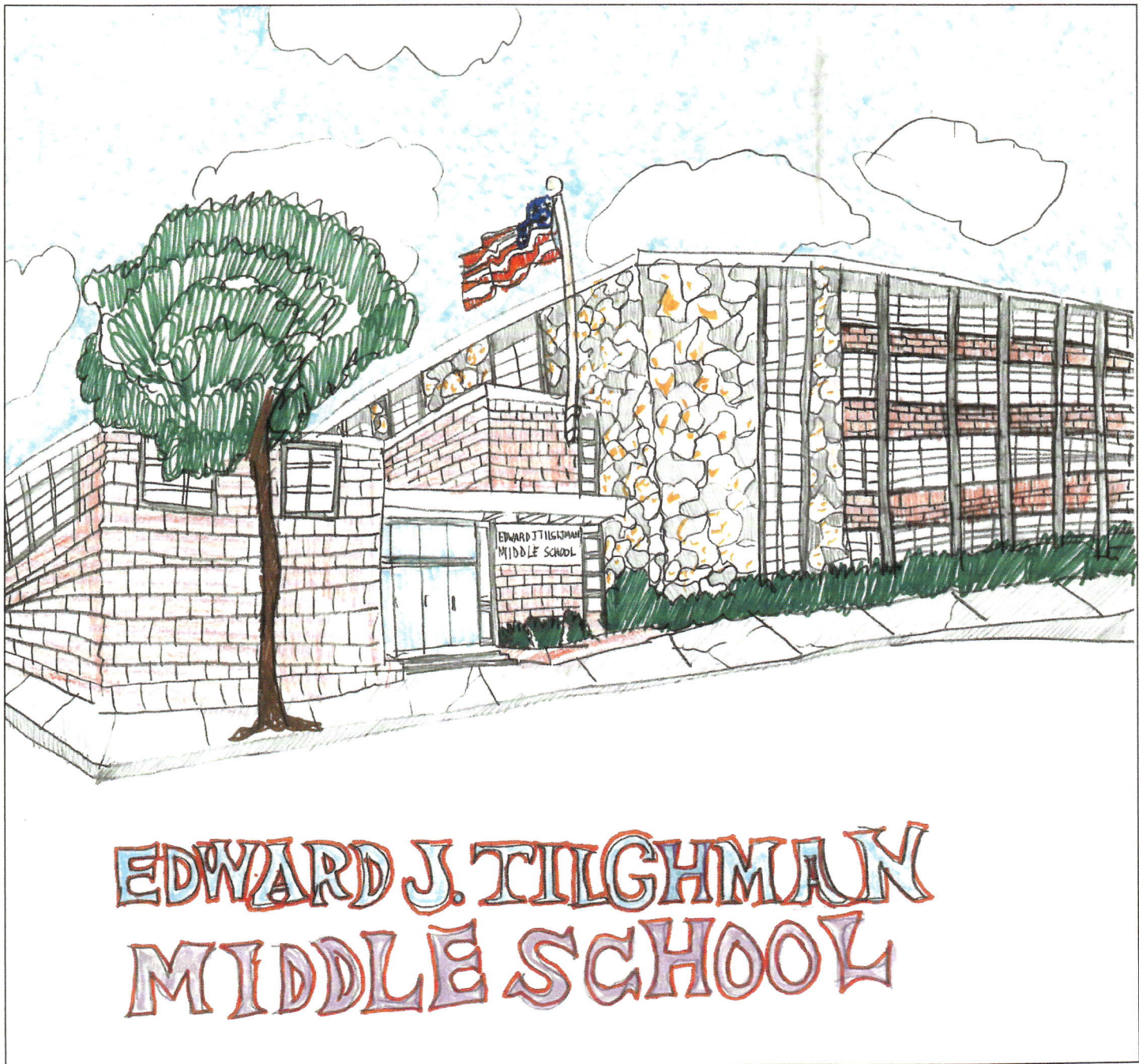

EDWARD J. TILGHMAN MIDDLE SCHOOL

Parenti wants a sizable group to work with, consisting of older kids—high schoolers, ideally. Bunny, who has practical experience with the boys and girls Parenti wants to work with, advises him to start with middle schoolers. Younger kids can still be diverted from negative ends, he reasons. And Tilghman has plenty of suitable participants.

Bunny, Parenti, and their team pull one of the most notorious corner kids, Namond, out of Prez's class for being disruptive and move him into Bunny's classroom—where, at first, the most he can contribute are frequent outbursts of "fuck you."

Once everyone settles in, Namond joins the others in offering Bunny and the academics some wisdom from their point of view. "We do the same thing as y'all, 'cept when we do it, it's like, 'Oh my God, these kids is animals!' Like it's the end of the world coming," he tells Bunny and the academics. "Man, that's bullshit, aight? 'Cause, this is like, what's it, hypocrite? . . . Hypocritical."

"Duquan may have basic shelter, but he isn't safe at home."

OPPOSITE TOP Namond (Julito McCullum, *left*) and Randy (Maestro Harrell, *right*).

OPPOSITE BOTTOM Carver (Seth Gilliam, *left*) and Cutty (Chad L. Coleman, *right*) both take an interest in helping Namond (McCullum, *center*) escape a life on the streets.

TOP An illustration of Edward J. Tilghman Middle School taken from a special yearbook created for the cast and crew of season four of *The Wire* at the end of the shoot.

Soon they cut through the hypocrisy, with the educators figuring out how to spark the kids' intellectual curiosity by asking them to explain what makes an effective corner boy or corner girl. When the kids act up—overturning school desks, getting physical with each other or their educators—they aren't suspended. Instead, the academics use de-escalation tactics, taking them on walks to cool down before returning each kid to class to resume their lessons.

Eventually these "problem" students figure out how to collaborate, how to communicate more effectively, and how to be around other classmates without derailing school for everyone. But the pilot program is shut down anyway.

(In one of life's tiny coincidental ironies, the abandoned school where the fourth season was filmed is now the city's first public Montessori school, devoted to some of the one-on-one learning techniques Bunny attempts to implement.)

Prez also meets his kids at their own level, teaching them math in ways they can understand, such as using dice games to help them learn about mathematical probabilities. He takes a particular shine to Michael, Randy, and especially Duquan, to whom he grants access to the classroom's computer.

He still views them as kids who should be free to enjoy childish pursuits. They love sweets and street fashion and are thrilled to excel at math. Soon his students shift from ridiculing him by calling him "Prezbo" to respecting him and even enjoying his classes.

But beyond Prez's and Bunny's reach, small decisions doom each of the boys. Tilghman's administrators, in a theatrical move meant to persuade the state that they've made progress, shuffle Duquan off to ninth grade midway through the year. They present this as a reward. To him, it means losing the support system he has in Prez and his friends and entering a realm of unknown terrors. He drops out instead.

Michael trades his safety for that of his younger half-brother, persuading a neighborhood hit man named Chris Partlow to beat his abusive stepfather to death in exchange for agreeing to work for Marlo Stanfield, West Baltimore's new kingpin.

Randy unwittingly sets up one of Marlo's rivals by sending him to a decrepit playground, where the man is killed. Then he agrees to be a lookout for two boys who go into a bathroom with a girl who ends up accusing them of rape. To avoid getting in trouble for that schoolhouse crime, he offers to tell the cops about the murder.

Detective Ellis Carver takes his statement—a stroke of luck, because Carver knows these kids and their neighborhood, and has empathy for their lot. His mistake is in making a small yet enormously consequential decision to trust his friend and former partner Herc to deliver Randy to Bunk in homicide.

Bunk has the know-how to protect Randy and, helpfully, he sees him as a child. But Herc is a lunkhead who's drunk on a toxic combination of ambition and stupidity. He grills Randy, poorly, and goes on to let it slip on the streets that Randy talked to the cops. Randy is branded a snitch and run out of school; Miss Anna's home is firebombed, and she's critically injured. His reputation follows him to the group home where he's warehoused.

RIGHT (*Left to right*) Michael (Tristan Wilds), Randy (Maestro Harrell), and Namond (Julito McCullum) hit the streets.

In every way imaginable, these kids are the least cared for. While they're together, they try to care for one another in the best way they're able.

None of that matters.

Not to the city council members, the mayor, and the cops who don't know their neighborhood. Not to state government officials more dedicated to maintaining their hierarchal rank than doing the best they can by the people who elected them.

Carcetti, who wins the election, discovers that his predecessor bequeathed him an educational system with a $54 million deficit. Maryland's Republican governor dangles a bailout, but it comes at a political cost either way. If Carcetti takes it, Council President Nerese Campbell tells him, he's selling out the teachers. If he doesn't, he's selling out the kids. Eyeing a political future that would be dimmed by kowtowing to the other party, he declines the funds, leaving Baltimore's schools to continue rotting.

People tend to think about *The Wire* in expansive literary terms when, as the fourth season shows us, its extraordinariness is enshrined in collections of small moments adding up to a series of massive events, each with lasting consequences.

The season begins with bits of possibility for these boys, albeit the kind that depends on the pathways adults allow for them. By its end, the one who gets that shot at rising above it all receives it by the grace of one man's decision. Even that involves luck and the wisdom to circumvent the system: Bunny goes directly to Wee-Bey to obtain his blessing to take in Namond. Carver tries to do the same for Randy but cannot because he makes the mistake of calling Social Services instead of simply taking him home. Once the sprawling bureaucracy is activated, nothing can stop it. Protocol must be followed, even if that means Social Services' inefficient machinery chews up another child.

In a city that starves out and mismanages its public educational resources, which describes the state of affairs for most major municipalities, the options available to these boys and other kids like them are depressingly few. Whether any of them will survive beyond adolescence is anyone's guess by the fourth season's end. Sadly, the impediments that hold them back, and send them down, are with us even now.

To reference "the system" is to utilize an admittedly nebulous term to describe the machinery upon which the world runs. That's why the least conscionable of us would rather deny that such structures exist or refuse to countenance critiques explaining the ways that system works for some people and against many others. Clinging to the illusion of equal opportunity seems simpler.

But you cannot watch this fourth season and deny the injustice in knowing the Duquan Weemses of the world never stood a chance. Their only mistake was being born into a game that has been set up to ensure that they cannot win.

TOP In season four, Carver (Seth Gilliam, *second from left*) tries to take Randy (Maestro Harrell, *seated center*) under his wing and keep him out of trouble. Also pictured are Corey Parker Robinson (*far left*) and Domenick Lombardozzi (*far right*).

OPPOSITE BOTTOM LEFT Major for the Western District Cedric Daniels (Lance Reddick, *left*) and his partner, Rhonda Pearlman (Deirdre Lovejoy, *center*), have lunch with Tommy Caretti (Aidan Gillan, *right*).

LEFT (*Left to right*) Carcetti (Gillen) meets with Landsman (Delaney Williams), Kima (Sonja Sohn), and Freamon (Clarke Peters).

# ED BURNS

## Interview by Nikki Stafford and Robert Thompson

A former BPD narcotics and homicide detective and Baltimore public school teacher, producer, writer, and cocreator Ed Burns brought a formidable level of authenticity to *The Wire*. The coauthor of *The Corner: A Year in the Life of an Inner-City Neighborhood*, Burns is David Simon's longtime creative collaborator and has also partnered with him on the HBO shows *Generation Kill*, *The Plot Against America*, and *We Own This City*.

**I believe many people didn't think the circumstances portrayed in *The Wire* would still be essentially unchanged twenty years later. How do you feel when you look at the social situations documented in the show and see that they're still going on?**

When David and I finished *The Corner*, I had these speaking engagements, and I would always say to the audience, "If you record my talk, you can play it twenty years from now, because nothing is going to change." I'm not cynical about it; it's the nature of what this country has become. But until enough of us realize that sitting on our asses is not going to work, things aren't going to change.

**You come at this as a police officer, an educator, and a writer. Cops are sometimes conservative in their vision of policing. How did you start seeing**

**things in the way you just described?**

I don't think it's that difficult for me, personally. When I started at the police department, I didn't know the world of the inner city, so I relied on people telling me about it. But the more I got involved in it, the more I began to understand it. And after a while, I did what we portrayed in *The Wire* and figured out a way to actually do something to stop homicides. I got a bunch of case folders, took them in to the captain and said, "I can solve these if you let me." Of course he said no, which I expected, so I went to the state attorney's office and made the same pitch. He said go for it, and for the next twelve years, that's what I did. It was very rewarding, because I was taking down the sharks, but I could never get anybody to see that this was probably the way to do it.

In fact, the command staff, when I was there, didn't even believe there were gangs in Baltimore,

Baltimore, which was kind of amazing to me. We had longstanding gangs; they just weren't Crips and Bloods. I made a lot of very big cases, and I generated a lot of animosity between Narcotics and Homicide, because when I was taking these guys down, I was also taking down large drug operations.

**We were talking to George Pelecanos about this, and one of the things he found really intriguing about writing for *The Wire* was developing the characters. He said that gone are the days of the traditional police show, and instead there are shows like *The Wire*, where the perceived bad guys—the Marlos, the Stringer Bells, the Barksdales—are not one-dimensional. I'm sure some of that comes from David Simon and the writing crew, but it sounds like you didn't see things as simple either.**

Well, the original guys, like Stringer Bell and Avon Barksdale, were second generation; their parents had jobs. And when the industries left Baltimore in the late '60s and early '70s, there were no opportunities for these sons and daughters coming up right, so they ended up in the drug world. And then the following generation, which was the Marlos, was totally disconnected from the straight world.

Like Marlo, he's a bit calculating, very cold. I had Bubbles run into Marlo's car, and the line that

I thought was appropriate was "Do it or don't, but I have someplace to go." Killing Bubbles made not a blip on his radar.

**Jamie Hector, who played Marlo, seems to think he was a sociopath.**

Yeah. You can call him a sociopath. I'm not a big fan of psychiatry, but you can label him that. We're mass-producing them. In this particular world, they're adapted to survive. So [yes], you could say Marlo was a sociopath, but we bred him to be that. We allowed that system to make him what he is today.

**The fourth season shows, from both a political perspective and an educational perspective, how these kids end up in these situations. How much of your experience as an educator do you see in this season's depictions of the Baltimore school system?**

All of it. When I got to Hamilton Middle School, which was an anomaly in itself, it was set in a white working-class neighborhood, and the kids were bused up from the inner city so that 98 percent of the kids in the school were Black and from very, very impoverished neighborhoods. Of about 230 kids, there were maybe twenty of them who were sort of like the happy bluebird class that you could actually try to teach.

And all the rest were just chaos. So after the first year, I proposed the idea to the principal, which

we did in the show, of separating the "stoop kids" and the "corner kids." Most of these kids were stoop kids, but we couldn't do anything, because if you have four or five corner kids in the classroom, there is no teaching. She asked, "How would we figure out who was corner and who was stoop?" I replied, "Well, it's simple. The kid who can sit in his chair is a stoop kid. If he can't, he's a corner kid." We divided them up, and I ended up on a team with the stoop kids, so I had like forty-five kids in my class, and the teachers teaching the corner kids had maybe six or eight in a class. We worked with them, and we followed them through seventh and eighth grades.

Before, the kids passing math, for example, would be like 3 percent. We bumped it up to 12 percent. Kids in reading: Maybe 5 percent passed, and we got it up to like 20 percent. It was numbers nobody had ever seen before. But at the end of the second year, the program was ended. Next, I went to what was called City College, which is sort of the main liberal arts high school in Baltimore. And it's there that I found the greatest tragedy of all: The school was probably 80 percent girls, and the freshmen I taught were a good four or five years behind their peers in the county. Every one of them had straight A's from first grade straight on through, but they couldn't write a sentence. We had some real gnashing of teeth and tears flowing like crazy, because I had to get them up and running. It was a really interesting challenge.

OPPOSITE *The Wire* producer, writer, and cocreator Ed Burns on set.

BOTTOM A floor plan for the Edward J. Tilghman Middle School set.

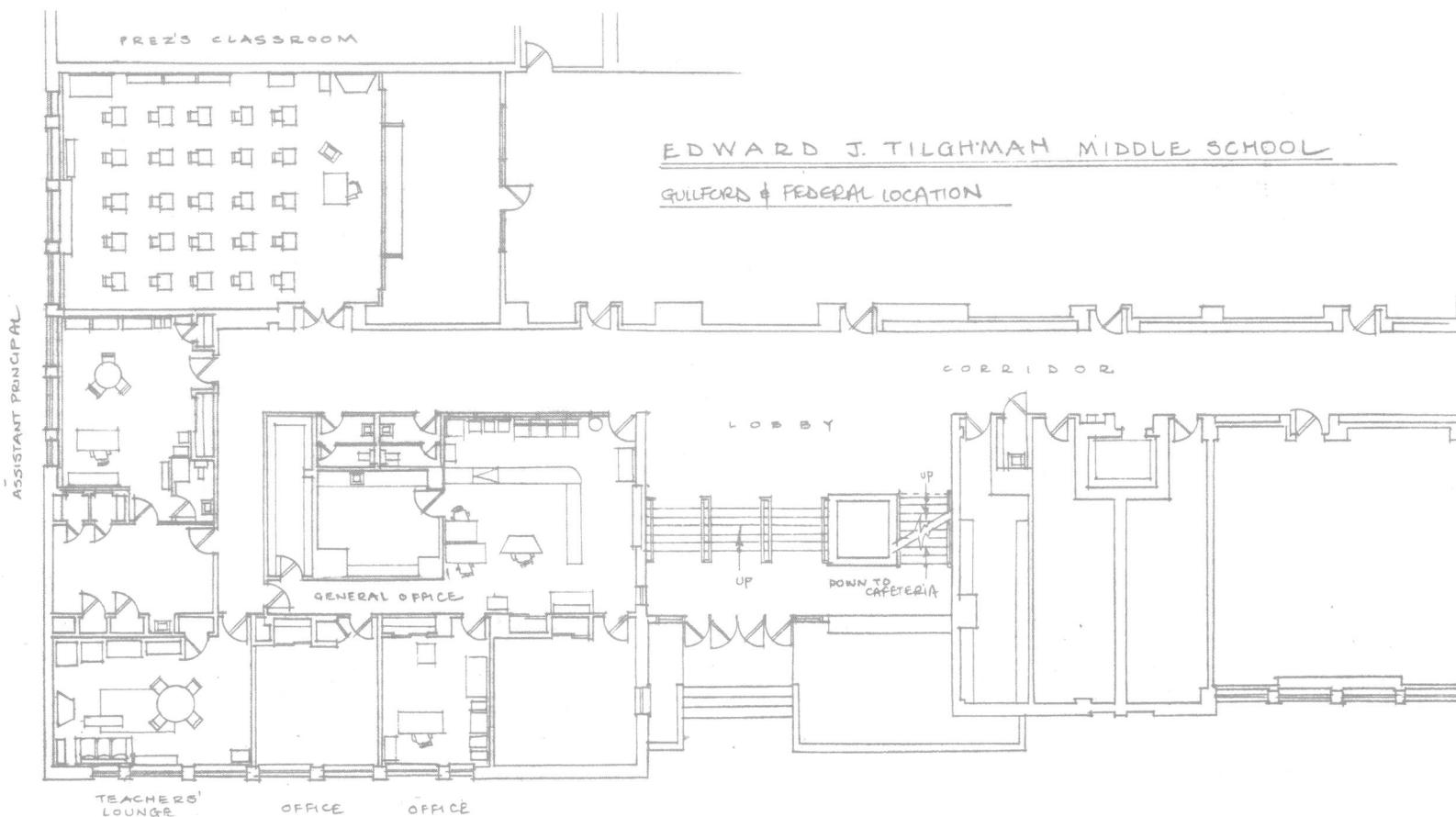

EDWARD J. TILGHMAN MIDDLE SCHOOL
GUILFORD & FEDERAL LOCATION

PREZ'S CLASSROOM

ASSISTANT PRINCIPAL

CORRIDOR

LOBBY

UP

UP

DOWN TO CAFETERIA

GENERAL OFFICE

TEACHERS' LOUNGE     OFFICE     OFFICE

# JERMAINE CRAWFORD

## Interview by Nikki Stafford and Robert Thompson

Actor Jermaine Crawford got his break playing street kid Duquan "Dukie" Weems in season four of *The Wire*, reprising his role in season five. He's also been seen in numerous other productions, including the Joel Schumacher feature *Twelve* (2010) and David Simon's *We Own This City*.

**What was it like to audition for *The Wire*?**

There were quite a few auditions initially. It was a very intense auditioning process, even for children, but now I understand that they intended to literally make the children the leads of this huge HBO show. It was kind of the biggest audition I've ever done, and I remember just giving that audition everything I had and waiting by the phone every day for the following two weeks. And then I got the call, and the rest is history.

**Robert F. Chew, who played Proposition Joe, was the acting coach for many of the young people on the show. Was he someone that you leaned on, on the set, while you guys were all working?**

Not so much on the set. The writers were very secretive, and they would introduce the script to us episode by episode, so that we wouldn't know

exactly what was going on. At the top of the episode, we would meet with Mr. Chew at the production office, myself and the other three boys, and we would rehearse all our scenes with him before we would even get to set.

Robert was such an amazing actor. He was just so cool, so personable. He really made you like him. And he was kind of a theater legend in Baltimore, so it's great that he got to impart some of that wisdom to us prior to every episode. Everyone might say that we all did a great job as children, but that's because we really had some adults that were guiding us to make sure that we stepped up to the opportunity.

***The Wire* tended to mix up the cast a lot: There were professional actors but also real people playing background characters. What was it like**

OPPOSITE Jermaine Crawford as Duquan "Dukie" Weems.

TOP Namond (Julito McCullum, *second from left*) faces off with assistant principal Marcia Donnelly (Tootsie Duvall) as Michael (Tristan Wilds, *far left*) and Dukie (Crawford, *center*) look on.

to perform scenes with regular kids?

It was very interesting for me because I grew up kind of lower middle class, but my parents did the best they could to give me what they could. I had two loving parents who supported my childhood dreams very much, and that's most of what I knew growing up. When I got into the classrooms and really started to get my hands on this Dukie character, it was a lot at the age of twelve, thirteen to wrap my head around the fact that this kid is homeless, and his parents are addicted to drugs. If that's not your reality, it kind of takes a bit of time to click.

And when we were in the classrooms, I believe Ed Burns pulled me to the side once and said, "Some of these guys and gals in this classroom are real-life Dukies. What you're acting, this is their life." It clicked with me that there was no cut, no wrap, no checking the gate for these kids. And it was because of this that I kind of committed my life's work to advocating for homeless youth, one step at a time. So hopefully, as the future comes, I can continue to raise awareness and funds for youth in America who are experiencing homelessness,

because there's a great deal of them. A great, great deal of them.

**It's incredible how many people from *The Wire* have gone on to do that kind of work because it really stuck with them in such a big way.**

It was so real. David Simon, Ed Burns, George Pelecanos, and Nina [Kostroff Noble, producer], made it their business to make the show as real as possible. It's almost uncomfortably real. We were shooting in real vacant houses, real blocks. We were in the thick of it, and once you're sitting in it, you kind of take it on. It speaks to you, you know?

**You were also a very, very young actor. Did you find yourself struggling with any of these scenes?**

Well, before *The Wire*, I was fortunate enough to do a lot of theater. So I was able to differentiate between what was pretend and what wasn't. But at that young an age, I didn't understand the necessary time it would take to recover from these scenes.

Doing the performance in itself was not hard, and I will say that I remember Ed Burns, and

especially Nina, were very, very good. They were like, "Do you want a closed set? Are you okay? Do you want people watching you? How are you? Do you need a moment?" And I understand why they were so [cautious] about it, because that's some serious shit for a thirteen- or fourteen-year-old. But they made it as easy for me as they possibly could.

### Things get worse for Dukie in season five. How did that season feel different for you?

Season four was very much child's play. Five was work. We knew at the top of season five that not everybody was going to return as they once were. So I was very grateful to be returning in the way that I was, and I understood that it was for a reason. The show had aired, we heard the reception, and we were seeing the connections with the audience. So I knew that this season was like, all right, this is a big deal, let's do it, let's hit it, this is not a game, this is not a joke, let's work.

I think the hardest part for me was the ostracizing that happened to the character. It was kind of inadvertently done, but there was a certain type of separation between me and the boys, even in public, because it was like people really thought that I was this character. After a while, it kind of wore on me.

### What do you think is the lasting legacy of this show?

I think the lasting legacy of *The Wire* is that it's the greatest American exposé on television of all time. It tells you everything you need to know about our culture: pop culture, government, streets, drugs, police—everything. And the reason it's just as good now is because no changes have been made. Maybe one day we can look back at it like something that once existed in a different world, but until we start to see reform, a lot of this stuff is going to continue.

OPPOSITE BOTTOM Omar (Michael K. Williams, *left*) and Proposition Joe (Robert F. Chew, *right*) undertake a business transaction, Baltimore style. Chew also served as an acting coach for the young performers on season four.

TOP Dukie (Jermaine Crawford, *left*) and Randy (Maestro Harrell, *right*) out on the stoop.

# NATHAN CORBETT AND TRAY CHANEY

## Interview by Brandon Easton

A native of Baltimore, Nathan Corbett plays Donut in season four of *The Wire* and reunited with David Simon for a role on the series *We Own This City*. Tray Chaney also appears in *We Own This City*, as police officer Gordon Hawk, a very different role from that of Poot Carr, the Barksdale organization drug dealer he played across five seasons of *The Wire*.

TOP (*Left to right*) Poot (Tray Chaney), Little Kevin (Tyrell Baker), and Bodie (J. D. Williams), whose clashes with the Stanfield organization form a major plotline in season four.

OPPOSITE Accomplished car thief Donut, played by Nathan Corbett.

**Can you tell me about the most positive aspect for you of working on *The Wire*?**

**NATHAN CORBETT:** The most positive aspect for me while working on *The Wire* was seeing the faces of the people and the environments that we were shooting in. The young kids saw me and said, "You know, I can do that. I can do this." We were shooting in the trenches, and crowds and crowds of people saw that you don't have to go to Hollywood or to different places for [acting] opportunities [as long as you are] are genuine, positive, focused, and your mind is where it's supposed to be. [If you are], then these opportunities will crash into you.

[Since I was young myself and from Baltimore,] just seeing [the kids] being so happy and talking to them while on set was amazing. You would have thought that *they* were filming. They were just so happy to see somebody who looked like them, who came from the same place they [did], and who was doing such crazy things. You have to remember, I was stealing cars on set, and they would see me hopping out of the car wearing sunglasses like Ethan Hunt in *Mission: Impossible*, which [was something] you just didn't see in Baltimore.

And [we filmed] before you could simply go to Instagram and view behind-the-scenes shots. So to know that somebody saw me one day and thought that they could do it [like me]—in addition to the opportunities that were granted to me by the writers and directors of the show—that's one of the biggest [positive] things [for me]. To this day, people are still [talking about] the work that I did back then. Words cannot express the humility that it gives me, because I didn't write the character Donut; I just played him.

TOP Poot (Tray Chaney, *left*) bumps heads with Herc (Domenick Lombardozzi, *right*).

The show was great because the writers allowed it to be authentic.

**TRAY CHANEY:** For me, it was just being on [the series], working and seeing all these up-and-coming and amazing actors at the time. All of us have done so many amazing things, and we are still [continuing to act]. [I also appreciate] the camaraderie, how the whole cast was a family. I've never been on a cast where I really considered them like brothers and sisters, like my family, both on and off screen. And one thing about *The Wire* was that it told the truth—and sometimes the truth hurts. That we could build upon [the hard truth] and really uplift our community the best way possible—and to be talking about it twenty years later—that's the positivity that came out of it. [It is] still one of the most critically acclaimed shows ever made. Not to take anything away from other shows, but when you watch them, you understand where their blueprints came from: *The Wire*. I mean, just look at what it's doing for us now.

All of us are still in the business in our own ways, and a bunch of us are working on some of the same projects together, like HBO's *We Own This City*. J. D. Williams and I are regulars on *Saints & Sinners* on Bounce TV.

**NATHAN CORBETT:** A number-one show.

**TRAY CHANEY:** Yeah, number-one show. And the hip-hop community embraces it. Nate and I are fortunate to be able to do music in this business and

tour with different national mainstream artists. And to be able to still talk [about the series] twenty years later when a lot of people don't make it past two or even ten years . . . it's like we are still here, and we *still* got it. We still have so much further to go and are leaving legacies for our families. It's just a beautiful thing.

**Since the actors filmed in different units, how did you manage to bond together as an acting ensemble? Was there a process to it, or did you just chill after hours?**

**NATHAN CORBETT:** I'll let the vet who was on all five seasons speak.

**TRAY CHANEY:** Well, you pretty much answered it. When you looked at the call sheet, you knew a certain actor was shooting that day. When I first got on set and saw Wendell Pierce, I remember thinking, "That's the guy from *Waiting to Exhale* and a whole bunch of other [roles]!" I would sit around and just wait to see [which next famous actor would appear]. You also ended up running into each other in between takes, in hair and makeup, on set, or in wardrobe. [You would] bump into each other, and you felt the energy. It felt like, "Oh, man, we are a family, and we are going to be on this set together." I vividly remember asking Lawrence Gilliard Jr. thousands of questions, since *The Wire* was my first job as an actor and also my first audition. [It was incredible] to come out of the gate and be on a show like that and run into guys like Wood Harris and

J. D. Williams, who I had watched on television and who I was fans of. [We became] a family, brothers. We got to know each other's families, and it was all love, always—all the way up until now. It's still that way.

**NATHAN CORBETT:** And to piggyback on what Tray is saying: When we joined for the fourth season, everybody welcomed us with open arms. Robert F. Chew was the acting coach [for us] young'uns, and we received a big, warm welcome from one of the greatest thespians of all time. He coached us like a teacher and wanted us to do well. It doesn't get more embracing. Everybody was just so welcoming. There was nothing but love from all the cast members. There was *not one* cast member who I got a weird vibe from. [When I would] see the camaraderie the older veterans had among themselves, I was just so thankful to be a part of the show. It's deeper than us; it transcends. Everybody was just so cool.

### What would you say is the ultimate legacy of *The Wire*?

**NATHAN CORBETT:** Well, I believe that the legacy of *The Wire* is the raw and gritty stories that were told *before* today's censoring—and we won't see anything like it again. Certain things [that were] said, jokes, [and even] characters just wouldn't be allowed to fly in this day and age, [which makes the series serve as] a time stamp of when television was raw. I also believe that the legacies [of actors] Michael B. Jordan, Idris Elba, and Michael K. Williams are *The Wire's* legacy, too. The show has given us so many awesome entertainers who we enjoy with our families. Even the character arcs [are incredible] for only a five-season show with just ten to twelve episodes per season. I mean, the character arc of Bubbles, come on, now—and those of Brother Mouzone, Felicia "Snoop" Pearson, and

Michael Lee. All the questions and [plot] holes were closed—and they only needed five years to do it.

Even the one-liners. For example, when Snoop asks Mike, "How my hair look, Mike?" "You look good, girl," [he responds]. One of my personal favorites is when Omar says to Brother Mouzone, "[With] this range, and this caliber? Even if I miss, I can't miss." That's something you would hear Muhammad Ali say before a fight. And the music! The [writers] really knew what they were doing. It's like they brought the spaghetti Western to Baltimore, but with way better writing.

**TRAY CHANEY:** The ultimate legacy of *The Wire* is [that it is] a study guide. You can learn so much from it. It's like an open book. I always called *The Wire* the first reality television show ever—and not in the sense of reality TV today. We're talking about a pivotal moment that hit in 2002 that nobody was really ready for, because [the series] was before its time. [Viewers] learned about certain things that need attention: the educational system, the war on drugs, why cops operate the way that they do—or why they *should* operate a certain way but aren't. Within five seasons, it gives you a [deep] insight into these issues. It's crazy, because we still get asked, "Is *The Wire* ever coming back?" It could go on forever.

**NATHAN CORBETT:** A spin-off?

**TRAY CHANEY:** There are so many stories. I think David Simon—but I don't know 100 percent—wanted to end [the series] on top, and he ended it on the highest note possible.

TOP LEFT Donut (Nathan Corbett) in his natural environment: the seat of a stolen car.

TOP RIGHT Wallace (Michael B. Jordan, *left*) with Poot (Tray Chaney, *right*) in a scene from season one.

# SEASON FOUR EPISODES

**S04E01:** Boys of Summer

**Written by:** Story by David Simon and Ed Burns; teleplay by David Simon

**Directed by:** Joe Chappelle

**Original airdate:** September 10, 2006

**Epigraph:** "Lambs to the slaughter here." –Marcia Donnelly

**Description:** In the season four premiere, four boys from West Baltimore play out their summer vacation in the streets. Meanwhile, Marlo has solved the problem that baffled Stringer Bell: how to maintain discipline–read: murders–without getting police attention.

**S04E02:** Soft Eyes

**Written by:** Story by Ed Burns and David Mills; teleplay by David Mills

**Directed by:** Christine Moore

**Original airdate:** September 17, 2006

**Epigraph:** "I still wake up white in a city that ain't." –Carcetti

**Description:** Herc's soft-duty job with the mayor takes an unexpectedly hard turn. Despite the potential damage to her career, Pearlman provides Freamon and Sydnor with subpoena ammunition for their "grizzly bear" hunt in city hall.

**S04E03:** Home Rooms

**Written by:** Story by Ed Burns and Richard Price; teleplay by Richard Price

**Directed by:** Seith Mann

**Original airdate:** September 24, 2006

**Epigraph:** "I love the first day, man. Everybody all friendly an' shit." –Namond Brice

**Description:** With his lead dwindling, Royce resorts to extreme measures to stall Carcetti's momentum. At Bodie's corner, Michael proves adept as a runner, with Bodie and Marlo taking notice. A re-up bodega is put under surveillance by Omar and Greggs.

**S04E04:** Refugees

**Written by:** Story by Ed Burns and Dennis Lehane; teleplay by Dennis Lehane

**Directed by:** Jim McKay

**Original airdate:** October 1, 2006

**Epigraph:** "No one wins. One side just loses more slowly." –Prez

**Description:** With Freamon and Greggs moved to Homicide, Herc and Dozerman join Marimow in the stripped-down Major Crimes Unit. Cutty gets a "custodial" job at Tilghman School mopping up truants but can't make headway in his efforts to mentor Michael.

**S04E05:** Alliances

**Written by:** Story by David Simon and Ed Burns; teleplay by Ed Burns

**Directed by:** David Platt

**Original airdate:** October 8, 2006

**Epigraph:** "If you with us, you with us." –Chris Partlow

**Description:** Valchek leaks details of the Braddock case to Carcetti, who contemplates how to best leak it to the press. The ensuing negative attention turns Royce against Burrell, who takes the heat while Rawls comes to the rescue.

**S04E06:** Margin of Error

**Written by:** Story by Ed Burns and Eric Overmyer; teleplay by Eric Overmyer

**Directed by:** Dan Attias

**Original airdate:** October 15, 2006

**Epigraph:** "Don't try this shit at home." –Norman Wilson

**Description:** With Election Day approaching, the three mayoral candidates make last-minute appeals. Carcetti wrangles for votes as he responds to a potentially devastating smear. Norris and Greggs get a lead on the Braddock case but end up being detoured.

**S04E07:** Unto Others

**Written by:** Story by Ed Burns and William F. Zorzi; teleplay by William F. Zorzi

**Directed by:** Anthony Hemingway

**Original airdate:** October 29, 2006

**Epigraph:** "Aw yeah. That golden rule." –Bunk

**Description:** With a bounty on him, Omar calls in a favor with Bunk. The election over, Royce and Carcetti make peace and contemplate their futures. At school, Prez tricks his students into learning math. Finally, Greggs uses "soft eyes" at a crime scene.

**S04E08:** Corner Boys

**Written by:** Story by Ed Burns and Richard Price; teleplay by Richard Price

**Directed by:** Agnieszka Holland

**Original airdate:** November 5, 2006

**Epigraph:** "We got our thing, but it's just part of the big thing." –Zenobia

**Description:** To monitor the pulse on the street, Carcetti makes the rounds with members of the force. With Marimow on his case, Herc resorts to strong-arm tactics to retrieve his pinched camera, but Marlo isn't impressed.

**S04E09:** Know Your Place

**Written by:** Story by Ed Burns and Kia Corthron; teleplay by Kia Corthron

**Directed by:** Alex Zakrzewski

**Original airdate:** November 12, 2006

**Epigraph:** "Might as well dump 'em, get another." –Proposition Joe

**Description:** Poot returns to the corner after a stint in prison— and is welcomed back. Carcetti engages in a testy budget battle with City Council President Campbell, promotes Daniels, and hits a snag in his efforts to relieve Burrell of his duties.

**S04E10:** Misgivings

**Written by:** Story by Ed Burns and Eric Overmyer; teleplay by Eric Overmyer

**Directed by:** Ernest Dickerson

**Original airdate:** November 19, 2006

**Epigraph:** "World goin' one way, people another." –Poot

**Description:** Acting on Clay Davis's advice, Burrell seeks to burnish his reputation by ordering the department to double their street arrests. The mandate does not sit well with McNulty, who sets his sights instead on cracking a string of church robberies.

**S04E11:** A New Day

**Written by:** Story by David Simon and Ed Burns; teleplay by Ed Burns

**Directed by:** Brad Anderson

**Original airdate:** November 26, 2006

**Epigraph:** "You play in dirt, you get dirty." –McNulty

**Description:** After flexing his muscles around the city, Carcetti faces his first dilemma when a group protests Herc's mistreatment of one of their own. Later, the mayor reverses Burrell's mass-arrest mandate, but Burrell still has some cards to play.

**S04E12:** That's Got His Own

**Written by:** Story by Ed Burns and George Pelecanos; teleplay by George Pelecanos

**Directed by:** Joe Chappelle

**Original airdate:** December 3, 2006

**Epigraph:** "That all there is to it?" –Bubbles

**Description:** On the trail of missing bodies, Freamon turns to a higher authority after being rebuked by Landsman. Carcetti finds his promises of prosperity undermined by the school debt, forcing him to contemplate groveling before the governor in Annapolis.

**S04E13:** Final Grades

**Written by:** Story by David Simon and Ed Burns; teleplay by David Simon

**Directed by:** Ernest Dickerson

**Original airdate:** December 10, 2006

**Epigraph:** "If animal trapped call 410-844-6286." – Baltimore, traditional

**Description:** In the season four finale, the bodies from the vacants pile up while Burrell offers his support to Daniels and admonishes Rawls for crossing him. A distraught Bubbles finds himself at his wit's end after his revenge plan backfires.

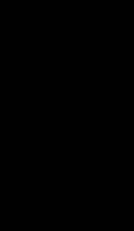

SEASON

5

# AN INTRODUCTION TO SEASON FIVE

By D. Watkins

LIGHT FOR ALL

"Respectable newspapers have turned into outfits that will publish anything to survive . . ."

Season five of *The Wire* predicted the future by shining a light on what was happening and what was going to happen to newsrooms all across the country. While *The Wire* was filming, the *Baltimore Sun* had over three hundred people working in the newsroom. That number now is under seventy. Respectable newspapers have turned into outfits that will publish anything to survive, hungry to come up with content in the sea of online publications that seem to have popped up overnight.

The need to compete carved out a perfect path for a character like season five's *Sun* journalist Scott Templeton (Tom McCarthy) to make up stories and constantly be rewarded for it. Templeton starts out by inserting small lies into his stories to make them more exciting, but by the end of the season, he has created an imaginary serial killer. He's caught in his web of lies multiple times but is protected because his popular stories have created a readership in a failing industry. Templeton even receives a Pulitzer. Mike Fletcher (Brandon Young), a general assignment reporter for the Metro desk, indirectly rivals Templeton by doing the job the correct way. He talks to people, takes real notes, and never lets his ambition corrupt the integrity of his stories.

In this season, we see Bubbles's journey come full circle, as Fletcher profiles his road to recovery. Viewers examining the dynamic between

TOP A version of the *Baltimore Sun*'s logo created by the art department of *The Wire*.

OPPOSITE When season five begins, Bubbles (Andre Royo) has been clean for a year and sells issues of the *Baltimore Sun* to make ends meet.

TOP Key players in the Stanfield organization: (*left to right*) Snoop (Felicia Pearson), Marlo (Jamie Hector), and Chris (Gbenga Akinnagbe).

RIGHT Marlo (Hector), drug kingpin and sociopath.

OPPOSITE TOP Freamon (Clarke Peters) raids Marlo's operation and recovers a huge quantity of heroin.

OPPOSITE BOTTOM Back on the case: (*left to right*) Kima (Sonja Sohn), Bunk (Wendell Pierce), and McNulty (Dominic West).

the reporter and the addict develop even more empathy for Bubbles after seeing the hard work it takes to beat a drug problem, especially when drugs are everywhere, and you have little or no support.

And our officers are nearing the finish line as they try to bring down ruthless kingpin Marlo Stanfield. Stanfield is Stringer Bell and Avon Barksdale rolled into one, but younger, smarter, and even more vicious. Unlike Avon, Marlo kills for sport. Of course, the Baltimore Police Department arrests Marlo, but they do so illegally and lose the case—allowing him to retire from the drug game free and clear with millions of dollars. Marlo is so smart that, if they rebooted *The Wire*, I wouldn't be surprised if they brought him back as the city's mayor.

And just like in real life, a few cops were promoted from patrol to sergeants and lieutenants, a few street guys were promoted from corner boys to bosses, new addicts were birthed, and the game continues.

It's been twenty years, and in Baltimore, absolutely nothing has changed. As a matter of fact, it may be worse—but we will continue to fight.

# WENDELL PIERCE

## Interview by Nikki Stafford and Robert Thompson

Actor Wendell Pierce has enjoyed a hugely varied career, appearing in projects including Spike Lee's historical drama *Malcolm X* (1992); *Selma* (2014), directed by Ava DuVernay; and Amazon Prime's hit series *Jack Ryan*. But he might be best remembered for his key role in *The Wire* as Detective William "Bunk" Moreland, the hard-drinking comrade of Jimmy McNulty. Pierce also starred in David Simon's *Treme*, a role that took him back to his native New Orleans.

**You've told the story about how you got into an argument with the cab driver on the way to your audition and came in complaining loudly about it. Do you remember the audition well?**

I read with Dominic, and this man came in ready! I made a joke to him about that: I said, "Oh man, you make me look bad. You are American, and I don't sound American at all."

Weeks later, when we were finally shooting, I remember David saying, "Man, I'll never forget that story you came into the audition with about your taxi ride there. That's where you got the job. That was Bunk." He told me that my telling of the story said it all. And then my rapport with Dominic as we were trying to get the scene together, the way we were reading different scenes and complaining to each other about each other—we had a great rapport. David told me, "You got the part not because of what you did with your words, but what you brought in on your own, in your own words." And that's how I came on *The Wire*.

**How fully baked was Bunk's character when you got your hands on it? Was it complete in terms of the backstory and how they wanted you to approach the role?**

No, it wasn't wholly complete. For the most part, it was, but I think of that role as a three-legged stool: a combination of what I brought to the role, what I learned researching the role, and then what was on the page.

I brought a wryness to the character, but the most important part of developing how I played Bunk was researching Black detectives. Especially Rick Requer [the real-life Baltimore detective who Bunk was based on].

OPPOSITE Wendell Pierce as William "Bunk" Moreland.

TOP Pierce sits at Bunk's desk between shots on *The Wire*.

## BALTIMORE POLICE DEPARTMENT

### DET. WILLIAM MORELAND
**HOMICIDE DIVISION**
C.I.D

OFFICE 410-396-1212          CELL 410-276-6266

TOP Omar (Michael K. Williams, *left*) is picked up from Harford County Detention Center by Bunk (Wendell Pierce, *right*) in the season four episode "Know Your Place."

ABOVE A business card prop created for the Bunk character.

He was at the courthouse at the time, and he showed me around it. He was gregarious and outgoing, he knew everyone, and he had a real rapport with people, and I picked up on all of that. Even when it was antagonistic! If there was a sealed-off section, it was like, "Why can't we go down there? Listen, I'm taking this man around, I'm showing him around, we can go through this door, that's not going to be a problem." He could be very humble, soft-spoken, and fun. I watched the way he treated people, and I said, "That's Bunk." That was the quality I wanted to have.

Rick came to the set on my first day of work. He pulled up in his long Cadillac, smoking a cigar, and looked across the yard quizzically from a distance. He looked at me, and his face contorted into this look of

disgust. He tilted his head left, then he tilted his head right, and then he got back in his car and just drove off. And that was the last time I saw him for five years. I talked to him during that time, on and off, but I was terrified. I was thinking, "This man came to the set, took one look at what I was doing, and was just disgusted." Near the end of the show, I went to his retirement party, gift in hand, and from across the hall, he gave me the same look. Face contorted, disgusted, the same expression. I walked up to him, and suddenly his whole demeanor changed. He put on a big smile and said, "Boy, come here, you made me a star! That's my boy!" I told him I hadn't spoken to him because I was afraid, because I thought he hated what I was doing, and he said, "No, man, I loved it! You were great!" I told him he'd come to set and had a look of disgust, and he said, "No, man, I just couldn't see what the hell y'all were doing! I was trying to figure it out from that far away!" It was just a complete misunderstanding.

In my research for the role, I met so many Black police officers who became police because the crime that affected their neighborhoods did not reflect the good people in them. They wanted to make sure they represented 99 percent of the people in all these underserved communities who worked every day—the working poor, living paycheck to paycheck, disproportionately affected as victims of crime. That motivation defined how I portrayed Bunk and led to my greatest scene, the one with Omar on the bench.

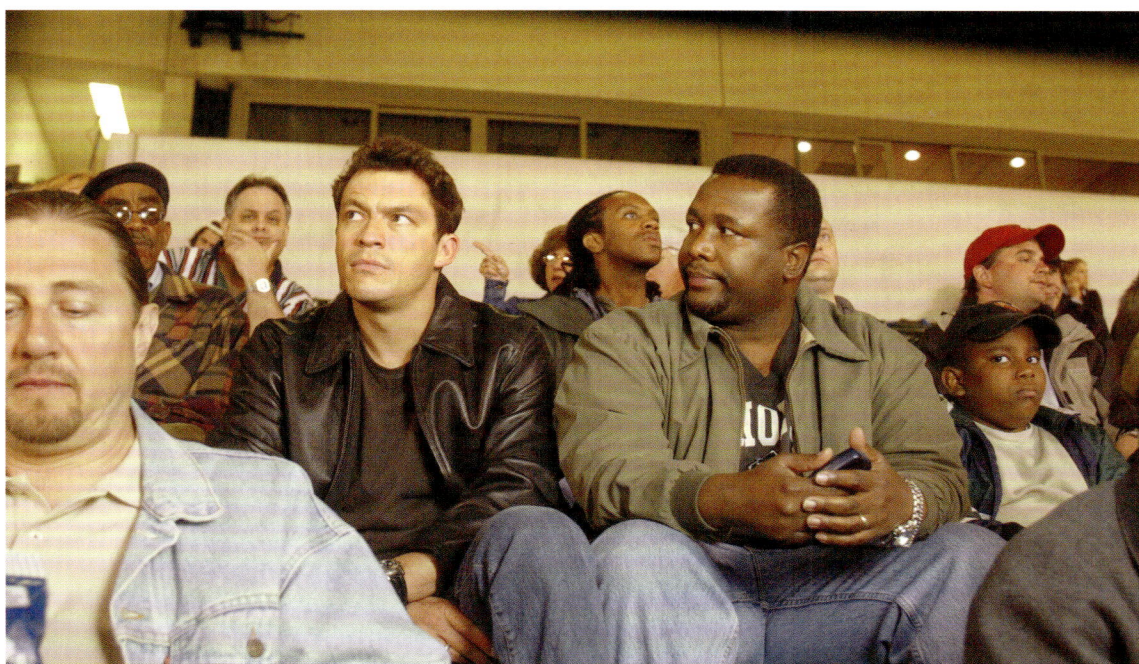

That is a staggeringly good scene. Michael K. Williams was soft-spoken, friendly, and outgoing, and he inhabited an iconic character that wasn't anything like him. In your interaction with Michael, did you get a sense of how he pulled that off?

That is the epitome of what all great artists strive for, and great artists like Michael attain: the ability to tap into a humanity that you can then draw from, draw upon, and be so specific in your choices and so specific and strong in the development of the world around you that it induces the behavior, pulls it out of you—you make that connection as simple and as affecting to the human condition as possible. It does the work for you.

And Michael did that in abundance. He had a connection to his humanity that allowed him to portray so many different people and go a lot further and deeper than most people and most actors can and do. That's exactly what made him great. He was able to transform, but be truthful, specific, and authentic. The more specific you are, the more universal you become—the more you shine light on the complexities of humanity. After *The Wire*, you'll never look at a corner boy in Baltimore the same way again.

There's a whole world and humanity that created the person that brought them to that place. You never just flippantly look at someone making a choice to be where they are without understanding the multitude of variables, conditions, and parts of their humanity that brought them there.

That's what Michael's absolute genius was. This kind, quiet, shy, introverted, insecure at times person tapped into his humanity, and it made him a fuller person, a more complex character, a more engaging artist.

The scene on the bench was rewritten by George Pelecanos after overhearing a conversation you were having. It must have been interesting to have your personal experience translated into writing and then handed back to you to interpret in a theatrical way.

Yeah, but it wasn't just my personal experience. It was an amalgam of so many different experiences that I had studied, had heard, and was working on.

David and the writing room actually had an edict that actors were never supposed to know where the storyline was going. He believed that we're all hams, and if we knew where the storyline was going, then we'll tip the hat all the time. I disagreed with him—I told him that we're actors, and we know where we're going. If I know where I'm going, I can set it up even better. I was complaining because I didn't know where my storyline was going. I only knew that I was chasing one piece of evidence, which was a gun that was connected to a homicide.

I was frustrated because I didn't even know why I'm getting the gun or what it connects me to. All I have to play is the frustration of wondering what this is about. And meanwhile, I talked to all these police officers, and they're telling me how their community is not reflective of its crime. I remember my girlfriend's father saying that even in the '30s—and even earlier than that, at the height of Jim Crow—their communities took care of them . . . Everyone knew this guy over here was going to school because his father

TOP (*Left to right*) Freamon (Clarke Peters), Bunk (Wendell Pierce), and McNulty (Dominic West) enjoy a "taste" after a hard day of police work.

OPPOSITE BOTTOM Kima (Sonja Sohn, *left*) and Bunk (Pierce, *right*) work a case.

was the principal, for example, and even the thugs in the neighborhood were making sure that he stayed on the straight and narrow because they knew he was going to be something. They'd say, "Hey, schoolboy, you're not supposed to be here."

I had all these rich stories about communities, how we come together, what we do during a crisis, and that's the stuff I want. And here I am chasing this gun. And George turned to me and said, "Hey, Wendell, I heard you talking—do you mind if I use some of that?" I didn't mind at all; that's what I wanted to see. He said, "The gun is arbitrary: It leads you to Omar, and you finally get to have that conversation with him, and I'm going to use what you were talking about for it."

George did such a wonderful job as a writer. I thought he was going to ask me to come back and give more details, but he just wrote a tremendous scene. It really is one of the high-water marks of my career.

**I think one of everyone's favorite scenes in *The Wire* is the moment where Bunk and McNulty examine a crime scene using only profanity. How was it set up, and how did you feel when they told you, "Wendell, you're just going to walk around the room going 'Fuuuuuuuuuuck?'"**

David came to us around the second episode of the show. He said, "I know automatically that I'm going to get some feedback about the language in our show." I agreed, and he said, "I want to talk to you about a scene I'm writing." Then he said, "You're gonna come in, you're gonna go back to an old crime scene, and you have the file. You open the file and realize, 'Oh, man, this is really not well put together,' and you're like, 'He's an idiot; he doesn't know what he's doing.' And you're gonna see a picture of a young girl totally shot up. A bloody scene where you look at the pictures and it just breaks your heart, Wendell, you know?"

He described it all for us. He said, "When you guys start doing the scene, you're doing the ballistics and it's not making sense. The shooter would have to be ten feet tall, judging by the trajectory. It makes no sense. You lay out the pictures, and you're like, 'This is where she fell.' And if this is where she fell, it makes no sense that he's standing there. You comb through the room and discover glass on the windowsill. Wendell, you realize that it's on the windowsill, so if it was a bullet coming from the inside to the outside, the glass would be outside. You point it out to McNulty. He comes over and you agree that it came from the outside, and you both scramble and look for the bullet. They must have missed it, because it wasn't on the list of evidence. You comb the room looking for it—you realize based on the trajectory, measuring it, that it would be near the refrigerator, but there's nothing near the refrigerator. McNulty says, 'What if they were standing with the refrigerator open?' You open it, and you see the refrigerator's been patched up, and they find a bullet. McNulty says, 'Wait a minute, the bullet's here, and they thought the shooting happened inside, so they didn't look outside—maybe there's a casing.' So you go out, Bunk, and here's the casing. And in the scene, we see that no matter how crazy and drunk Bunk gets and how dysfunctional McNulty is, this is what they share in common. It's a demonstration of how good you guys are as police."

And then he says, "But you're only going to say one word: *fuck*." I said, "What?" He said, "Yeah, they're going to get on me about cursing, so we're going to do a scene where it's nothing but cursing. I want you do this whole scene saying 'fuck,' or any variation of it. 'Fuck me,' 'fuck you up,' anything, right?'" So he wrote out the whole scene and put "fuck" exactly where he wanted it.

We did it exactly that way, and they shot it exactly that way. Then they said to do whatever we wanted, to ad-lib it. It turned out brilliant.

In a way, it's a gibberish exercise. In acting classes, you do an improvised scene in gibberish, and the audience has to understand what the scene is about even though we don't know what the hell you're saying. It's one of the best acting exercises.

The scene originally ended differently. We were going, "Fuck, fuck, fuck, fuck," and then I got to the casing, and then all of a sudden, the landlord went, "Fuck me!" It was really funny, man. They cut it, but it was so great.

### After all these years, how would you describe *The Wire*'s legacy?

It's a classic. A classic speaks to our humanity across time and place. Long after we are gone, *The Wire* will speak to people, because it was the canary in the mine. It's relevant. Although humankind changes its ways, it will always be relevant how the dysfunctions of the whole destroy the individuals, and how we let oppression reign, thinking that keeping others down will free us when it's actually self-destruction. I said it best in the opening of one season: The bigger the lie, the more they believe.

When we were making the show, we thought it was just about what was happening then, but you cannot tell me that it's not a more prevalent lie right now. The bigger the lie, the more they believe. I'm watching the destruction of our democracy. *The Wire* will live and be relevant long after we're gone.

# THE WIRE SEASON FIVE: A FAILING MEDIA FOR A BROKEN CITY

by Eric Deggans

"...one of its most impressive traits is the show's tendency to build landmark scenes around little moments other series wouldn't even dream of showing."

**T**he Wire distinguishes itself from other, more conventional TV shows in many ways. But one of its most impressive traits is the show's tendency to build landmark scenes around little moments that other series wouldn't even dream of showing.

There is one such moment in the fifth season—during the second episode, "Unconfirmed Reports"—that not only authentically captures the spirit of its righteous journalist protagonist, but also helps explain why creator (and former *Baltimore Sun* cops reporter) David Simon gave the press so much space in the show's final run.

Clark Johnson—an alum of NBC's *Homicide: Life on the Street* who directed *The Wire*'s first two episodes and its finale—plays *Baltimore Sun* city desk editor Augustus "Gus" Haynes, a fictional character. He's the kind of newshound who looks out of the *Sun*'s office windows, sees smoke from a fire on the other side of town, and wonders why one of his reporters hasn't

jumped up to chase down what's happening. But in this particular scene, Haynes wakes up in a panic at 1:10 a.m., grabbing a phone to call the *Sun's* newsroom. He's convinced he mixed up the numbers in a story for the next day's paper; after a quick conversation with a bemused overnight news editor, Haynes is assured that he got it right after all.

"You had the usual deadline nightmare to no actual purpose," says overnight editor Jay Spry, played by actor Donald Neal. (Spry is a character who bears the name of an actual rewrite man at the real-life *Baltimore Sun* during Simon's time there as a reporter.) "I guess you're better at this than you thought."

Any journalist who has put in a little time in the game can relate a similar story; the scene is so true to the reporting life that watching it gave me flashbacks. It also quickly establishes Haynes as one of Simon's Characters Who Care—working stiffs who are good at their jobs and just wish the incredibly dysfunctional institutions where they are employed would get out of their way and let them take care of business.

Alas, the story of *The Wire* is mostly about seeing these characters ground down and chewed up by institutions to which they have already given too much of their heart, sweat, and devotion.

So it makes sense that Simon—who spent thirteen years at the *Sun*—would center *The Wire*'s final season on the last institution to let down the great American city of Baltimore: the news media.

"Sometimes I say season five is the stepchild of *The Wire*," says Michelle Paress, who plays up-and-coming young *Sun* reporter Alma M. Gutierrez,

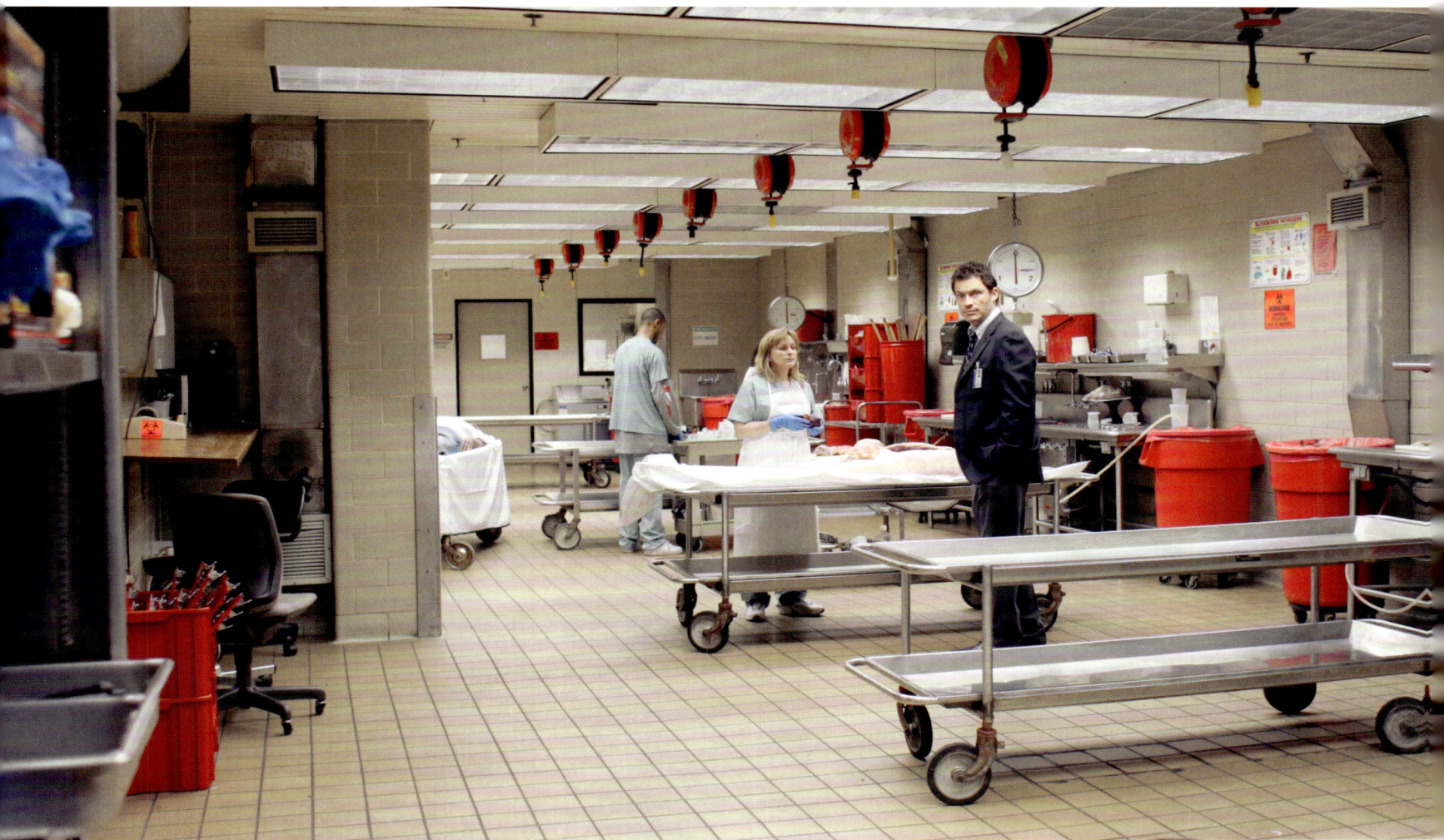

in Jonathan Abrams's oral history book *All the Pieces Matter: The Inside Story of The Wire.* "I don't know that we got as much love as all the other seasons, but it was a great storyline."

Indeed, many fans of *The Wire* will argue that the fifth season is its least regarded. Derided as a rushed, ten-episode conclusion filled with disappointing turns—ferocious robber of drug dealers Omar Little killed by a middle school–age kid? In a convenience store? Really? The season is also sometimes dismissed as a platform for Simon to grind his axes against real-life managers he tangled with at the *Sun* before his departure.

But a more measured look reveals that the fifth season is also the culmination of Simon's wider story, which deconstructs how a host of major institutions have failed the city of Baltimore. While other TV storytellers focus their energies on characters, Simon often focuses on systems and, particularly in the case of *The Wire*, how those systems have decayed and fallen apart just when the city needs them most.

The broad outlines of season five's story fit *The Wire*'s jaundiced outlook perfectly. Self-destructive Detective Jimmy McNulty, frustrated that the city's fiscal troubles have led police brass to shut down an investigation into twenty-two murders ordered by remorseless West Baltimore drug kingpin Marlo Stanfield, hits on a plan to force the department to cough up the resources he needs.

McNulty fakes evidence, leading his superiors to believe that a serial killer is targeting the city's homeless folks, secretly rerouting the resources he gets for the made-up case to revive the investigation into Stanfield,

PAGE 202 The *Baltimore Sun* newsroom in season five: (*left to right*) reporters Bill Zorzi (William F. Zorzi), Scott Templeton (Tom McCarthy), Alma M. Gutierrez (Michelle Paress), unknown, and city desk editor Augustus "Gus" Haynes (Clark Johnson).

PAGE 203 In season five, Marlo (Jamie Hector) feels the net closing in on his drug empire.

OPPOSITE TOP Freamon (Clarke Peters, *standing*) and McNulty (Dominic West, *seated*), who in season five embark on a desperate scheme that will ultimately curtail their careers.

OPPOSITE BOTTOM Reporter Scott Templeton (McCarthy), who prefers a good story to facts.

TOP At the pathology lab, McNulty (West, *right*) begins to formulate the fake serial killer scheme that will eventually get him in hot water.

among others. But one reason the cop's gambit works is that an ambitious *Sun* reporter—seemingly guilty of inventing quotes and sources to make his stories more impressive—dips into the homeless killer story, fabricating details of his own to make his narrative more compelling.

It's telling that Simon and his writers focus the media end of their storytelling on newspapers and not local TV. Even though cutbacks and advertising pressure arguably debilitated television newsrooms even more during this period—and more people got their news from local TV than print, even then—the newspaper stands as a symbol of in-depth, factual watchdogging intended to keep police and politicians on the up and up.

No one expects local TV to be substantive. But when the paper of record misses the big stories—nearly all the big stories in the final season—it's the last nail in urban America's coffin. Because when the public isn't even aware of the major problems of its cities, how can it actually address them?

Simon wrote as much in a column for the *Huffington Post* published about a week after *The Wire*'s last episode aired. He noted that most TV critics, even those who praised the show's final season, missed the subtextual critique that was so obvious it was nearly left lying in plain sight.

As Simon detailed, his fictional version of the *Sun* missed that the city's reformist mayor wound up forcing police to cook up bogus crime stats just like his predecessors; the city's schools taught students mostly to do better on standardized tests to ease political pressure and cover up their own failings; police were shutting down key investigations on major crimes over political and financial issues; a major drug figure was assassinated—rest in power, Prop Joe!—with little notice.

And then there was that whole "police officers faking a serial killer" thing.

Simon wrote: "That was the critique. . . . The season amounted to ten hours of a newspaper that is no longer intimately aware of its city. . . . In Baltimore, where over the last twenty years, Times Mirror and the Tribune Company have combined to reduce the newsroom by forty percent, all of the above stories pretty much happened [author's note: except the bogus serial killer thing] . . . Amid buyout after buyout, the *Baltimore Sun* conceded much of its institutional memory, its beat structure, its ability to penetrate

TOP LEFT Lester Freamon (Clarke Peters) is a vital part of *The Wire* ensemble across all five seasons of the show.

TOP RIGHT Proposition Joe (Robert F. Chew, *right*) with his nephew and lieutenant Cheese (Clifford Smith Jr., *left*). Cheese betrays his uncle to Marlo in season five, leading to Prop Joe's death.

municipal institutions and report qualitatively on substantive issues in a way that explains not just the symptomatic problems of the city, but the root causes of those problems."

In *The Wire*'s world, disconnection is the ultimate sin. There is no more pitiable and contemptible sight than a cop who doesn't know his post, a drug dealer who doesn't understand his market, a teacher who can't connect with his kids or a newspaper reporter who doesn't know his city. (In the world of *The Wire*, it's also almost always a "he," which we'll get to a little later.)

Simon and his writers knew the world of newspapers well enough to render it with heartbreaking accuracy. Mid-level editors and senior reporters commiserate while smoking a few butts at the newspaper's loading dock; a young reporter gets up early to find an edition of the *Sun* she expects will feature her first front page story; editors grouse about not getting "art"—a photo—to go with a big story; newsroom leaders constantly tell staffers they will have to do more with less resources.

On screen, the *Sun* reflects the changes transforming newsrooms across the country. Owned by a chain with leadership in Chicago, its newsroom is buffeted by cutbacks and buyouts even as elitist, out-of-touch top executives focus on stories aimed at winning prestigious prizes—protecting that same ambitious reporter suspected of faking sources.

It's here that some critics suspected *The Wire*'s narrative veered into axe-grinding territory. Simon had been vocal in his criticism of leadership at the *Sun*—he took a buyout himself in 1995. I watched him give a speech at the then–*St. Petersburg Times* (now known as the *Tampa Bay Times*) in 2007 directly criticizing former *Sun* editors John Carroll and Bill Marimow for enabling cutbacks that hobbled the newspaper,

TOP An ID badge created for the Alma Gutierrez character, played by Michelle Paress.

BOTTOM McNulty (Dominic West, *left*) meets with Gutierrez (Paress, *right*) to discuss Baltimore's "serial killer."

TOP Scott Templeton (Tom McCarthy, *right*), meets with the *Baltimore Sun*'s managing editor, Thomas Klebanow (David Costabile, *center*).

ABOVE An ID badge created for the Scott Templeton character, played by McCarthy.

OPPOSITE A page from the script of the season five episode "-30-," in which Templeton finds someone passed out drunk on the street and then falsely claims that the man was the victim of an attempted kidnapping.

while tolerating little dissent, calling it "a very cynical and insecure way of doing business."

Simon had already named a character on the show Marimow—a jerk of a police lieutenant who crippled an investigative unit's look at political corruption. But in the fifth season, *Sun* executive editor James Whiting and managing editor Thomas Klebanow seem like thinly veiled versions of Carroll and Marimow; on *The Wire*, Whiting and Klebanow eventually exile Haynes to the copy desk for daring to suggest their ace reporter might have invented material.

I asked Marimow about this conflict back when I was TV critic for the *St. Petersburg Times*. He told me then he was unsure why Simon hated him so much and defended his tenure at the real-life *Baltimore Sun*.

In a story published by the *St. Petersburg Times* in 2008, Marimow said: "A year ago, when he named a loathsome character on *The Wire* Marimow, I decided to take the high road and say David Simon was an excellent journalist . . . I still say he's a brilliant and creative journalist who has this obsession about John Carroll and me that, instead of demeaning us, it demeans him."

The three also famously clashed over Simon's final story for the paper, a sympathetic look at addicts who stole scrap metal for money to fund their drug habit.

Still, in the same way that *The Wire* presciently depicts the failure of the war on drugs—a memorable scene from an earlier season features disillusioned police Major Howard "Bunny" Colvin telling a young sergeant how that war has disconnected cops from the neighborhoods they protect—the show also identifies how newspapers were crippled by rampant cost-cutting implemented by big chains.

To be sure, it's the way the Internet ate away at advertising, especially sites like eBay and Craigslist, that really put newspapers' economic engines

> TEMPLETON
> Couldn't see it from where I was.

> MCNULTY
> Describe the driver?

> TEMPLETON
> White.  Six foot.  Not heavy, but
> not skinny either.

> MCNULTY
> Clothes?

> TEMPLETON
> Nothing I noticed.  Kinda non-
> descript.

> MCNULTY
> Non-descript?

> TEMPLETON
> I was surprised, I guess.  I just
> thought, whoa, what's he doing?

MCNULTY stares at TEMPLETON for a beat.

> MCNULTY
> Funny it bein' you to see this.

> TEMPLETON
> It's weird.  If an interview doesn't
> go late, I'm not even out here
> tonight.

MCNULTY eyes him: Yeah, sure.

> TEMPLETON (CONT'D)
> You mind if I get inside?  I gotta
> check in with my desk.  Anything
> else you need, you got my number.

MCNULTY nods, TEMPLETON exits.  MCNULTY moves to ambo,
assesses DRUNK, talks to UNIFORM #1, who is standing by.

> UNIFORM #1
> Smokehound can't remember a thing.
> Only motherfucker he remembers messin'
> with him is the fella found him.
> Whatever happened before that is
> anyone's guess.

MCNULTY turns to DRUNK.

(CONTINUED)

in a tailspin. But brutal cutbacks and a lack of innovation among industry leaders didn't help things. And as *The Wire* ably notes, disconnection from the community and the job can bring dire consequences.

The fifth season wasn't even going to happen initially. Simon has spoken in the past about how HBO originally argued to cancel *The Wire* after its critically acclaimed fourth season, eventually agreeing to a truncated fifth season that would shave two episodes off the total he wanted.

It was a tough situation; Simon was also developing *Generation Kill* for HBO, the seven-episode limited series about a Marine Corps battalion engaged in the 2003 invasion of Iraq. His longtime partner on *The Wire*, Ed Burns, had already shifted his focus to work on *Generation Kill*, and George Pelecanos, the vaunted crime novelist who was also a key contributor in *The Wire*'s writers' room, had returned to writing books. But in Simon's mind, he was getting seventeen hours of storytelling time on HBO between the two series, and he was glad to have it.

Aside from following a highly regarded season centered on the educational system, the show's fifth season also faced the challenge of wrapping up the series' most convoluted and dark storylines.

This is the season that claimed the life of not only fan favorite Omar Little, but also Stanfield's charismatic assassin and enforcer "Snoop" Pearson, played by reformed drug dealer Felicia "Snoop" Pearson. Her final line before she is shot by a man she was planning to kill for Stanfield—"How my hair look, Mike?"—has to have gone down in TV history as the most gangsta finish ever. (The novice actor's work was so good that famed novelist Stephen King called her "perhaps the most terrifying female villain to ever appear in a TV series" in *Entertainment Weekly*.)

It's also in season five that viewers learn kindhearted but weak street kid Duquan "Dukie" Weems is headed for a life of addiction and squalor.

And our stalwart hero McNulty is forced into retirement—along with Clarke Peters's super savvy investigator Lester Freamon—the inevitable penance for working a con so outlandish, his bosses couldn't publicly fire him, prosecute him, or allow him anywhere near a courtroom on a fresh case.

Even Stanfield, played with a simmering, relentless ambition by Jamie Hector, doesn't land well, though he evades prosecution and sells his drug connections for millions. To keep McNulty and Freamon's deceptions secret, officials cut a deal agreeing not to prosecute Stanfield, as long as he never attempts to sell drugs again. Barred from ever getting back in the game, Stanfield is now sitting on a pile of money with no desire to operate in legal society—and no clue how. For him, a fate worse than death.

Among the few characters to get a truly happy ending is longtime addict Reginald "Bubbles" Cousins, who stays clean and sees his story told accurately and fairly by a young *Sun* reporter. And let's not forget fabricating reporter Scott Templeton—played by Tom McCarthy, who would later win an Oscar for writing the 2016 film *Spotlight*—who is honored with a Pulitzer Prize while city editor Haynes is shipped off to the copy desk.

Some criticisms of *The Wire*'s final season ring true. It is among the most obvious and didactic of the show's seasons, both because it has to wrap up so many storylines so quickly and because its conclusions are pretty plain. (Wendell Pierce's gruff homicide detective Bunk Moreland provides the money quote to kick off the first episode: "The bigger the lie, the more they believe.")

The season also continued the show's unfortunate habit of centering most of its agency on male characters, despite impressive turns by Pearson, Sonja Sohn as homicide detective Kima Greggs, and Deirdre Lovejoy as prosecutor Rhonda Pearlman.

But the final season also earned the show's second-ever Emmy nomination for its writing—along with a Best Drama Series nomination from the Writers Guild of America and a Heritage Award from the Television Critics Association—indicating lots of folks felt differently about the series' conclusion.

The plunge into the *Sun*'s newsroom culture may have felt awkward to some viewers—and it was impossible to avoid a sense of score-settling, given how harshly top managers at the newspaper were portrayed.

Looking back, however, the fifth season's turn toward the media seems inevitable, as the show that made TV history by examining the rot in America's urban institutions finally got around to taking a peek at why that decay wasn't publicly exposed in the first place.

# FELICIA PEARSON

## Interview by Nikki Stafford and Robert Thompson

Born in Baltimore and raised in a foster home, Felicia "Snoop" Pearson fell into drug dealing as a teenager and served time for second-degree murder. After she was released, a chance meeting with Michael K. Williams led the actor to invite her to the set of *The Wire*, where she met the creative team and was later offered a role on the show. Pearson's character, the cold-blooded assassin Snoop, quickly became a fan favorite.

**How did you end up being cast on *The Wire*?**

I met Michael K. Williams in a nightclub called Club One in downtown Baltimore. Mike was looking at me all crazed, and I didn't know who he was. I mean, I knew about *The Wire*, but I hadn't watched it because I was living outside in the streets and stuff like that. So I told my homeboy, "This man keep looking at me kinda crazy." And he said, "Man, that's Omar. He plays a gay character on *The Wire*. He's a big gangster." I said, "Oh, for real? Well, why he keep looking at me like that?" By the time I finished saying that to him, Mike came over and introduced himself to me. We exchanged numbers and then the next day he called me to come on to the set. He told me where it was,

and I was like, "Yeah, that's like a block away from my house," where I was living with my grandmother at the time.

I just got in the shower, and then I went up there to see what he was talking about. I was just sitting outside of Mike's trailer, talking and stuff, and I guess, I don't know how it happened, but I think Ed Burns and Nina [K. Noble] and David [Simon] probably were walking past, and that's how I started.

**You didn't have any training as an actor at the time. Was it difficult to figure out how that world functioned?**

Not really, because they had started me off slow,

OPPOSITE AND TOP
Felicia Pearson as
Stanfield organization
soldier Snoop.

you know, trying to see if I could remember lines. My first lines were with Jamie Hector as Marlo. Marlo was in the pigeon coop, and he says to me, "Your turn, girl." And I say, "It's about time." [They just wanted to see] if I could remember lines and how I looked on camera.

**David Simon and the other creators didn't give you much background on the Snoop character or where she would end up—she just kind of pops in and out of things. Did that take some getting adjusted to? Not necessarily knowing what would become of your character?**

Yes. I didn't know anything, you know? Like, Ed and David kept saying, "We want you on the show." I'm coming from the streets and so the acting deal—it most definitely was crazy. Because you got to think about it: I mean, I knew it was a hit show, but I didn't know that it was a hit like that, you know. After season three, people were coming up to me [because they recognized me from the show], and I was like, what the fuck's going on? Before season four, Ed and David and Nina asked me, "You ready to be a star?" I was like, "Man, I'm already a star." But I was only a star in my head and in my neighborhood, so I had to adjust really quickly. Whenever I went to New York or wherever, people were just running down on me: "Snoop! Snoop!" I'm like, "Aw, man!" I started loving it.

**Did you find that some people confused the real-life Snoop with the one on the show?**

Yes, I was playing a character. Because I come from the streets, people assume that I'm like the character on *The Wire*. Nah. The character on *The Wire*, she and Chris are putting people in boarded-up houses. I wasn't doing nothing like that. I wasn't sitting here murdering half of the damn city, you know? I just come from the streets, and my charisma and my swagger, that's the same as the character's, but everyone thought we were the same person.

**How did you feel about Snoop's death scene in season five, where she asks Mike how her hair looks before he shoots her?**

I didn't like it. That scene when I got shot—I come from the streets, so I had to separate acting from the real life—I didn't like that part. So that's why they just had the flash go off. [But] the writing was excellent. You live by the sword; you die by the sword. Snoop knew that something was going to go down, you know, be it prison or [death].

**Given your connection to the city, do you feel that Baltimore has changed in the twenty years since *The Wire* first aired? Do you think the show is still a true reflection of the city?**

I mean, *The Wire* wasn't a reflection of what Baltimore is. Baltimore is a beautiful city, and we have crime just like everybody else has crime. *The Wire* was written up so good, you know, that you would think that people around here are putting people in abandoned buildings and things like that, but nah. [The show made it seem] like in Baltimore they just want to leave you where you're standing; if you're standing on the corner, and they want to shoot you, you're gonna be dead right there on the corner, you know? But *The Wire*, the writers, man, they wrote that motherfucker up so good, you would think Baltimore is like that, but, when I was growing up, we had rules. No kids, no old people, no women, things like that. Now today it's like, these kids, they don't have no rules. So it's just crazy out here. But like I said, they're not putting anybody in abandoned buildings or nothing like that.

OPPOSITE TOP Chris Partlow (Gbenga Akinnagbe, *left*) and Snoop (Felicia Pearson, *right*) carry out a hit.

OPPOSITE BOTTOM (*Left to right*) Marlo (Jamie Hector), Snoop (Pearson), and Darius "O-Dog" Hill (Darrell Britt-Gibson), another Stanfield enforcer.

BOTTOM Pearson as Snoop, who became one of the show's most beloved characters after her debut in season three.

# DEIRDRE LOVEJOY

## Interview by Brandon Easton

Appearing in all five seasons of *The Wire*, Assistant State's Attorney Rhonda Pearlman was the lead prosecutor in the Major Crimes Unit, building cases against Baltimore's criminal organizations, including the Barksdale gang. Played by actress Deirdre Lovejoy, also known for her work on *Bones* and *The Blacklist*, Pearlman brought a considerable knowledge of Baltimore's legal system that was vital to the MCU's work.

**When you first heard about the premise of the series, what drew you to a drama about the complexities and corruptions within the city of Baltimore?**

It was an audition that came in just like any other. I [thought] that I didn't have a chance in hell to get the job, because I was sure that I was *not* going to be one of the two women on this new HBO series. I didn't have that sort of view of myself, and I wasn't placed in any position professionally to think that [it would be a] high possibility. So, I just went in. It was one of those situations where I didn't have any nerves because I just sat in the present moment and was able to do the scene. I think that I was what they were

looking for, but they didn't know until they saw me. There's no reason [they picked] me over any other actress. Sometimes you walk into a room and people go, "Oh, yeah, there she is!" And I think that's what happened with Rhonda Pearlman, quite frankly, and I was just sort of secondary in the equation.

I knew the story was going to be gritty, because *Homicide: Life on the Street* had been a predecessor, so I knew the storytelling wouldn't pull any punches. I don't think I had a sense of the breadth, complexity, or the wide net of the cast. That's the refreshing thing about the show: Every time you watch it, more layers of the onion reveal themselves, which is the brilliance of [David Simon's] writing. I would be lying

OPPOSITE Deirdre Lovejoy as Assistant State's Attorney Rhonda Pearlman.

TOP Pearlman (Lovejoy, *right*) with Ilene Nathan (Susan Rome, *left*), deputy state's attorney of the Major Crimes Division.

TOP Pearlman (Deirdre Lovejoy, *left*) discusses a case with Freamon (Clarke Peters).

actors, crew, writers, and the people involved, but also the viewing audience.

What I mean by "exponential" is that as the years went on and we were able to do positive outreach in the neighborhoods and communities and tried to become involved in giving back and supporting causes that were reflected in the show, it impacted the circumstances and illuminated [the struggles the series depicted]. Systemic racism and systemic rotting of the system are not generally pleasant things to reveal. I think the fact that anything positive was achieved [is due to] the depth of storytelling that David Simon and company created. There aren't many television shows that are taught in Harvard and Yale classes—talk about a positive impact! The dialogue reached hundreds, and hundreds, and hundreds of people, [and continues to attract] new audience members every day through streaming. [The series'] positive impact has far outlived the initial lifespan of the series, which is an amazing thing.

**Because many actors filmed in different units, did you ever find it difficult to bond with your fellow actors?**

That's a great question. I think it was something that we all craved . . . that together time. So it was a joy to be able to sit down and watch the show, because we could see all of us together at the same time. We [only] got to experience [togetherness] on very rare occasions and marking points, such as opening and wrap parties. It's interesting [that our characters] could share storylines and yet never share screen time. I personally always wanted more screen time with anyone I could get, and because the storytelling was so rich, I was always looking forward to finding out what was going to happen every single week. I cherished the screen time I had in season one during the detailed room scenes. It laid the foundation for a lot of great friendships and a lot of great scenes throughout the years.

**Did you do anything special to prepare for the role?**

I took it upon myself to do a lot of research about district attorney offices. I spent some significant time at the Manhattan DEA [office], which was very accommodating, and I really got to see the belly of the beast in terms of the day-to-day [processes]. I spoke to some attorneys in Baltimore. At one point in season one, I found out that there was a "real" Rhonda Pearlman, but I was encouraged to not go there. I didn't do anything other than suit up and show up—and get a haircut. I tried to do my due

if I said I always knew what was coming, because David really liked to keep the actors just on the page that they were on. He didn't want anyone thinking ahead or looking behind, [but rather] just staying in the moment. He didn't give you too much of an idea of where you were going.

**Did you try to pick up a Baltimore accent?**

I was told to not try to adopt the Baltimore accent. Thank goodness, because it's the toughest. Although I consider myself fairly adept at [accents], I could not give you an accurate Baltimore accent if my life depended on it—and I've spent a lot of time there. I could make fun of it a little, but I couldn't deliver anything.

**Although *The Wire* had many dark and sometimes bleak plots and themes, what were some of the more positive or heartwarming experiences you had while working on the show?**

Well, they were exponential as the years rolled on. I think as the show began to air, the enthusiasm for the kind of storytelling we were doing was so genuine that it was contagious, which was a very positive thing. [In fact,] the whole vibe on the set was very positive. I think anyone would be lying if they said that by episode one of season one, they knew [the series would be a] big hit. We all just showed up to go to work. But I think the storytelling had such a fresh eye that it ignited something in not only the diligence in terms of what my character's lawyering abilities were, which were plenty. It is such a huge plate. I have such respect for all those attorneys. They're not just courageous, but also have to be so well versed. It's impossible for them [to know] all the subjects they are expected to be experts in, but they do an amazing job.

**You mentioned earlier that you were one of only two women in season one. How did you feel about the lack of women characters in the show?**

Well, it's an interesting thing through the lens of hindsight. I think the show is illuminating in that regard, as opposed to necessarily keeping pace or holding up. There's a lot of very real behavior. Would it have benefited from having [more] women-centric storylines? Yes. I completely agree. [But] that's not the story we were telling, nor was it the story [David Simon] was telling. I think it holds up pretty darn well.

**What do you think the legacy of *The Wire* will be twenty years from now?**

First of all, I have to say with complete humility that I am honored to have been an actor on *The*

*Wire* and to have been part of the story. I think the perspectives of all the characters were so shockingly vital and so real that people got to see a side of the system, a side of society, in a way that shook them. *The Wire* tells [authentic] stories of human beings trapped in a rotted system that people [would rather] turn and look away from, write off, or claim they aren't participating in. But *The Wire* pulled that rug out from under everyone and said, "No, look." Its lens shifted, and the spotlight [slightly] turned ninety degrees each year. It was crazy brilliant.

I [never would have thought] a show twenty years ago would still be so impactful to this day. It's evident in the actors [and writers] who have gone on to incredible careers. There's an extended *Wire* family, and we have reunions. It's a family because there's something that really bonded all of us in the process of creating the characters and telling the story in that way at that time. It was so specific to Baltimore and so specific to the people in the story—they're intertwined and richer because of it. The storytelling is beautiful, and I'm grateful to have been a part of it.

BOTTOM Deirdre Lovejoy (*second from left*) between takes on a scene. Also pictured is Lance Reddick (*far right*), who plays Pearlman's partner, Cedric Daniels.

# DONA ADRIAN GIBSON

## Interview by Brandon Easton

After working on the pilot of *The Wire* as key costumer, Dona Adrian Gibson returned as the tailor on season two before becoming costume supervisor for seasons three, four, and five. Following *The Wire*, the Baltimore-based costumer has gone on to work on a wide range of high-profile projects including *Treme*, *The Walking Dead*, and *Iron Fist*.

**What does being a costume supervisor entail?**

Managing the costumes on set, being the liaison there. Every single department matters, and that's exactly what drew me to this business. I looked at the back of a call sheet the first time I ever stepped on set, and I thought, "All these people help make this happen. I really want to be a part of this." It was *Homicide: Life on the Street*, another David Simon [show].

I always feel that costumes make the character. But it's not just the costumes. A character walks into a room and you get a feeling for who they are based on how they're dressed—where they are going, where they are coming from. Not to take anything away from makeup or production design, because it's all of that together that makes it work. And we did communicate with each other; we all became friends and family, and everybody was open to suggestions. Which is how it should be. Collaborative. It's not always that way, but it certainly was on that show.

**Were there any characters who had a specific visual palette?**

Oh, that's interesting. The one time that color palette really did enter was for Hamsterdam. Everything was gray. We overdyed everything. It was all [costume designer] Alonzo Wilson's vision—I can't take credit for designing the show, but it's certainly a team effort. Other than that, we didn't have specific color palettes for people. Once the first season was established, every character took on their own vibe. One of my favorite characters was Lester Freamon. And Bubbles, too, definitely Bubbles. Alonzo's whole philosophy about Bubbles was, who knows where he's getting his clothes from? And that's exactly how he looked. He had marching band pants, and it was just great. You can see why I learned so much from Alonzo: His perspective was just very farsighted.

OPPOSITE A continuity Polaroid featuring notes on McNulty's (Dominic West) costume.

TOP Additional continuity Polaroids for Idris Elba's Stringer Bell costumes.

COSTUME BREAKDOWNS - THE WIRE - 107 - A MAN MUST HAVE A CODE - 4/30/2002- 4:25 PM

| | | | | |
|---|---|---|---|---|
| PRODUCTION | | THE WIRE | ACTOR | 1 |
| | | 107 MAN MUST HAVE A CO | CHARACTER | MCNULTY |

| CHANGE | SCENE | DESCRIPTION | COSTUME |
|---|---|---|---|
| 1 | 1 | INT. DETAIL OFFICE | SHIRT "XMI"<br>BLUE W/GREY & WHITE PIN GRID<br>TIE "JOHN W. NORDSTROM<br>METALLIC BLUE W/ PRINT<br>PANT:<br>BLACK JEANS<br>BELT: BLACK W/2 ROWS<br>TOP STITCH<br>SHOE: BLACK SLIP-ON LOAFER<br>W/SILVER BUCKLE<br>SOCK: BLACK DRESS |
| 1 | 4 | INT. JUDGE'S CHAMBERS | |
| 1 | 9 | INT. JUDGE'S CHAMBERS | |
| 1 | 24 | EXT. STREET | |
| 1 | 26 | INT. RESIDENT APARTMENT | |
| 1 | 27 | EXT. STREET | |
| 1 | 33 | INT. HILLBILLY BAR | |
| 1 | 39 | INT. HILLBILLY BAR | |

| CHANGE | SCENE | DESCRIPTION | COSTUME |
|---|---|---|---|
| 2 | 43 | INT. DETAIL OFFICE | T-SHIRT - "OLD NAVY" (XL)<br>DARK DRAB OLIVE/BROWN<br>SHIRT: "JOHN W. NORDSTROM"<br>DARK TAN W/SHEEN SURFACE<br>(DRESS)<br>PANT: "LUCKY BRAND"<br>BLACK COTTON - THIN OFF BLA<br>BELT: BLACK 2/ROW TOP STITCH<br>SHOE: BLACK SLIP-ON LOAFER<br>W/SILVER BUCKLE<br>SOCKS: THIN DRESS BLACK |
| 2 | 44 | INT. WIRETAP ROOM | |
| 2 | 47 | INT. DANIEL'S OFFICE | |
| 2 | 49 | INT. GREGG'S CAR | |
| 2+ | 53 | EXT. STREET | |
| 2+ | 54 | INT. MCNULTY'S CAR | |
| 2+ | 56 | INT. MCNULTY'S CAR | |
| 2+ | 57 | EXT. STREET | |
| 2 | 61 | INT. HOMICIDE OFFICE | |
| 2 | 62 | INT. INTERROGATION ROOM | |
| 2 | 65 | INT. SQUAD ROOM | |
| 2 | 66 | EXT. PERLMAN DUPLEX | |

## What were the most heartwarming or best experiences you had during those years you worked on the show?

There are so many. All these people are like my family. I live in a city, but I have a really big yard. We invited over people who didn't go home for the Fourth of July, And the following year we said, let's do it again. And we did. And there had to be 150 people at my place. By the fifth season, there had to be about around 300. It was unbelievable. I would take off a couple days to get ready. We even had a table full of cakes and desserts. It was so much fun! It was the best.

## Did you serve crabs?

We did have crabs. Of course we had crabs.

## How did the school uniforms work with the kids in season four?

It's hard to pick a season, but I think I really do like season four the best. We pretty much modeled it after the school system in Baltimore. They wear khaki pants and have a different color for every year. It was not easy, but uniforms are easier than trying to dress every child in something different.

## Twenty years down the line, what do you think the ultimate legacy of *The Wire* is going to be?

I think when I was in the middle of it, I didn't realize that it was what it was. It didn't hit me until afterward, and I think I have now watched the show from beginning to end at least five times. Twice I was a convalescent, and I thought, "Eh, I'll just watch *The Wire*." And it wasn't until I was a little older that I even realized how it connected. Also, my daughter is in season one, episode twelve, and to this day people recognize her from that. For the scene read, she was holding a phone and rolling her eyes. I said, "David, this is my daughter. Nobody can roll their eyes better than her." And he said, "No, she's too pretty." I replied, "Are you saying there's no pretty girls in the hood?" So he relented.

OPPOSITE Costume notes for a McNulty costume in the season one episode "One Arrest."

LEFT Dominic West wears another McNulty costume: his Marine Unit uniform from season two of the show.

# JAMIE HECTOR

## Interview by Nikki Stafford and Robert Thompson

Playing cold-blooded drug kingpin Marlo Stanfield, actor Jamie Hector created a character who could strike fear into the hearts of even the Barksdale organization. Hector has gone on to enjoy a varied acting career, most notably playing a key role in Amazon Prime's hit detective series *Bosch* and reuniting with David Simon to play real-life Baltimore detective Sean Suiter in *We Own This City*.

**How did you get the role of Marlo Stanfield?**

I was part of a short film directed by Steve Mann—it was his thesis film for NYU. My manager got a clip of the short, and she just happened to be watching *The Wire* [at the time]. I think it was the scene where Wallace was killed, and she called me and said, "I have to get you on this show." So fast forward, my agent called Alexa Fogel, the casting director for *The Wire*, and her assistant picked up, and he said, "We don't really watch shorts," et cetera. But my manager convinced him, and she walked it over to his office and put it in his hands. After that, they called me in to read. I was [first] presented with the material for [the character] Cutty, but I was too young. Then they had Marlo in mind, but they didn't have any text for him, so they asked me to read Avon's dialogue. I made it

not too far out of the room before I got a phone call saying I was being considered for the role. That was a big deal for me.

**The way you play Marlo is fascinating; he's sort of unflappable and very difficult to read, and it would have been easy to overact the part. For a young actor, you seemed to pull back on that. Was that something conveyed in the material or a conclusion about the character that you came to on your own?**

It's funny, because the first line said it all; he's economic with words. And because of that, I was led to move in this direction. He's barely seen, but you always hear about him. When he speaks, it's very few words. And then you tap into all your

OPPOSITE AND TOP
Jamie Hector as
sociopath drug kingpin
Marlo Stanfield.

character-building resources and pull from his qualities as a leader and as a sociopath. He's like a high-achieving businessman. There were certain excerpts from books that I would pull from, and I would play certain songs and meditate on them. Because I was fresh out of [the Lee Strasberg Institute], I was also applying everything that I had learned. I was throwing everything against the wall.

**You saw him as a sociopath?**

When you think about it, what he was able to do and feel nothing about . . . I don't mean it with judgment, but I have to look at him and his actions. When that security guard was murdered—that's a telltale sign of a person who doesn't really measure right and wrong. You see him operating on this level where it's like, "You're down there; I'm up here. You're over there; I'm over here. You have the crown; I need it." So did I see him as a sociopath? I saw him as what some people might call a businessman, but when someone is actively taking lives to move people out of the way, you can't just call them that.

Marlo is much more complicated [than a typical villain]. He understands how he has to operate in the world in which he exists, and George, David, and Ed clearly saw that he's just a human being. Unlike in other writing, in *The Wire* you see that this person exists in a world among other humans who have emotions and qualities and personalities and orders and disorders, and these things exist in him as well.

**When you begin your career with a role like this, how does everything afterward compare? When you look at roles now, do you think about them in comparison to what you did on *The Wire*?**

No, everything is fresh to me. There's so much content out there. I look at the material, the director, the writing, the team I'm going to collaborate with. Do I enjoy it? Does it affect me? And then I move in that direction. But the bar is high.

OPPOSITE Marlo (Jamie Hector, *right*) with his trusted second-in-command, Chris Partlow (Gbenga Akinnagbe, *left*).

LEFT Marlo (Hector) is a force to be reckoned with.

BOTTOM The Stanfield organization circa season five: (*left to right*) enforcer Monk Metcalf (Kwame Patterson), Chris Partlow (Akinnagbe), Marlo (Hector), Snoop (Felicia Pearson), O-Dog (Darrell Britt-Gibson), and Cheese (Clifford Smith Jr.), who joins after betraying his uncle, Proposition Joe.

# WILLIAM F. ZORZI

## Interview by Brandon Easton

A former reporter who spent twenty years working at the *Baltimore Sun*, William F. Zorzi came to *The Wire* with a deep knowledge of the city's political culture. Joining as a staff writer on season three, he would go on to become a key part of the writing team for seasons four and five. He also played a *Baltimore Sun* reporter, named Bill Zorzi, in seasons one and five of the show.

### How did you become involved with *The Wire*?

I wandered into *The Wire* orbit during season one, back in March 2002. David Simon and I had worked together as reporters at the *Sun* as far back as the mid-1980s, and he invited me to audition for a cameo as "Newspaperman #1" in episode three of the first season of his new show. I passed the audition, and part of the scene even made the episode. That was just weeks before David finally lured me away from the paper to develop what became *Show Me a Hero*, the HBO limited series based on the nonfiction book of the same name.

Fast forward to July 2003, when David, Ed Burns, and George Pelecanos were at a *Wire* writers' retreat to go over the ideas, themes, and arcs for season three, in Tarrytown, New York, less than an hour north of Manhattan. As I happened to be in New York for a funeral, I figured I'd drop in before returning to Baltimore to see if I could learn something about this whole new world of scriptwriting, as I faced down *Show Me a Hero*. I did not know at that point that the political world—which I had spent my newspaper career covering—was next up on the *Wire* agenda. Well, I stayed the afternoon and then for dinner and, after shooting pool (and losing my shirt) against those three, I stayed the night. And the next day, too. I guess the rest is history. I was on the writing staff for seasons three, four, and five, first as a staff writer, then story editor, and finally as executive story editor.

### When deciding to focus on the cross-section of police, government, and the drug game on the street, were you ever concerned that you would be taking on "too big" of a story?

I don't think the world ever seemed "too big," no, at least until we were figuring out the final montage in the last episode, maybe. I came to see the story as the *Wire* universe simply expanding with each season, as a new dimension of life in Baltimore was examined and given context, like a camera pulling back and enabling the viewer to take in more of a scene.

### What did you learn about Baltimore during the production of the series?

I learned a lot of new [things], really, which I guess is what it's all about. But if I had to single out one thing, I'd have to say the city schools and the kids in them. As a reporter, I had not covered the schools, nor had I paid much attention to them; my focus had always been elsewhere. So in preparing for season four, I spent time in two Baltimore public middle schools on the Westside, to help me understand the dynamics of what went on between teachers and students in the classroom—and what was handed down from on high. I also spent a lot of time with some of the city's middle school kids, listening to what they said and thought, taking in their attitudes and the language they used, and becoming acquainted with their lives at home. To say that it was eye-opening falls well short of the insight it offered.

### What did you learn about yourself as a creator during the production of *The Wire*?

Professionally, I had always written nonfiction and counted on exposition to anchor those pieces—which is pretty much the opposite of what you do in writing a script. I learned in short order how to show rather than tell. I also learned to translate my own experience and observations into script form, and to shape various fictional characters as needed to fit the story. It's like using the other half of your brain to write.

### Did you have a concern that the series would lean into negative stereotypes of Black Americans?

We were all extremely aware of those potential pitfalls, especially given the nature of the story, which takes place in a city whose population is roughly 65 percent Black. I think more than race, *The Wire* examined the world through the lens of class—poor, middle class, and, to some degree, upper middle class, Black and white. Black drug dealers and white drug dealers, Black cops and white cops, Black addicts and white addicts, Black politicians and white politicians, Black teachers and white teachers, Black journalists and white journalists. The trick was to try to show that nothing is simplistic and then to convey that through character and story.

### Some of the critical acclaim for *The Wire* (as well as the postfeminist critique it has received) centers on the portrayals of women with flaws and virtues. Where did your writers' room draw inspiration for those characters?

BOTTOM William F. Zorzi (*seated*) with *Baltimore Sun* metro editor Steven Luxenberg (Robert Poletick, *left*) and city desk editor Augustus Haynes (Clark Johnson).

By the time I came aboard for season three, there were key women characters already established, and most would continue to be seen through the end. As the series moved forward, we did still need characters to populate the world and answer the needs of the widening story. In those cases, the characters—whether a politician, political wife, political consultant, or even the combustible mother of a schoolboy—were based on composites of people we had known or written about. One exception for me, though, was Felicia Pearson and her character, Snoop. She was, and is, unique.

**If you had a predominantly white and male writing staff, how did you manage to capture the local street dialect and colloquialisms so convincingly?**

Most of us had deep experiences in Baltimore and interactions with its residents, and I guess your ear becomes attuned to what you hear on the street. We weren't television writers, not really. We were ex-newspaper reporters, an ex-homicide cop turned teacher, and crime writers who did their homework on the street. We wrote in the voices that we had heard.

**After the series ended, were you surprised at how it was received as a critical darling?**

Absolutely surprised. I don't think anyone would have dreamed that *The Wire* would resonate so with viewers—and critics.

**Do you have an anecdote about a particular day or experience on *The Wire* that made you realize you were working on something special?**

Something seemed to happen almost every day to make me realize I was working on something special. At the risk of sounding like a cornball, I was constantly reminded of what a privilege it was to deal with so many real people as they lived lives—not in a studio or on a soundstage, but on the streets of Baltimore.

At one point, I remember turning to "Little" Melvin Williams, once a notorious Westside drug dealer, who portrayed The Deacon in season four, for help with something in which I had absolutely no knowledge or experience. Melvin was glad to instruct, and taught me how to shoot crap—including what the players would say—so I could write . . . overdub lines for a background scene where a dice game plays out in the street. I still have the dice he used to illustrate the finer points.

Another time, in season four, we shot a scene with Duquan "Dukie" Weems at a West Baltimore a-rabber's stable. As the sun set on a summer evening, an elderly man, who I believe was the stable owner, led a mule past me on his way up the alley, as what must have seemed like the Horde of Hollywood, with all its army of crew and equipment, descended on his little piece of West Baltimore real estate. He looked directly at me and shook his head. "Too much worriation," he said in my general direction as he slowly trudged up the alley with the mule in tow, headed for a tether away from the stable.

How can you not realize you're part of something special when things like that happen?

TOP Cutty (Chad L. Coleman, *left*) consults with The Deacon (Melvin Williams). In real life, Williams is a reformed Baltimore drug kingpin who William F. Zorzi turned to for advice when writing an episode of the show.

# NINA K. NOBLE

## Interview by Chris Prince

A highly experienced producer who oversaw all five seasons of *The Wire*, Nina K. Noble has gone on to work closely with David Simon on his subsequent projects, producing the HBO shows *Generation Kill*, *Treme*, *Show Me A Hero*, *The Deuce*, *The Plot Against America*, and *We Own This City*. Introduced to Baltimore through her work on her first project with Simon, *The Corner*, Noble moved to the city after season two of *The Wire* and has been based there ever since.

**How did you get your start in television?**

I started my career in feature film production. I worked my way up through all the positions and joined the Directors Guild eventually. Then, I sort of segued into television. I was working with Tom Fontana and Barry Levinson's company, The Levinson/Fontana Company, and they introduced me to David Simon, who was then preparing to do *The Corner*. Jim Finnerty was Tom's producing partner. I had done a bunch of shows for them, and so they set up a meeting with David and I. HBO was a little bit concerned about having first-time producer David Simon at the helm of *The Corner*, so they wanted to make sure he had a strong producing team. So, I came on and then eventually Bob Colesberry joined as well.

**What initially interested you in David's work?**

What interested me is the caliber of his writing. I read the book *The Corner* when I was considering doing the piece, and it's incredibly depressing. At the time,

I should say, I was preparing a show called *Ellis Island* for Tom Fontana and Jim Finnerty, which was very positive and uplifting. It was a network show, and they pulled the plug at the last minute, and that's how I became available to work with David. So, I went from this incredibly inspiring and uplifting show to *The Corner*. I started reading it and I just felt like I was descending into Hell. And then, when we were scouting the locations it became clear that that was exactly what we were doing. But, to this day, when people ask me what genres I'm attracted to, it's just the caliber of the writing. Bottom line, between David and his writing partners, whether it was David Mills, Eric Overmyer, George Pelecanos—I mean they're great writers, novelists, and journalists, so we always have great scripts. There's always a really in-depth fact-checking operation; they're not just like making stuff up and putting it out there without being able to back it up, so I've appreciated that.

OPPOSITE *The Wire* producer Nina K. Noble.

TOP Nina K. Noble (*center*) and Ed Burns (*second from left*) between takes on the set of *The Wire*. To Burns' left is actress Edwina Findley, who plays Tosha, a member of Omar's crew who is killed in a season three shootout.

TOP Producer Nina K. Noble on the set of the 2015 HBO miniseries *Show Me A Hero* which she produced alongside David Simon.

## Did producing *The Corner* prove to be a good trial run for *The Wire*?

Yeah, I mean *The Corner* was my introduction to Baltimore. I'm not from Baltimore so obviously I learned a lot about the city, the locations, and the people. And then, of course, *The Wire* was sort of a continuation of that. I should mention Ed Burns also, who was instrumental in both projects and very influential. So, yes, *The Corner* was actually sort of a small-scale project for me in certain ways, just working in Baltimore, which is a smaller market and smaller cast, and so it was a lot easier—when you get out of New York or LA it's always easier, it seems like. But I think it was very much a trial for David, Bob, and I in terms of our partnership. It was also a trial in terms of what we could prove to HBO, meaning that we delivered a high caliber project on schedule and on budget and that became something we were known. I always hoped that on *The Wire* that if I could come in on budget, it would make it an easier decision for HBO to pick up the next season.

## How was the work divided between you and David when you first started working together?

David was new as a producer at that time. He had a credit as a producer on *Homicide*, but he was really mostly just in a writing place. So, I kind of took it upon myself to teach him a little bit about producing, just in terms of the below-the-line stuff. He was curious about everything and wanted to learn. I mostly hired the crew for *The Corner* and I was involved with the locations and the logistics of the everyday. And also,

I think together we sort of built the culture of the show and the environment that we wanted to create, which then continued on *The Wire*. To this day, people still talk about *The Wire* in terms of it being a family and something that was worth dropping everything else for to come back if they knew [a new season had been] picked up. It was really a very supportive and inspiring environment. That was something David and I really set out to create. Because neither one of us came from television, we didn't necessarily know how things should be run and so we sort of made it up as we went along. I think both of us had a feeling of wanting to be respectful of everybody and wanting to be fair—now those are popular ideas, but in those days, it wasn't so much.

But Bob Colesberry was the creative producer on *The Wire* until his death. They'd say that David was the ears and Bob was the eyes. Bob was very much the visual producer and helped guide the directors because we had lots of different directors, some of whom were very new to the business and some of whom were just new to the material. And David was really intent on the words for the most part.

## Did your role change significantly after the passing of Bob Colesberry?

Oh absolutely. I mean first of all it was a big leap of faith with David and HBO to put me in that role and not bring somebody [new] in. But I had prepared myself—not that I knew Bob was going to die. I was somebody who is always trying to learn new things, and both Bob and David left the door open for that.

So, I was watching all the casting auditions and sitting in on editing and other things after-hours, just so I could learn. And when the time came that I had to step up, fortunately, I had some of the tools I needed. So, yes, I started really taking the helm on the casting, editing, as well as hiring all the directors and guiding them through.

**After your experiences on *The Corner*, what was it like working in Baltimore again? Were there any difficulties with getting access to locations?**

Oh no, it wasn't difficult on the first season. The second season on *The Wire* was the most difficult because we had gotten accustomed to working in neighborhoods that were extremely impoverished with a huge amount of vacant housing. I had gotten spoiled by just being able to walk into anywhere that we wanted to shoot—there was never any opposition because the places were mostly unoccupied. The hardest thing was just trying to find an owner of a building.

But on the second season, I went to Seagirt [Marine Terminal] and I said, "This season we're going to be focused on the port. We want to come in here and do this and this . . ." And they were like, "No thanks." It's private property, it's a business, and they don't have to allow us in there. That was a big wake up call. I was able to eventually gain their trust, and, through a few different maneuvers, we were able to shoot at the Port of Baltimore. We also rented a space at the port where we were able to build our container village. But dealing with the private sector and people who didn't really need our business or our money . . . was a challenge. I mean, every season has its challenges, but I have to say it was a show that we were incredibly proud of just because we felt like such underdogs, really.

**How did you feel about ending *The Wire* after five seasons. Would you have liked it to go to six seasons?**

I was happy that we ended while we still had something to say, you know? Because there's so many shows that just go on even though they don't really need to go on. So, I respected David for making that decision. Everybody has their ideas about [a sixth] season and what it could have been, and I guess we could have easily done another season. But, no, I think it ended at a good point.

**David Simon has said publicly that you are the one responsible for keeping his production on schedule and on budget. What do you think is the secret to successfully producing a show?**

I don't know what the secret is. I wish I did. I think I still care about all the minutiae. I still look at efficiency at all levels of production, and I think the fact that I come from assistant directing means I have a good understanding of set operations. I can be on set for a day and kind of know how much that day cost before I even see the cost report from the accountants. I think [it comes down to] just having a good knowledge of every department and what people do and what things cost and what people really need to get their job done. I also think [it helps] when people see producers on the set, from call to wrap, eating the same food as the crew. David and I drive ourselves—we don't have drivers or fancy trailers. In fact, we typically share part of a double-banger trailer. We don't have, I guess, some of the indulgences, and when people see that it sort of sets the tone that we're here to put the money on the screen. A lot of people say that, but that's really honestly what we do.

Hiring people that have that same kind of attitude helps too. We couldn't really do this without having a great team and great people who have the same ideas as we do about efficiency. [It's also] about creating opportunities—that's the other thing that we're really known for. *The Wire* is the only show I've been on where people really want to spend time together on the weekends—like, every weekend, you know? They were playing softball or going to bars or whatever. People would have barbecues in the summer in their backyard and invite the whole crew over. You'd think you would want to get away from all those people you just spent 100 hours with, but that's really the way it was. I can't take total credit for that. I think part of it was just being in Baltimore and dealing with a subject matter where people had so little and were suffering so much. A lot of the activities that we did were fundraisers and things where we'd go out and we'd build a playground in an inner-city school or have a guest bartender night. We were always doing something for charity, and I think that's what sort of bonded us together and made us feel incredibly grateful for doing that job and for what we had.

# SEASON FIVE EPISODES

**S05E01:** More with Less

**Written by:** Story by David Simon and Ed Burns; teleplay by David Simon

**Directed by:** Joe Chappelle

**Original airdate:** January 6, 2008

**Epigraph:** "The bigger the lie, the more they believe." –Bunk

**Description:** Season five premiere. As McNulty and the detail continue staking out Marlo's crew, recently promoted Sergeant Carver is welcomed by a cauldron of discontent from officers coping with unpaid overtime.

**S05E02:** Unconfirmed Reports

**Written by:** Story by David Simon and William F. Zorzi; teleplay by William F. Zorzi

**Directed by:** Ernest Dickerson

**Original airdate:** January 13, 2008

**Epigraph:** "This ain't Aruba, bitch." –Bunk

**Description:** Although he tells Sydnor the Davis investigation could be a "career case," Freamon keeps a wary eye out for Marlo, who takes care of some unfinished business and strikes a business deal with Barksdale.

**S05E03:** Not for Attribution

**Written by:** Story by David Simon and Chris Collins; teleplay by Chris Collins

**Directed by:** Scott Kecken and Joy Lusco

**Original airdate:** January 20, 2008

**Epigraph:** "They dead where it doesn't count." –Fletcher

**Description:** Carcetti's master plan for the police department is leaked to the press, sending the brass into a panic. Marlo turns to Proposition Joe to help with an enviable problem. Whiting and Klebanow drop a bombshell on the newspaper staff.

**S05E04:** Transitions

**Written by:** Story by David Simon and Ed Burns; teleplay by Ed Burns

**Directed by:** Dan Attias

**Original airdate:** January 27, 2008

**Epigraph:** "Buyer's market out there." –Templeton

**Description:** Campbell tries to smooth out the transitions in the police department. The newspaper scrambles to confirm surprising news from city hall but loses out to the TV media in scooping a high-profile grand jury appearance.

**S05E05:** React Quotes

**Written by:** Story by David Simon and David Mills; teleplay by David Mills

**Directed by:** Agnieszka Holland

**Original airdate:** February 3, 2008

**Epigraph:** "Just 'cause they're in the street doesn't mean that they lack opinions." –Haynes

**Description:** Marlo forges an alliance with a drug connection, who shows him a new communications trick. McNulty's case receives increased attention from the newspaper, in large part thanks to the addition of Templeton to the reporting team.

**S05E06:** The Dickensian Aspect

**Written by:** Story by David Simon and Ed Burns; teleplay by Ed Burns

**Directed by:** Seith Mann

**Original airdate:** February 10, 2008

**Epigraph:** "If you have a problem with this, I understand completely." —Freamon

**Description:** Mystified by Omar's disappearance, Marlo and Chris ramp up their efforts to locate their nemesis. After a sparsely attended waterfront ceremony, Carcetti fires away at a larger press event—and recasts himself as a champion for the homeless.

### S05E07: Took

**Written by:** Story by David Simon and Richard Price; teleplay by Richard Price

**Directed by:** Dominic West

**Original airdate:** February 17, 2008

**Epigraph:** "They don't teach it in law school." —Pearlman

**Description:** An unexpected call puts Templeton back in the spotlight—and gets McNulty more attention than he expected. Bunk bucks at Landsman when ordered to help with the force's most recent red ball.

### S05E08: Clarifications

**Written by:** Story by David Simon and Dennis Lehane; teleplay by Dennis Lehane

**Directed by:** Anthony Hemingway

**Original airdate:** February 24, 2008

**Epigraph:** "A lie ain't a side of a story. It's just a lie." —Terry Hanning

**Description:** Baltimore's renewed police commitment brings fresh recruits to Daniels and McNulty, starting with Carver. Facing a new political challenge, Carcetti is forced to make dangerous political deals.

### S05E09: Late Editions

**Written by:** Story by David Simon and George Pelecanos; teleplay by George Pelecanos

**Directed by:** Joe Chappelle

**Original airdate:** March 2, 2008

**Epigraph:** "Deserve got nuthin' to do with it." —Snoop

**Description:** With Steintorf ordering Rawls to initiate "creative" remedies for the rising crime rate, Freamon's vigilance pays off with a promising lead, sending Sydnor and the department into overdrive.

### S05E10: -30-

**Written by:** Story by David Simon and Ed Burns; teleplay by David Simon

**Directed by:** Clark Johnson

**Original airdate:** March 9, 2008

**Epigraph:** ". . . the life of kings." —H. L. Mencken

**Description:** In the series finale, Carcetti maps out a damage-control scenario with the police brass in the wake of a startling revelation from Pearlman and Daniels. Their choice: Clean up the mess . . . or hide the dirt.

# A TRIBUTE TO MICHAEL K. WILLIAMS

Tragically, on September 6, 2021, actor Michael K. Williams passed away at the age of 54. Playing stickup man Omar Little across five seasons of *The Wire*, Williams left an indelible mark on the series. Off screen, he was adored by the cast and crew, a rare mix of phenomenal talent, humility, and generosity. Here, Williams's friends pay tribute to the actor's brilliance and compassion, on and off screen.

**SONJA SOHN:** Oh, Lord. He and I were so close. It was kind of like love at first sight, in terms of Mike's soul. He had seen *Slam* and fallen in love with my work and me from that. He called my name in the cafeteria—my character name from *Slam*—and we bonded so immediately.

We both had this effervescent childlike quality, this innocence, and he was the only other adult I knew who kept that up front. So we bonded in this place of being understood and alive—there was such a joy in just being alive and that we could be so blessed to have come from where we had and have made it to where we had made it. We never lost sight of that. We both had this intention to keep discovery and innocence alive in ourselves. So we bonded in that place from the moment we met. We had a beautiful, beautiful journey together that we are still having, because our spiritual bond is very deep.

When he passed, it was like I lost a part of me that shared that space. I'll never be the same again.

I'll tell you a story. Michael and I shared a perspective about how characters transform us a certain way. Characters teach us, heal us—it is an intricate dance that is very psycho-spiritual. Michael's work is so palpable and real because he's in a real relationship with the character he's playing. You're not simply seeing the character—you're seeing the relationship he has with the character. You know he's giving you what the character is giving him.

It's very ethereal sometimes, and I don't want to speak for him, but I know that landscape because we inhabited it together. We would process our work together, and when the character would give us certain information about ourselves or we would

OPPOSITE The beloved Michael K. Williams as Omar Little, an iconic role for an iconic actor.

TOP Omar (Williams, *right*) sticks up Marlo's (Jamie Hector, *seated right*) card game in the season four episode "Refugees."

TOP Omar (Michael K. Williams), a badass stickup man with a heart of gold.

have a discovery, we would talk to each other. I mean, who do you talk to about those things but other folks who understand that?

That is how Michael delivered the quality of work he was able to deliver. He was in a relationship with these characters.

**ED BURNS:** I was on set the day Michael did his first scene—in which Omar and his lover are in a small room, gearing up to go out and rob a drug dealer. A prop master comes over to Mike and hands him a sawed-off shotgun, turns, and walks away, and Michael calls to him and says, "How do you open this?" When Michael was told he was on, a persona came over him, just like with Jamie Hector. They went from being two of the nicest guys I've ever met to two ferocious individuals.

**DONA ADRIAN GIBSON:** Losing Michael was a devastating blow. When he came to *The Wire*, his only hope was that maybe he would be able to come back and be on the show [again]. In season five, when Michael's character was going to be shot, I went to see him, and he broke down and cried. It was the end of an era for him because he literally embodied

that character. I think he never imagined that he was going to rise to that kind of success. I remember three or four years after we shot the show, I was in a Gap store, and his picture was on the wall. I called him and said, "Oh my God, I can't even believe this!"

He was gone too soon. His heart was so big. Before he passed in September, we were trying to get together, and I said, "Well, why don't you just come by for lunch tomorrow?" I didn't really think he was going to make it, and he totally made it. He came. I'm so happy that I had time with him; he was there for about three hours. We had a really long, leisurely lunch. That was my last memory of him, so I'm really happy that I had that. He truly always remained humble and kind. He really did.

**JAMIE HECTOR:** It was fun [to work with Michael]. It was like watching a master class on sensitive vulnerability on display. He had an ability to dive into that character, but when you met Mike and you knew him, you found that he was such a humble, beautiful soul. I felt that as soon as I saw him, I knew him. That's the thing—when you join a show that's already in existence, you think you know everybody, but you don't realize that no one knows you. It was a blessing to have known him, to have worked with him, and to have been friends with him. He was a true supporter. And I still can't believe he's gone.

**JERMAINE CRAWFORD:** He is one of the greatest actors of all time. Michael, it was such an honor to share this space with you. I'll never forget doing Michael Jackson at the season four wrap party with you. And thanks for dancing with me.

**ALEXA FOGEL:** It's still so hard to talk about him. I think everybody feels the loss so profoundly. Obviously because of the pandemic I hadn't seen Michael in a while, although I had spoken to him. I consider him a brother, and he was in a really good place. I miss him.

**ANDRE ROYO:** I knew Michael K. Williams from Brooklyn. Michael was an ex-dancer for Crystal Waters. He got cut in the face in real life and didn't shy away from it. He was a very, very fearless, sweet person. He'd be so worried and very soft-spoken until they said action, and then he'd be like whistling and ready to punch you in the face. And when they yelled cut, he'd be, like "Was that good? How was that?" He was so sweet. What made Michael and I connect outside of the show was the reality that we both realized we've taken on these stereotypical roles that back then would end your career. If you played a junkie, you stayed a junkie. Nobody believes you can be a leading man if they see you looking that hapless. If you play a gay man in Black America, you're done. You're not working again, or it's gonna be hard-pressed for people to believe, because they don't want to see a Black man kissing on somebody and then being in a romantic comedy. Back then, they were not buying it. You were stereotyped. The show that helped Michael K. Williams quickly get out of the stereotype was *Boardwalk Empire*. Once he jumped on that, it was a different game. When I got out to LA, I was [typecast as] a junkie. They were like, "Oh, you're that junkie on the show?" So Michael and I really bonded on that aspect of, "Is this gonna hurt our careers moving forward?" But what was great about Mike [was that he helped me realize] we can't worry about it. We're going play this character the best way we know how and not worry about, you know, what's coming on down the line.

**SNOOP PEARSON:** Oh, yeah, I get emotional talking about Mike. Man, he was my angel. He said that I saved his life, and I'd say that he saved mine. Man, I miss him. I love him. Lord, have mercy, there's just so many words that could describe him.

He wasn't like his character. He was so soft, so sweet, so intelligent. As an actor, man, he could adapt to whatever roles that you put on him. I watched him transform into a lot of characters, just reciting lines with him, you know? But him as a person? That man would give you the shirt off his back. Like, if you didn't have a shirt, and it was cold outside, he would give you the shirt off his back. Mike was just the life of the party. He was a dancing motherfucker, you know what I'm saying? He wasn't my friend; he was my brother. Blood couldn't make us closer.

TOP An off-duty Omar Little (Michael K. Williams).

# EPILOGUE

By D. Watkins

**"...the show had a strong message, but I don't think the writers intended to transform Baltimore into Emerald City."**

TOP Author D. Watkins in Baltimore. Photograph by Devin Allen.

OPPOSITE (*Clockwise from top left*) McNulty (Dominic West); Omar (Michael K. Williams); Kima (Sonja Sohn) and Carver (Seth Gilliam)—just four key players in *The Wire*'s rich tapestry of characters.

PAGE 240 A parody version of the *Baltimore Sun*'s logo created by the art department for internal use during season five of *The Wire*.

I sat across from a young reporter in a café situated quaintly in a gentrified section of West Baltimore. She fumbled around inside her oversized purse in search of an iPhone charger.

"I'm so sorry, Mr. Watkins," she said, "My battery is the worst."

"No worries," I said, patting my pockets for a cigarette. I found one, plucked it, and stepped outside into my ever-changing city, full of new shops, pricy apartments, and unfinished construction—the sum all equaling displaced residents. I sparked the cig and took a long, slow pull into my lungs, and then quickly blew my anxiety out of my nostrils. The reporter walked out.

"Got another?"

I passed her my last. She wasn't profiling me but was new in town, and someone had told her that I could help her understand Baltimore. I don't think anyone can help anyone understand Baltimore, but I always try to show love to new reporters: After all, they control our city's narrative.

"I think I asked you everything I needed," the reporter said. "Oh well, I guess nothing has really changed since *The Wire*?"

"I guess not."

"That bothers me," she said with a playful pout, holding her cigarette away from her face. "I love that show and really thought it would change the city."

To me, her statement was the biggest compliment a person could give to any piece of art, film, *or* television show. The fact that the project is so powerful that it has such an impact on you, your life, and the way you think, which leads you to question why it didn't change the world, or in this case, the city where it is based.

"Why does it bother you?" I asked. "You know it was just a TV show."

"I know but . . ."

I took another pull, which ended up being the final pull, and explained to her that the show had a strong message, but I don't think the writers intended to transform Baltimore into Emerald City. Did *Law & Order* stop crime in New York? Did *Oz* bring about criminal justice reform? Absolutely not, because television is meant for entertainment.

"Those writers were real cops and journalists," she pushed back. "They used so many real stories and so many real names. I'm not saying that the writers or HBO failed to save Baltimore, but you get where I'm coming from."

"Sometimes, I think it's a matter of perspective. Maybe looking for change on a grand scale isn't the answer, but I'll leave you with something that might make you feel better."

"I'm interested," she said.

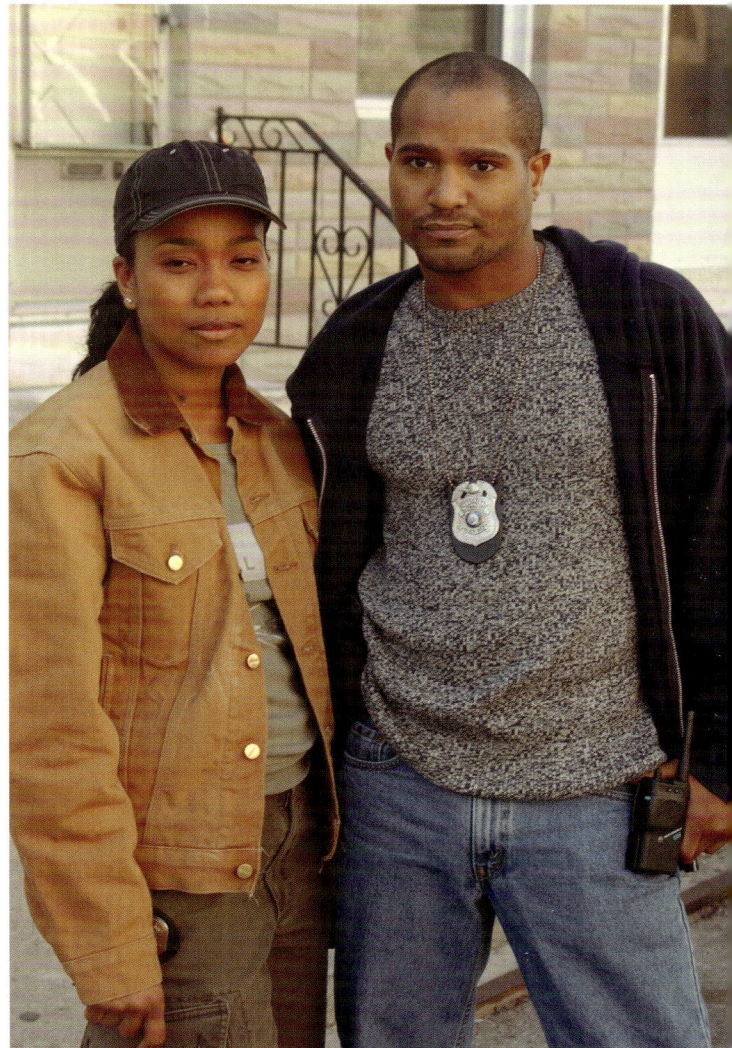

I told the reporter about my friendship with Sonja Sohn, who played detective Kima Greggs on all five seasons. Sohn has been an activist in Baltimore for over twenty years, and she and I have had many conversations about the impact of *The Wire*. During one of those exchanges, she said, "Once I was having lunch at that restaurant Miss Shirley's. An older white guy kept staring at me and then looking away. I thought he was just a fan of the show. And then he made his way over to my table, so I started preparing to take a picture, but he stopped me, saying he doesn't want a picture."

"What did he do?" the reporter asked me.

"He told her that he was a judge and that watching *The Wire* gave him a fresh perspective on Baltimore and its problems, even though he had lived in the city his whole life," I said. "And then he told her that the show was so powerful that it had changed the way that he sentenced people convicted of crimes, because he finally understands what Black people in Baltimore are forced to deal with."

The reporter's jaw dropped.

"*The Wire* did that," I said.

# LIGHT FOR ALL

# THE WIRE

## TITAN BOOKS

144 Southwark Street
London SE1 0UP
www.titanbooks.com

Find us on Facebook: www.facebook.com/TitanBooks
Follow us on Twitter: @titanbooks
Follow us on Instagram: @titanbooks

**HBO**
HOME BOX OFFICE.

Published by Titan Books, London, in 2022.

Published by arrangement with Insight Editions, PO Box 3088, San Rafael, CA 94912, USA. www.insighteditions.com

A CIP catalogue record for this title is available from the Britsh Library.

ISBN: 9781803363516

Publisher: Raoul Goff
VP of Licensing and Partnerships: Vanessa Lopez
VP, Creative: Chrissy Kwasnik
VP, Manufacturing: Alix Nicholaeff
VP, Editorial Director: Vicki Jaeger
Designer: Matt Girard
Executive Editor: Chris Prince
Editorial Assistant: Savannah Jensen and Emma Merwin
Managing Editor: Maria Spano
Senior Production Editor: Elaine Ou
Senior Production Manager: Greg Steffen
Senior Production Manager, Subsidiary Rights: Linas Palma-Temena

Additional editing by Justin Eisinger, John Foster, Savannah Jensen, Sadie Lowry, and Elizabeth Ovieda.

ROOTS of PEACE ✿ REPLANTED PAPER

Insight Editions, in association with Roots of Peace, will plant two trees for each tree used in the manufacturing of this book. Roots of Peace is an internationally renowned humanitarian organization dedicated to eradicating land mines worldwide and converting war-torn lands into productive farms and wildlife habitats. Roots of Peace will plant two million fruit and nut trees in Afghanistan and provide farmers there with the skills and support necessary for sustainable land use.

Manufactured in China by Insight Editions

10 9 8 7 6 5 4 3 2 1

Insight Editions would like to thank David Simon and his team, including Laura Schwarzmann at Blown Deadline Productions, for all their help in the creation of this book. We would also like to extend our gratitude to Michele Caruso at HBO for all her guidance and assistance on the project. Thanks also to Stacey Abiraj, Tara Bonner, Andrew Kelley, and Arielle Mauge at HBO for all their help. In addition, we would like to thank all our interviewees for sharing their memories of their time on *The Wire*: Paul Ben-Victor, Ed Burns, Tray Chaney, Chad L. Coleman, Nathan Corbett, Jermaine Crawford, John Doman, Idris Elba, Alexa L. Fogel, Dona Adrian Gibson, Jamie Hector, Deirdre Lovejoy, Nina K. Noble, Felicia Pearson, George Pelecanos, Wendell Pierce, Michael Potts, Andre Royo, Pablo Schreiber, David Simon, Sonja Sohn, Robert Wisdom, Debi Young, and William F. Zorzi. Special thanks also to Halina Gebarowicz for kindly sharing her archive of production design art from *The Wire* and to Debi Young for allowing us to publish her personal photos from the show.